'The substantially revised edition of this pioneer combines the formidable expertise and wisdc respected leaders with the fresh perspective of Students will love the fascinating illustrative da cases from five continents.'

Diana Eades, *Univer*

C000257182

Praise for the First Edition

'Seldom do introductions to any field offer such a wealth of information or provide such a useful array of exercise activities for students in the way that this book does. Coulthard and Johnson not only provide their readers with extensive examples of the actual evidence used in the many law cases described here but they also show how the linguist's "toolkit" was used to address the litigated issues. In doing this, they give valuable insights about how forensic linguists think, do their analyses and, in some cases, even testify at trial.'

Roger W. Shuy, *Distinguished Research Professor of Linguistics, Emeritus, Georgetown University, USA*

'This is a wonderful textbook for students, providing stimulating examples, lucid accounts of relevant linguistic theory and excellent further reading and activities. The foreign language of law is also expertly documented, explained and explored. Language as evidence is cast centre stage; coupled with expert linguistic analysis, the written and spoken clues uncovered by researchers are foregrounded in unfolding legal dramas. Coulthard and Johnson have produced a clear and compelling work that contains its own forensic linguistic puzzle.'

Annabelle Mooney, *Roehampton University, UK*

An Introduction to Forensic Linguistics

An Introduction to Forensic Linguistics: Language in Evidence has established itself as the essential textbook written by leading authorities in this expanding field. The second edition of this bestselling textbook begins with a new introduction and continues in two parts.

Part One deals with the language of the legal process, and begins with a substantial new chapter exploring key theoretical and methodological approaches. In four updated chapters it goes onto cover the language of the law, initial calls to the emergency services, police interviewing, and courtroom discourse. Part Two looks at language as evidence, with substantially revised and updated chapters on the following key topics:

- the work of the forensic linguist
- forensic phonetics
- authorship attribution
- the linguistic investigation of plagiarism
- the linguist as expert witness.

The authors combine an array of perspectives on forensic linguistics, using knowledge and experience gained in legal settings – Coulthard in his work as an expert witness for cases such as the Birmingham Six and the Derek Bentley appeal, and Johnson as a former police officer. Research tasks, further reading, web links, and a new conclusion ensure that this remains the core textbook for courses in forensic linguistics and language and the law. A glossary of key terms is also available at https://www.routledge.com/products/9781138641716 and on the Routledge Language and Communication Portal.

Malcolm Coulthard is Emeritus Professor of Forensic Linguistics at Aston University, UK, and Visiting Professor at the Federal University of Santa Catarina, Brazil. He is the co-editor of the recently launched international journal *Language and Law, Linguagem e Direito* and author of many books including *An Introduction to Discourse Analysis* (1985).

Alison Johnson is Lecturer in English Language at the University of Leeds, UK. She is the co-editor (with Malcolm Coulthard) of *The Routledge Handbook of Forensic Linguistics* (2010) and an editor of *The International Journal of Speech, Language and the Law*.

David Wright is Lecturer in Linguistics at Nottingham Trent University, UK, and Reviews editor of *Language and Law, Linguagem e Direito*.

An Introduction to Forensic Linguistics

Language in Evidence

Second edition

Malcolm Coulthard, Alison Johnson and David Wright

Routledge
Taylor & Francis Group

LONDON AND NEW YORK

Second edition published 2017
by Routledge
2 Park Square, Milton Park, Abingdon, Oxon OX14 4RN

and by Routledge
711 Third Avenue, New York, NY 10017

Routledge is an imprint of the Taylor & Francis Group, an informa business

First edition published by Routledge 2007

British Library Cataloguing-in-Publication Data
A catalogue record for this book is available from the British Library

Library of Congress Cataloging-in-Publication Data
Names: Coulthard, Malcolm, author. | Johnson, Alison, 1959- author. |
Wright, David, 1948 December 10-Title: An Introduction to forensic
linguistics/ by Malcolm Coulthard, Alison Johnson and David Wright.
Description: Abingdon, Oxon ; New York, NY ; Routledge, [2016] |
Includes bibliographical references and index.
Identifiers: LCCN 2016007458 | ISBN 9781138641709 (hardback) |
ISBN 9781138641716 (pbk.) | ISBN 9781315630311 (ebook)
Subjects: LCSH: Forensic linguistics.
Classification: LCC K2287.5 C68 2016 | DDC 363.25–dc23LC
record available at http://lccn.loc.gov/2016007458

ISBN: 978-1-138-64170-9 (hbk)
ISBN: 978-1-138-64171-6 (pbk)
ISBN: 978-1-3156-3031-1 (ebk)

Typeset in Times
by Cenveo Publisher Services

This book is affectionately dedicated to our families

Contents

11 Conclusion   **215**

List of illustrations

Figures

Tables

Acknowledgements

We are deeply indebted to Krzysztof Kredens, who read and commented in detail on an early draft of Part II and to David Woolls not only for his superb work in harmonising the varied referencing styles of the authors with that of the publisher but also for substantially computerising the normally labour-intensive task of creating the index especially for the book. We also thank Peter French who not only produced the spectrogram in Figure 7.1, but has also been a constant source of information and encouragement for the past 25 years. Finally, we are grateful to Dominic Watt who reviewed Chapter 7 for this edition.

Most of the material in this book has been presented over the past 20 years to literally thousands of students on undergraduate and postgraduate courses at the Universities of Aston, Birmingham, Cardiff, Leeds, Nottingham Trent and the Federal University of Santa Catarina in Brazil, and it has benefited immensely from their perceptive observations. We learned a great deal from innumerable colleagues who have discussed texts and responded to ideas following papers at conferences and university research seminars. Particular thanks for insights, stimulation and critical comments must go to our friends in the 1990s Birmingham Forensic Linguistics Research Group: Sue Blackwell, Janet Cotterill, Tim Grant, Chris Heffer, Charles Owen, Frances Rock and Michael Toolan. And last, but by no means least, Janet Ainsworth, Ron Butters, Diana Eades, John Gibbons, Roger Shuy, Larry Solan, Peter Tiersma and Teresa Turell, whose friendship, perceptive writings and generous personal communications have influenced the whole book.

Permissions

1 Introduction

Jaffa Cakes – definitely not biscuits – prepare to take on imitators
… McVitie's was determined to prove it [the Jaffa Cake] should be free of the consumer tax. The key turning point was when its QC highlighted how cakes harden when they go stale, biscuits go soggy. A Jaffa goes hard. Case proved.

(The Telegraph, 5 December 2015)

Shipman jailed for 15 murders
Family GP Harold Shipman has been jailed for life for murdering 15 patients, as he goes down in history as the UK's biggest convicted serial killer. He was also found guilty of forging the will of Kathleen Grundy, one of his patients.

(BBC News, 31 January 2000)

Court rejects Da Vinci copy claim
The *Da Vinci Code* author Dan Brown did not breach the copyright of an earlier book, London's High Court has ruled.

(BBC News, 7 April 2006)

Google successfully defends its most valuable asset in court
The 'Google' trademark regularly ranks as one of the most valuable in the world […]. Recently, Google's opponents in a court case claimed [it] had become 'generic' […] [T]he court decisively rejected the challenge, confirming that 'Google' remains a valid and protectable trademark.

(Forbes, www.forbes.com, 15 September 2014)

Man remanded in Ripper hoax probe
A 49-year-old man has been remanded in custody charged with being the infamous Yorkshire Ripper hoaxer known as Wearside Jack. The clerk at Leeds Magistrates' Court read the charge to Mr Humble, which said he was accused of sending the letters and audiotape between 1 March 1978 and 30 June 1979 [27 years earlier].

(BBC News, 20 October 2005)

Legal words, murder, plagiarism, trademarks and a voice hoax

Linguistic aspects of legal stories often make headline news around the world, indicating the high profile given to such material by newsmakers. Five such headlines and reports taken from news media form the epigraphs for this introduction. The first story involves the now famous – Jaffa cake – biscuit or cake? – court case between United Biscuits and Customs and Excise over value added tax (VAT). The case revolved around the legal definition, in tax law, of 'food' versus 'confectionary'. 'Cake' is defined as an essential food, whereas 'biscuits' are luxuries. This case and a similar one involving whether Pringles are crisp-like or non-crisp-like are discussed in Chapter 3, drawing our attention to the differences between the legal meanings and ordinary meanings of words.

The second refers to the case of Harold Shipman, a doctor who was convicted in January 2000 of the murder of 15 of his patients. The judge, the Honourable Mr Justice Forbes, observed that 'there has never been another case in this country [Britain] which has required the investigation of as many possible murders committed by a single individual as needed to be investigated in this case' (The Shipman Inquiry 2001). In Chapters 4 and 5 we deal with material from the Shipman case when we analyse police interviews and courtroom testimony.

The third story relates to the alleged copying of material by Dan Brown, the author of *The Da Vinci Code*, from an earlier work of non-fiction, *The Holy Blood and the Holy Grail* (*HBHG*). This claim for damages, brought by the authors of the earlier work, delayed the launch of the film of the same name and thereby raised the profile of copying, plagiarism and copyright violation in the minds of the general public. The headline in the epigraph (*Court rejects Da Vinci copy claim*) reports the ruling in favour of the defendant, Random House, that they (and Brown) did not infringe copyright in the novel. The judge's conclusion was that 'there is no copyright infringement either by textual copying or non-textual copying of a substantial part of *HBHG* by means of copying the Central Themes' (*Baigent v Random House*, 7 April 2006). Plagiarism is treated in more detail in Chapter 9.

The fourth story – about trademark protection for the Google name – is concerned with the interesting question of how far companies can claim to 'own' words and have the right to decide who can use them and in what circumstances – and it gives an insight into the process of continually needing to defend a trademark, which involves preventing the protected word(s) from slipping into common usage as a generic meaning, which they are liable to do. If that happens, anyone can use the word(s) and benefit from all the investment in marketing and publicity. In Chapter 6, we show McDonald's' and others' vigorous defences of their marks.

The final story is about the uniqueness of voices and whether a tape recording of a speaker committing a crime a quarter of a century earlier can be successfully matched with the contemporary vocal output of a recently arrested suspect, in spite of the passage of time and its effect on the voice. It draws us into the world of forensic phonetics and speaker identification. The most significant case in England is that of 'The Yorkshire Ripper', a serial killer who, between 1975 and 1979, murdered

13 women in the Leeds and Bradford area of Yorkshire. In June 1979, Stanley Ellis, a phonetician, dialectologist and lecturer at the University of Leeds, was called in by police after a tape recording, purporting to be from 'The Ripper', was sent to them. At the same time Jack Windsor Lewis, another linguist, was employed to analyse three letters sent to the police apparently from the same person (see Windsor Lewis 1994). Ellis's analysis led him to report to police: 'in my opinion the man's voice represented someone who had been brought up in the Southwick or Castletown areas [of Sunderland]' (Ellis 1994: 202). Ellis and Windsor Lewis became concerned that the letters and tape recording could be a hoax and that therefore eliminating from the murder investigation all suspects who did not have a north-eastern accent was a mistake. In 1981, Peter Sutcliffe, a lorry driver from Bradford, pleaded guilty to manslaughter on the grounds of diminished responsibility, but Sutcliffe did not have a Sunderland accent, so, as Ellis noted, 'the identity of a man who sent [the] tape and letters ... has never been discovered' (1994: 206). However, in October 2005, 26 years after the tapes had been sent, a Sunderland labourer, John Humble, was arrested and charged with sending the hoax letters and the tape to the police. Not only did Humble's genetic profile match a saliva sample taken from one of the original hoax letter's envelopes, but forensic phoneticians were able to match the voice on the 1979 hoax recording with Humble's voice as recorded in his 2005 police interview. Humble's address was given in court as Flodden Road, Ford Estate, in the suburb of South Hylton in Sunderland, half a kilometre away from Southwick and Castletown, which had been identified by Ellis as the two likely places of origin. This case highlights the way that forensic phoneticians' work is used alongside other investigative processes – see French *et al.* (2006) for a report by the phoneticians involved and Chapter 7 for more forensic phonetic cases. The Yorkshire Ripper case is also the focus of recent interest. The convicted killer is reported to be a potential suspect in other unsolved cases (Meikle, 2015) and the 'Wearside Jack' story is being made into a movie (Child, 2015).

These five headline stories highlight some of the media interest in legal cases and some of the concerns of forensic linguistics and phonetics. These and others that will be treated in subsequent chapters are:

- the language of legal documents;
- the language of the police and of law enforcement;
- interviews with children and vulnerable witnesses in the legal system;
- courtroom interaction;
- authorship attribution and plagiarism;
- forensic phonetics and speaker identification;
- linguistic evidence and expert witness testimony in courtrooms.

Who is this book for?

The book is designed for students on taught undergraduate and postgraduate courses in forensic linguistics, law and language and legal linguistics, but could, equally well, be used by advanced students and researchers as a stand-alone introduction to forensic linguistics and by lecturers planning such courses. In addition, we know that forensic linguistics is taught as a topic on a diverse range of courses, such as: applied linguistics, corpus linguistics, criminology, education, law, psychology, sociolinguistics, sociology, translation, and many more. This book will form a useful resource for students and lecturers there too. Equally, not all the researchers to whom we refer in this book would identify themselves within a field called forensic linguistics (they might identify as criminologists, psychologists, lawyers, sociolinguists or sociologists), but their work is, nevertheless, included in bibliographies of forensic linguistics.

Organisation of the book

The book is divided into two parts: 'The Language of the Legal Process' and 'Language as Evidence'.

Part I, Chapters 2 to 5 of the book, offers a thorough grounding in forensic approaches to language analysis and explores key ideas in legal language (Chapter 3), emergency service calls and police interviews and courtroom discourse (Chapters 4 and 5). Students and researchers are equipped in Part I to carry out research tasks on understanding the legal language of terms and conditions, statutes and contracts, the language of emergency calls and police interviews, and the use of questions in courtroom examination and cross-examination activities. This work is underpinned by the introduction to theoretical and methodological issues in Chapter 2. Part II, Chapters 6 to 10, discusses forensic linguistic and phonetic casework, research and practice. The cases in which expert evidence has been commissioned from linguists range from disputes about the meaning of individual morphemes in a trademark dispute and of individual words in jury instructions, through the 'ownership' of particular words and phrases in a plagiarism case, to accusations in certain murder cases that whole texts have been fabricated. Students and researchers are equipped in Part II to carry out research tasks in relation to authorship attribution, speaker identification, plagiarism and trademark law.

Descriptive linguistics and forensic linguistics work hand-in-hand: corpora and real data, though they are often limited in size and availability, are central to our endeavour. All of the texts used in this book are authentic, and the majority have been the focus of teaching or research, or are taken from cases where linguistic expertise has been called upon. The text extracts used in each chapter promote critical analytical discussion and the chapters are designed to develop an understanding of current research, field-specific vocabulary, skills and knowledge as well as to stimulate reflection and discussion. The book represents the authors' belief in the centrality of the text as the basis of teaching and research.

Reading and research tasks and how they function

Each chapter ends with Suggested Readings. These vary in number, but are intended as a fairly comprehensive starting point for students and researchers at all levels. Since it is impossible to guess what any given reader knows already, we suggest that you concentrate on those texts that are new to you. For some readers, for example, law students with no linguistic background, there will be a need to select more, and for others, fewer readings. We intend each chapter to be an introduction to one particular area of forensic linguistics and expect readers to use the follow-up readings, as well as items selected from the references, to develop a wider knowledge. After completing the first edition of this book in 2007, Coulthard and Johnson edited *The Routledge Handbook of Forensic Linguistics* (2010), which was designed specifically as a companion volume. It has 39 chapters produced by 40 internationally recognised authors and therefore many of the suggested readings are from there. At the same time, the discipline is continually developing, but books can only be updated occasionally, so you are advised to become a regular reader of the discipline's two major journals: the *International Journal of Speech, Language and the Law* and *Language and Law – Linguagem e Direito*.

Each chapter also contains a set of related Research Tasks. Sometimes they suggest research that replicates a published study, sometimes a more detailed analysis of a text referred to in the chapter, while yet others propose investigations that could be the basis of undergraduate or postgraduate projects or theses. Individual tasks can be used by students for independent research or set by teachers as tasks to be reported on in class. Equally, they could be set or adapted as assignment or project questions. Research tasks are intended to engage readers in two central ways: in a reflective response to the ideas raised in the chapters and in a practical response, through applying the critical ideas and methodologies outlined in Chapter 2.

The second edition

In this edition we have been joined by David Wright who has contributed his expertise on authorship attribution and phonetics. All of the chapters have been substantially rewritten and updated, drawing on texts and case examples from a wider range of countries; this book now features examples and material from: Australia, Brazil, Canada, China, England, Japan, New Zealand, Northern Ireland, Spain, and the USA. Parts of Chapters 1 and 3 from the first edition have been incorporated into other chapters, making space for the completely new Chapter 2 on critical, theoretical, and methodological approaches to language in legal settings. We have also written a new conclusion in which we point to some new directions in the field and the potential for continuing and increased collaboration between forensic linguists and, for example, lawyers, psychologists, sociologists and other legal professionals.

Part I
The Language of the Legal Process

2 Critical, theoretical, and methodological approaches to language in legal settings

Introduction – Powerful professionals and ordinary people

The legal process all over the world involves a wide range of people, what Agar (1985) and Mayr (2008: 4) call 'experts' and 'non-experts'. These people are members of a wide variety of professions – barristers, clerks, emergency services call-takers, judges, legislative drafters, police officers, prison officers, probation officers, solicitors, writers of legal information leaflets and notices – and the members of the public who come into contact with them at any stage of the process. That might be when they report a crime, provide a witness statement for use later in legal proceedings, or become a suspect accused of a crime. Linguists and other qualified professionals are also sometimes called upon to provide expert opinion in legal cases, thereby achieving some kind of in-between status, neither legal professional nor ordinary lay person, but someone with expert status within the judicial process. This complex mix of professional and lay participants results in multilayered interaction at the interface between the legal world and the world of ordinary people. Rock, Heffer and Conley (2013: 25) argue that the legal-lay or lay-legal pairing is, in fact, a reductionist distinction, as 'even where the communication is solely between legal participants, as in the Supreme Court [of America] written briefs and oral arguments, some of the oppositionists' narrative voice remains' and 'this suggests that the lay voice is still present in what is, from a pure roles perspective, an example of legal-legal communication'. Tracy and Delgadillo (2013: 228–29) 'trouble' the distinction too, asking: 'Is "legal-lay" a descriptor for the talk that occurs in particular institutional sites, or is it better thought of as a style of thinking, speaking or writing?'. The second option suggests a dynamic definition that takes us into the domain of 'institutional interaction' or 'institutional discourse' (e.g. Drew and Heritage 1992; Sarangi and Roberts 1999), a hierarchical social order in which 'participants' institutional or professional identities are somehow made relevant to the work activities in which they are engaged' (Drew and Heritage 1992: 3–4). Conceiving of discourse as an institutional style marks it as a specialised, professional discourse in which dominant and powerful identities are played out in a whole range of 'activity' that is 'goal-defined, socially constituted' and which features 'events with *constraints* on participants ... but above all on the kinds of allowable contributions' (Levinson 1992: 69). This means that legal and lay speakers operate within unwritten, but discursively perceived, constraints on what is appropriate and the activity – police interview, cross-examination – determines 'how what one says will be "taken" [and] what inferences will be made from what is said' (Levinson 1992: 97).

Roberts (2011: 83) makes a useful distinction between institutional discourse and professional discourse, saying 'the latter is acquired by professionals as they become teachers, doctors, human resources personnel', or police officers and lawyers. The term implies 'some notion of autonomy or freedom as a result of acquiring a body of knowledge through rigorous training'. It is 'a form of "habitus" (Bourdieu 1991), a set of linguistic practices and conventionalized behavior and values that the professional has to acquire mastery over'. Institutional discourse, on the other hand, 'is formed both by the wider ideologies and relations of the ruling apparatus' (Roberts 2011: 83). Therefore, rather than the autonomy inherent in professional discourse, institutional discourse involves an orientation to the rules, ideologies, and systems of the institution, which Drew and Heritage (1992: 22) describe as having:

- core goals, tasks, or identity conventionally associated with the institution – 'goal orientations';
- constraints on 'allowable contributions' (cf. Levinson 1992);
- specific 'inferential frameworks' in the context (Levinson 1992: 72 refers to these as 'inferential schemata').

This means that the professional members of legal conversations – police officers in interviews or lawyers in court – are in control of the legal goals and agendas and are aware of constraints on the meaning of particular words or phrases, such as the police caution or 'right to silence', whereas lay members do not understand the talk in the same way, a situation that produces asymmetrical relationships, which we expand on below. Inferential frameworks, or schemata, refer to the ways that successive turns in talk can be interpreted. In Chapter 5, on courtroom discourse, we use an example from Levinson (1992: 83), from the cross-examination of a woman who alleges rape. Expertly phrased and sequenced questions that ask the woman why she was not wearing a coat on a cold night, in spite of still recovering from a cold, elicit answers that suggest the woman was more concerned with her attractiveness than her health and safety. This renders the rape complainant's narrative interpretable as implying a predisposition to consent rather than to resist 'advances', and the inference is that the woman was responsible, rather than a mere victim.

Professionals in the legal system are, therefore, always operating within these two parameters – habitual ways of being and ways of talking within an overarching system – formulating their professional words and worlds within the institutional frame and the schemata that circulate in the particular *speech community*. These rules and norms generate distinctive language through vocabulary or *register* choices, generic features of cross-examination, norms for interruption and politeness and so on.

The asymmetrical relationships produced by institutional discourse can lead to inequality and injustice. Eades (2010b: 153) describes a 1980s case in which she acted as an expert witness, where an 'Aboriginal English-speaking appellant alleged he had been verballed in [his] police interview, which provided an apparent confession to a gruesome murder'. 'Verballing' is a term used by suspects in both Australia and the UK to refer to the police putting words into their mouths or inserting them into written confessions. Eades' (2010b: 153) analysis 'showed how the allegedly verbatim answers attributed to this man, in the typed police record of interview, used English differently from typical Queensland Aboriginal English usage at the time, as well as from this man's speech patterns in other interviews' (Eades 2010b: 153). According to Agar (1985: 164) institutions produce 'socially legitimated expertise together with those persons authorized to implement it', leading to institutional power and control over lay persons, in ways that produce social inequalities and can lead to abuses of that power, such as verballing, and also false or unsafe confessions. In Chapter 8 (and below in our sections on sociolinguistics and corpus linguistics) we show how Coulthard's analysis of the 1950s Derek Bentley case uncovered a 'confession' that contained striking similarities to the language used by police officers in their witness statements.

Professional discourse, with its use of technical terms only fully understood by expert professionals, often excludes lay people, but experts can also work to assist them. Eades' research (e.g. 1994; 2000; 2006) on the 'communicative clash', 'silencing', and 'lexical struggle' between Aboriginal Australians and legal professionals in police interviews and the courtroom points to linguistic inequalities and, therefore, an unequal access to justice for this group of lay participants. However, in a 2014 post on the Forensic Linguistics discussion list (www.jiscmail.ac.uk), which readers might like to subscribe to, Eades reported on an Australian court hearing: *The State of Western Australia v Gibson* [2014] WASC 240 (http://www.austlii.edu.au/au/cases/wa/WASC/2014/240.html), in which Eades and a number of other expert linguists were consulted. The case was of an Aboriginal suspect who had been questioned about and accused of murder. The hearing sought to find out, amongst other things, whether he had needed an interpreter during his police interview and whether he understood the caution. Taking the expert opinion of his level of English and linguistic performance in the interview into account, in the matter of whether he needed an interpreter, the judge concluded that 'there was no reasonable excuse for not obtaining the assistance of an interpreter [when] all the objective indications were that an interpreter was required. Such inquiries as were made to determine the English language proficiency of the accused were inadequate' (para. 178). In relation to his understanding of the caution, the judge concluded that 'the accused received conflicting messages and that it is unlikely that he would have understood the caution. When the translated statements of Mr Butler [an 'interview friend', who supported the suspect in his first language and provided an interpretation of police questions for him] are taken into account, the message the accused received was not that he was *not* obliged to speak to the police but that he *was*. No adequate efforts were made by the police to ensure that the caution was understood' (para. 149; our emphasis). Following cases such as this one, police are now instructed in both Australia and the UK to insist on the use of interpreters, even if the suspect is willing to continue without one.

In the *Gibson* case the 'interview friend' was not a qualified interpreter, but even with qualified interpreters, disruption of the message can occur. Berk-Seligson's (2002) study of the role of interpreters in the courtroom shows how interpreter style and simply the presence of an interpreter, a third person in what is essentially dyadic interaction, has a potential impact on the ways that jurors evaluate witnesses. The multi-layered dynamic of the legal process is further complicated by the presence of non-native speakers and requires additional efforts by the police and by interpreters.

Complexity is also an issue in the reading of rights at the interview stage of the judicial process. The inherent complexity of the wording of the right to silence, or police caution, in England and Wales ('You do not have to say anything. But it may harm your defence if you do not mention when questioned something which you later rely on in Court. Anything you do say may be given in evidence') (Home Office 2013, S10.5: 34) or Miranda warning (in the USA), has implications for justice, as we just saw in the Australian case (see also, for example, Ainsworth 2008; Cotterill 2000; Leo 1996). Rock's ethnographic study of the caution, as well as a written notice that is given to detained persons about their rights shows that it is the institutional processes and practices surrounding the caution and notice which make them 'institutionally meaningful' (Rock 2007: 12). As well as delivering the caution, in the UK officers are encouraged to explain its phrases to detainees. From her analyses of police officers' explanations, 'you do not have to say anything', for example, is shown to mean different things to different police officers, from 'you have a right to total silence', to some, but 'you have a right to partial silence (silence in response to some questions)', to others (Rock 2007: 164). While it is one thing for detainees not to understand the caution – a study by Shepherd *et al.* (1995) (cited in Fenner and Gudjonsson 2002) found that 'you do not have to say anything' was understood by only 27 per cent of ordinary people – it is another thing for police officers not to fully understand it. The study by Fenner and Gudjonsson (2002: 83) found that although 'more than 96% (52) [of a group of people tested] claimed that they had understood the caution fully, after it had been presented to them as it would be by a police officer, none of them did so [in fact]'. Another study by Eastwood and Snook (2010: 366), investigating subjects' understanding of the two Canadian cautions – the right to silence and the right to legal counsel – presented both orally (as is usual practice) and in written form, found that only 4 per cent and 7 per cent respectively fully understood the cautions when they were delivered orally, whereas 48 per cent and 32 per cent understood them in written form. Rights are tricky things to fully understand and deliver, not just for lay detainees, but also for the expert professionals.

Rights are, worryingly, also difficult things to invoke. Ainsworth (2008: 1) argues that the way that suspects invoke their rights means that they have the right to remain silent or to ask for a lawyer 'but only if you ask for it just so'. Rather than interrogatives, such as *Could I get a lawyer?* or requests with softening language which renders them ambiguous, such as *It seems what I need is a lawyer,* which were deemed by the US courts not to have invoked the right to a lawyer (Ainsworth 2008: 7–8), suspects need to use a 'bald and completely unmodified imperative', such as *Give me a lawyer!* (Ainsworth 2008: 11). This state of affairs has come about through a series of judgments in the US courts. In an ideal world, Ainsworth (2008: 11) argues, a 'linguistically informed judge would recognize that speakers in powerless positions are quite likely to resort to indirect and hedged syntactic forms, in lieu of using unmodified imperatives, but that utterances in a "powerless" register are intended by their users to be no less unequivocal than those that are syntactically more direct'. The asymmetrical discursive context is what produces these less powerful invocations of rights, a situation judges, Ainsworth suggests, should understand.

Each of these studies ultimately shows how professional and institutional talk produces powerful institutional meanings both 'subtly and routinely' (Mumby and Clair, 1997: 184) to gain the institutional 'upper hand', but, as we have seen above, when abuses of power occur, expert linguists can have a role to play.

Forensic linguists transforming practice

Forensic linguists do not stop at describing and demonstrating powerful institutional practice; they also seek to transform it, whether by critiquing judicial language in law journals, working with police officers to increase their understanding of their own professional talk, or doing the difficult job of giving expert opinion as a witness in court. For example, Stokoe (2014) has developed a Conversation Analytic Role-play Method (CARM), a technique for training mediators and police officers in communication skills. Using her research with Edwards (e.g. Edwards and Stokoe 2011) into police interview interaction, and data from her large collection of transcribed police interviews in cases involving neighbour disputes, she has developed a workshop approach, working with trainees and 'selecting extracts from research findings about a particular practice (e.g., explaining a service)'. The workshops use animation software to play audio clips alongside her transcripts, so that 'workshop participants live through conversations without knowing what is coming next, and then role-play what they might do next to handle the situation' (Stokoe 2014: 256–57). They discuss what they might do to respond and then the actual response is played to them, allowing for identification and evaluation of effective practice. Research into police interview discourse can, therefore, have an impact on training and thereby influence future practice.

These interventions by linguists in the social world (expert opinions used in court, ethnographic work in police stations, and professional training) have a real impact on professions and individuals and transform practice and thereby people's lives. The CARM method has been used not just in police and mediator training, but also in other professions, bringing the linguistic principle of using real data and empirical evidence into the workplace. And in the *Gibson* hearing in Australia (referred to above) the outcome was that:

> the interviews between the accused and the police on 16 and 17 August 2012 are not admissible. Those interviews were not voluntary, were obtained in breach of the CIA [Criminal Investigation Act 2006 (WA)] and to admit them would, in any event, be unfair to the accused.
>
> (*The State of Western Australia v Gibson* [2014] WASC 240, para. 183)

This meant that the prosecution could not rely on any evidence obtained in the interviews and the unfair prosecution advantage that this might have produced was prevented.

Thus, we can conclude that forensic linguistics is a sub-field of linguistics that is particularly engaged with professional and institutional interaction in legal contexts. It is also an applied discipline, in that it has real-world applications and its findings can be applied in professional practice. In the remainder of this chapter we will situate forensic linguistics within the discipline of linguistics more generally and show how other linguistic sub-disciplines inform forensic linguistic research. At the heart of linguistics are the basic building blocks of language, its sounds, words, grammar, meanings and functions: *phonetics, phonology, lexis, syntax, semantics*, and *pragmatics*, which we use to describe what we see. There are many sub-fields of linguistics: sociolinguistics, pragmatics, discourse and conversation analysis, critical discourse analysis (CDA), and corpus linguistics, to name but a few. Each involves different concerns with the basic building blocks of language and gives us unique insights into language use in legal settings.

Sociolinguistics and forensic linguistics

Sociolinguistics is concerned with language in society and studies how language varies according to its users and the uses to which it is put. Users and usage are shaped by the variables of gender, ethnicity, age, geographical location, education, and profession and these variables combine and interact, rather than being discrete, but they also actively perform and 'enregister' these linguistic facets in everyday life (Agha 2003; Johnstone 2009). Because legal interaction takes place in specialised social settings rich in combinations of these and other variables, sociolinguistic theory is important for forensic linguistics. Think, for example, of the differences that might occur between a lawyer's language in their consultation with a client, compared with a chat with their daughter on the phone. Bogoch (1994: 70) found that Israeli lawyers in legal-aid consultations used an 'authoritarian', rather than 'participatory' approach, to their clients, which meant pursuing professional goals in a legal register over any of 'the social rituals of everyday encounters', such as performing greeting rituals or expressing emotion.

Groups of speakers, such as lawyers, can be said to form a *speech community* (Gumperz 1968; Labov 1972b) or a *community of practice* (Lave and Wenger

1991), groups of professionals who are 'characterized by regular and frequent interaction' (Gumperz 1968: 114), who create knowledge and 'participat[e] in a set of shared norms' (Labov 1972b: 120–21) and practices. This means that within these communities 'successive utterances are alike or partly alike' (Bloomfield 1926: 153–54), resulting in the same kinds of questions being asked, for example, or prioritising particular legal-professional goals over social ones.

Language not only differs at the level of the group (sociolect, dialect, gender-lect), but also at the level of the individual (idiolect), a concept which is also important for forensic linguists in terms of authorship attribution: determining who wrote a text (a topic which we explore in Chapter 8). The forensic linguist approaches the problem of questioned authorship from the theoretical position that every native speaker has their own distinct and individual version of the language they speak and write, their own *idiolect*, and the assumption that this *idiolect* will manifest itself through distinctive and idiosyncratic choices in speech and writing. The term seems to have been used first by Bloch in 1948, although McMenamin (2002) traces the underlying concept back to the *Biographia Literaria* written in the early nineteenth century by the English poet Coleridge. Every speaker has a very large active vocabulary built up over many years, which will differ from the vocabularies others have similarly built up – these differences will be manifested not only in terms of the actual items available, but also through preferences for selecting certain items rather than others. Thus, whereas in principle any speaker can use any word at any time, in fact they tend to make typical and individuating co-selections of preferred words. This implies that it should be possible to devise a method of *linguistic fingerprinting*, in other words that the linguistic 'impressions' created by a given speaker should be usable, just like a signature, to identify them. So far, however, practice is a long way behind theory, and no one has even begun to speculate about how much and what kind of data would be needed to uniquely characterise an *idiolect*, nor how the data, once collected, would be analysed and stored. Indeed work on the very much simpler task of identifying the linguistic characteristics or 'fingerprints' of single *genres* is still in its infancy (Biber 1988, 1995; Biber *et al.* 2009; Stubbs 1996).

In reality, the concept of the linguistic fingerprint is an unhelpful, if not actually misleading, metaphor, at least when used in the context of forensic investigations of authorship, because it leads one to imagine the creation of massive databanks consisting of representative linguistic samples, or summary linguistic analyses, of millions of idiolects, against which a given text could be matched and tested. In fact such an enterprise is, and for the foreseeable future will continue to be, impractical, if not impossible. The value of the physical fingerprint is that every sample is both identical and exhaustive; that is, it contains all the necessary information for identification of an individual, whereas, by contrast, any linguistic sample, even a very large one, provides only very partial information about its creator. This situation is compounded by the fact that many of the texts which the forensic linguist is asked to examine are very short indeed – most suicide notes, ransom demands and threatening letters, for example, are well under 200 words long and many consist of fewer than 75 words.

Moving beyond variation in terms of groups and individuals, sociolinguists are also concerned with the social contexts of language production and interpretation. Not only did the 1960s and 70s see a social and cultural revolution, but in linguistics, too, the landscape changed, particularly in sociolinguistics and discourse analysis. Gumperz and Hymes (1964, 1972) called their approach to language in society 'the ethnography of communication', grounding communication in close observation of its situations of use, moving theoretical argument away from hypothetical examples and firmly into real empirical data. Hymes (1974) developed the SPEAKING acronym to describe a range of components of the speech situation that need to be taken into account when examining what language is doing. The components are arranged under each of the eight letters: S (Setting and Scene), P (Participants), E (Ends, goals, and outcomes), A (Act sequence), K (Key, tone, and manner), I (Instrumentalities), N (Norms), G (Genre). Legal talk and texts are context-rich, with combinations of setting (courtroom, interview room, consultation), legal and lay participants, legal goals, speech acts that combine to produce a range of legal activities (e.g. cross-examination), a range of speech styles, video-linked testimony, audio and visual recordings, and professional norms and genres. Legal genres, their styles and modes of interaction and the social practices, roles, and participant relationships that they produce, constitute complex interrelationships between text and context. The communicative practices that they employ and the functions that they serve in legal and world contexts make them linguistically distinct. For example, police interviews and courtroom discourse are rich in spatial and temporal expressions (*this, here, now, earlier*) because of the work they do in situating the talk in space and time. If we want to fully account for how these texts work and what speakers are doing when using language, we have to take account of all the contextual variables that affect linguistic choices.

Holmes (2008: 9) builds on and condenses Hymes' model to describe the linguistic choices (who, where, what, why) made in any speech situation:

1   The **participants**: *who* is speaking and *who* are they speaking to?
2   The **setting** or social context of the interaction: *where* are they speaking?
3   The **topic**: *what* is being talked about?
4   The **function**: *why* are they speaking?

She also points out four social dimensions of the context, interrelated with these components:

1.   A *social distance* scale concerned with participant relationships
2.   A *status* scale concerned with participant relationships
3.   A *formality* scale relating to the setting or type of interaction
4.   Two *functional* scales relating to the purposes or topic of interaction.

(Holmes 2008: 10)

Social distance is important in professional discourse because speakers can move between distant styles with low solidarity to more intimate styles with high solidarity. This can be indicated through naming practices, for example. In a police interview with a UK murder suspect, Dr Harold Shipman, the interviewer referred to him mostly with the intimate *you* ('You attended the house at 3 o'clock and that's when you murdered this lady'), but in relation to specific coercive questions that attempted to achieve disclosure, he switched to a more distant *doctor*: 'I'd like to put it to you doctor, that you were the person who administered that lady with the drug, aren't you?'(Interview available online: BBC, 31 January 2000). Shipman's *status* as a doctor is also used to remind the suspect of his medical duty of care, so the distance and status dimensions move the question to a more formal footing, compelling the interviewee to respond. Solidarity or distance can also be understood in terms of 'social accommodation theory', which is seen as a 'contextually complex set of alternatives, ubiquitously available to communicators in face-to-face talk'. It can function 'to index and achieve solidarity with or dissociation from a conversational partner reciprocally and dynamically' (Giles, Coupland and Coupland *et al.* 1991: 2), through 'convergence' or 'divergence' (Giles 1973). The naming strategies, exemplified above (in the police interview and below in the lawyers' closing speeches in court), demonstrate the indexing of convergence with and divergence from Shipman's identity as a doctor. Speakers also accommodate to their audience in what Bell (1991) calls 'audience accommodation' or 'audience design' (Bell 1984). In audience design 'speakers accommodate primarily to their addressee' but also, to a lesser extent, to 'third persons – auditors and overhearers' (Bell 1984: 145). This becomes relevant in the courtroom as lawyers simultaneously address witnesses and the jury, as well as other overhearers, such as the public and the media.

To learn more about audience design in legal discourse, read Haworth's (2013) article on 'audience design in the police interview' and the 'interactional and judicial consequences of audience orientation'. Haworth investigates the communicative challenges interviewees face as they design their talk for the existing audience in the interview room. The police interview is fundamentally a 'transcontextual mode of discourse' (Haworth 2013: 45) in which police officers are eliciting responses that are intended for the future judicial context of the courtroom.

Status is important in forensic discourse as it can be given or taken away, with important effects. In the closing speeches by barristers in the Harold Shipman trial (Days 40-42, HMSO 2001) the prosecution do not acknowledge Shipman's status as a doctor in the way that the defence do. They only refer to him as *Dr Shipman* on 101 occasions (at a rate of 1.5 times per thousand words in a speech of 34,697 words), and in negative contexts, such as 'How is it that Dr. Shipman failed to tell these relatives?' (Day 40). However, 23 per cent of those occurrences are in quotations from witnesses' uses of the term, so the rate is nearer to once per 1,000. By contrast the defence refer to him as *Dr Shipman* four times as frequently (400 times at a rate of four times per 1,000 words in a speech of 51,569 words), using the term respectfully to give him status and making positive points, such as 'Doesn't that demonstrate precisely the point we are seeking to make, that in themselves the actions of Dr. Shipman are not sinister?' (Day 41).

These choices contribute to the construction of the barristers' arguments, painting a contrasting picture of the defendant: as a wicked man capable of murder (the prosecution) and as a caring doctor assiduously tending to his patients (the defence).

Formality is a dimension that could be used to describe the register of written police statements but, as we show in Coulthard's analysis of the Derek Bentley confession (in Chapter 8), the frequency and position of the temporal adverb *then* in Bentley's confession, which, the prosecution claimed, he dictated in his own words to police officers, contained a striking number of *I then ...* sentences, with *then* positioned after the pronoun, rather than before (*Then I ...*), which is more usual in ordinary speech. This gave parts of his statement the formality and style of *policespeak* (Fox 1993) and contributed to Coulthard's opinion at the posthumous appeal hearing that the presence of this feature added support to Bentley's claim that the statement was a document co-constructed by the police and Bentley, undermining the credibility of the police officers and the safety of the 'confession' as evidence.

Holmes's *functional* dimension emphasises two broad functions of language: referential and affective. Most forensic discourse is referential in that it has high information and low affective content, as the example from Bogoch (1994), above, in research with Israeli lawyers in consultations with clients illustrates.

We extend this brief introduction to sociolinguistic theory in Chapters 4 and 5, where we deal with issues of narrative and storytelling in discourse, bilingualism and multilingualism, non-native speakers, and child language in police interviews and courtroom discourse. As we show in Chapter 5, the 'sociolinguistics of narrative' (Thornborrow and Coates 2005) brings storytelling out of the literary domain and into the social world. Law is full of stories and storytelling, and the narrative mode is as important as the legal argument mode, as Harris (2005) and Heffer (2005) explain. Since we live in a multilingual world, bilingual speakers and non-native speakers of English are important constituents of social variation in the justice system, and these speakers are also considered, as are issues of questioning in relation to children and vulnerable witnesses. In Chapter 8, on authorship attribution, we also return to and develop the notion of idiolect.

To read more on sociolinguistics and the legal process, see Gibbons (2003) and Eades (2010b). Gibbons (2003: 1) begins his book by telling us that 'law represents a society's value system, in that it attempts to impose both rights and obligations, proscribing and punishing behavior that goes against a society's norms' and he ends it by saying 'linguistic evidence is of social importance [...] because it may reveal problematic miscommunication, or contribute to the conviction of the guilty and the freeing of the innocent' (2003: 309). Eades (2010b: 11) also casts light on the answers to important sociolinguistic questions, including: 'How can a lawyer destroy a witness's version of events? What impact does cultural difference have on a person's participation in the legal process? Is it fair to subject children to questioning in police interviews or courtroom hearings?' It is apparent from these questions that Eades, like Gibbons, sees sociolinguistic analysis of the legal process as a potentially transformative endeavour, but she also explicitly states what her approach is, saying:

> rigorous sociolinguistic analysis can help us understand the workings of the law and to see its shortcomings as well as its strengths. [...] sociolinguistics can make important contributions to the central question about how social inequality is reproduced both in the legal system and through the legal system.
>
> (Eades 2010b: 12)

A sociolinguistic approach to forensic linguistics is therefore one that seeks to analyse interaction in terms of socially-situated language use and to use that analysis to reveal and transform professional practice and society.

Pragmatics and legal language

Pragmatics is about what we do when we use language, and, as we have already seen, powerful things are done in legal settings, making pragmatics and power something that forensic linguists are keen to identify and explain. Since language is always socially situated, pragmatics and sociolinguistics overlap. Using pragmatic knowledge, we understand meaning in context, so, for example, we understand address terms (titles: *Mrs, Dr*; kinship: *mum, granny*, and endearments: *love, babe*) depending on the context we are in. We would not expect to be called *love* in a formal encounter with the police, and if used in this context it might lead to a feeling of being patronised, but in intimate contexts offence is unlikely. There are frequent news stories on this topic, such as 'Don't patronize me, Darling' (Crabb 2014).

It is often the little words that do the biggest job, as in the case of *discourse markers* which are function words and interjections such as: *but, so, well, you know,* and the ubiquitous *like* (Schiffrin 1987). As Green (1990: 250–51) points out, 'these little words are often overlooked, because they do not refer to observable properties or events, but, in their own way, they may speak volumes about the person who uses them' and/or the significance of the utterance. They are pragmatic 'as their presence or absence can affect the illocutionary force of the utterance' (Hale 1999: 58). They are usually in turn-initial position and they mark the pragmatic force of the turn. Hale's innovative (1999) study examined interpreters' treatment of discourse markers (DMs) in courtroom questions (see also Hale 2004), and she found that in lawyers' questions they served as 'devices of argumentation, combativeness and even control' (Hale 1999: 59). Not surprisingly, perhaps, since they can easily go unnoticed, she also found that 'these markers tend to go missing in most of the interpreters' renditions of the lawyer's talk' (see Extract 2.1 below). She examined the occurrence of *well, see,* and *now* and found that while *now* was more prominent in examination-in-chief, *well* was much more prominent in cross-examination and *see* only occurred in cross-examination. Extract 2.1 (from Hale 1999: 62–63) has examples of *well, now, but, right* and *so* being used in cross-examination.

Extract 2.1

Interpreted courtroom cross-examination

Q = lawyer; INT = interpreter; A = witness; *italics* for Spanish language use; (brackets) for English translation. Our emphasis of DMs in **bold**.

Q1:	Uh do you accept that you filled out a claim, an insurance claim for the car on the 23 July?
INT	*Acepta usted de que usted llenó un formulario de reclamo de seguros el 23 de julio?*
	(Do you accept that you filled out an insurance claim form on 23 July?)
A1	*Mm, que lo llené sí, que sea el 23 no estoy seguro.*
	(Uhm, that I filled it out, yes, that it was on 23, I'm not sure.)
INT	I accept that uh I filled it up but I'm not sure whether it was the 23rd.
Q2	Uhm, **well** when you filled out the insurance claim, your wife did that on your behalf, is that correct?
INT	*Cuando usted llenó el formulario de reclamo de seguro su esposa lo hizo por usted, verdad?*
	(When you filled out the insurance claim form your wife did it for you, right?)
A2	*Cuando, cuando se llenó, no cuando lo llené. Creo que fue ella porque buscaba la ayuda de otra gente que hablaba mejor que, mejor que ella todavía.*
	(When, when it was filled out, not when I filled it out, I think it was her because I was looking for help from people who'd speak better than, better than her even.)
INT	Uh when it was filled up not when I filled it up, uh, I remember that it was her because I was also looking for the help of other people that would speak English better than her even.
Q3	**Now**, in relation to the day you filled out the insurance claim form can you be more specific as to when the police told you that your car had been found.
INT	*En cuanto al día que usted llenó la aplicación, o que se llenó la aplicación, puede ser más específico en cuanto a la fecha que la policía le dijo de que había encontrado el coche?*
	(With regards to the date you filled out the application, or that the application was filled out, could you be more specific regarding the date the police told you that they had found the car?)
A3	*Tal vez no pueda ser más específico porque hace mucho tiempo de eso que no no tengo una secuencia de datos exactos (something else inaudible).*
	(Maybe I can't be more specific because it's been a long time since then and I don't don't have a sequence of the exact details.)
INT	Uh, perhaps I cannot give you uh, I cannot really be more specific because it's been so long ago and I have not in my mind a precise sequence of events, I wasn't prepared for this.

[...]	[Two more questions and answers: Q4 introduces a new theme of where the form came from and Q5 asks 'So did the insurance agent come round to your house on the 23rd?']
Q6	**But** you filled out the form on the 23rd?
INT	**Pero** *usted llenó ese formulario el 23.*
	(**But** you filled out that form on the 23rd.)
A6	*¿No le he dicho que no estoy seguro? ha pasada tanto tiempo.*
	(Haven't I told you that I'm not sure? It's been so long.)
INT	I have said I am not sure, it was so long ago.
Q7	**Right**, uh, **well** you accept that you filled out the form on the 23rd.
INT	*Acepta usted que usted llenó el formulario el 23?*
	(Do you accept that you filled out the form on the 23rd?)
A7	*No tengo la ..., you no sé exactamente la fecha en que lo llenaron.*
	(I haven't got a, I don't know exactly the date they filled it out.)
INT	I don't know exactly the day it was filled up.
Q8	**Well**, where did you get the form from to fill out?
INT	*Dónde obtuvo el formulario para llenarlo?*
	(Where did you get the form from to fill it?)

The lawyer prefaces his turns with *well* in questions 2, 7 and 8, pragmatically signalling his rejection of the witness's previous answer and 'provok[ing] him/ her by proposing something different, which [is] generally contentious' (Hale 1999: 60). Hale (1999: 60) also notes that '"well" often tends to act as a sign of contradiction and confrontation, expecting disagreement', because 'questions beginning with "well" can be said to be "negative conducive" (Hudson 1975)'. The use of *now* in question three dismisses the witness's answer, by moving on, and the use of *so* in question five attempts 'to finalize the question about the date' (Hale 1999: 64) and, as Schiffrin (1985) notes, comes at a possible completion point. The *but* in question six is particularly argumentative, restating the date issue. As Hale (1999: 65) notes, 'not once does the interpreter translate the discourse marker "well"'. Only *but* is translated in question six. The effect of these omissions, Hale (1999: 65) suggests, is that 'the interpreter seems to act as a shield, where the message is muted by an unofficial filtering, deflecting the aggression that comes from both sides' and also the *illocutionary force* (the speaker's intention in producing the utterance) of the message is altered, misrepresented, or lost. The pragmatic functions of these little words to reject, dismiss, argue, and provoke are therefore important.

Pragmatics also allows us to explain principles that operate in conversation and in legal conversations in particular. Grice's cooperative principle (CP) (Grice 1975 in Jaworski and Coupland 2006) is a pragmatic principle, which presupposes that one's conversational contribution should be 'such as is required, at the stage at which it occurs, by the accepted purpose or direction of the talk exchange in which [one] is engaged' (Grice 1975: 45). Clearly, the courtroom (and the police interview room) is a place where interaction is not always inherently cooperative, as Levinson (1992) points out, and may be deliberately argumentative. Of interrogation, Levinson says: 'it is unlikely that either party assumes the other is fulfilling the maxims of quality, manner, and especially quantity (requiring that one say as much as is required by the other)' (1992: 76). Cross-examination is an activity where witnesses expect to be challenged and even tricked, and cooperating with the questions would play straight into the lawyer's hands. In Extract 2.1, for example, the witness tries to resist the lawyer's argument and does not cooperate in providing the quality or quantity of information the lawyer requires.

Pragmatics is a fascinating and necessary field for us to explore, as pragmatic usage influences the ways that lawyers and other legal professionals' attempt to control witnesses and are resisted, the ways that speakers indicate meaning, the ways that politeness and impoliteness are used, and the ways that professional speakers coerce and confront lay speakers in talk. Pragmatic competence is an important component of professional discourse and therefore integral to forensic discourse and conversation analysis.

(Critical) Discourse and Conversation Analysis

In the 39 years since *An Introduction to Discourse Analysis* was published (Coulthard 1977) descriptive linguistics has been transformed. The creation of massive corpora, the rapid development of the worldwide web, and technological innovations in mobile communications have contributed to major changes in the way that language itself is viewed and have increased the availability and varieties of real language for analysis. In 2003, Michael Stubbs, in The Third Sinclair Open Lecture (Stubbs 2004), asked the question: what happened to discourse analysis? The term 'discourse analysis' is now found preceded by a wide range of modifying adjectives: *anthropological, child, cognitive, critical, educational, ethnographic, feminist, legal, medical, multimodal, political, psychotherapeutic* and, of course, *forensic discourse analysis.* The answer, then, to Stubbs' question is clearly that discourse analysis has proliferated and branched off into a number of specific sub-domains, one of those being forensic discourse analysis. It is concerned with specific institutional functions of language both above the level of the sentence in turntaking, topic creation, and text structure, and at the level of the word or particle in the use of discourse markers, terms of address, pauses, hesitations, and even laughter. Discourse analysis (DA) takes account of intonation, *paralinguistic* features (gesture, gaze direction, facial expressions) and examines pragmatic features, such as interruption, politeness, and question design. Forensic DA is chiefly concerned with *dyadic* interaction, conversations between two speakers (e.g. lawyer/witness; police officer/suspect), though, as we have seen, there are sometimes three people in the interaction in interpreted talk (see discussion of the impact of this in Russell's 2002 article, 'Three's a crowd: shifting dynamics in the interpreted interview') and there is often a solicitor present, making occasional interventions (see Stokoe and Edwards 2010).

A key conversation analytic (CA) study was Atkinson and Drew's (1979) analysis of courtroom cross-examination interaction, in which they show in detail how cross-examination questions are designed to perform actions that can allocate blame to a witness. DA and CA are sometimes seen as discrete subdisciplines, but there are many overlaps and commonalities (see Wooffitt 2005). Both are concerned with what language does in interaction, but CA restricts itself to the microanalysis of talk (see, for example, Stokoe and Edwards's 2010 analysis of lawyers' interventions in police interviews), while DA analyses broader functions of both talk and text.

A guiding principle of CA is that speaking turns should run smoothly, in line with Sacks *et al.*'s (1974: 700) 'simplest systematics' of turn-taking: only one person speaks at a time, meaning that 'overlap is usually brief' and interruption is constrained; 'order and distribution are not determined in advance'; 'size of turn varies'; and 'what is said and done is not determined in advance'. The principles of legal discourse vary from ordinary conversation in that in courtroom and police interview discourse turns are allocated equally (in terms of number of turns), but the amount of talk is constrained and controlled. In terms of topic, this is usually tightly controlled by the police officer or lawyer's questions. While we would expect the professional to lead the talk, because of this activity's 'turn-type pre-allocation' (Atkinson and Drew 1979) where questioning and answering are pre-allocated to the professional and the lay person respectively, lay people can influence topic and turn length by taking control.

DA is not just a descriptive endeavour; it is also applied. In Part II of this book we look at cases where institutional practices have been disputed and where DA is employed through the reports and evidence of experts to uncover what might have happened. Chapter 6 discusses a number of cases that use discourse and pragmatic analyses of notes and interview records. Forensic discourse analysis is, therefore, concerned with activities involved in the collection and interpretation of evidence. Some of these activities are later disputed, usually by a lay participant. In the first volume of the journal *Forensic Linguistics*, Shuy (1994) reports how he acted as an expert in a civil lawsuit against a car dealership in which a deaf man brought charges of false imprisonment and fraud. Because he was deaf, the interaction, which involved inquiring about purchasing a car, had been carried out through handwritten notes, which both the dealer and the customer produced. Each of the 101 separate pieces of paper consisted of a two-part exchange as in 22:

> Ex. 22. *Salesperson:*   Which one do you like? Lower Price. Demo.
>   *Bien:*   Demonstration model.
>   (Shuy 1994: 134)

Shuy's task 'as an expert linguist' was to produce a report that analysed the exchanges 'for clues to temporality and to either verify or correct the sequence they [the plaintiff and his attorneys] proposed' (Shuy 1994: 134). To do this Shuy looked at topic and response, speech acts, and the sequence of service encounters, to uncover what the judge called 'an anatomy of a car sale' (Shuy 1994: 148). Linguistic evidence using DA supported the plaintiff's case; the jury found in his favour and he was awarded $6 million in damages.

Critical discourse analysis (CDA) is a form of discourse analysis that seeks to bring to our notice:

> how discourse is shaped by relations of power and ideologies, and the constructive effects that discourse has upon social identities, social relations and systems of knowledge, and belief, none of which is normally apparent to discourse participants.
>
> (Fairclough 1992: 12)

It also aims to bring about change in the social world through the results of its close textual analysis. Forensic discourse analysis becomes 'critical' when it comments on the discourse practices of judges, lawyers, police officers, and other legal professionals. Heydon (2005) combines CA and CDA methodologies in her study of Australian police interviewing. She demonstrates the police interview's power in creating 'a police version of events' out of the suspect's version and 'in favour of a competing suspect version' (Heydon 2005: 145). The critical analysis highlights police interview myths (e.g. that the police interviewer understands the interviewee and vice versa) and the ways that the institutional voice produces assumptions which have 'the potential to seriously undermine the success of the interview', resulting in 'failure to obtain a voluntary confession' and 'the potential to erode the case for the prosecution in court' (Heydon, 2005: 191–92). Police interviewers have powerful narrative-transforming skills (Johnson 2008), which, Heydon tells us, are able to 'introduce alternative versions which cast the suspect's actions as remiss or deficient and emphasis[e] the violent or otherwise socially undesirable aspects of the narrative" (Heydon, 2005: 146). CA and DA, therefore, have important messages to transmit to the communities of police interviewers around the world, work which Heydon (2012) and others are engaged in.

We said that gender was a variable in sociolinguistics; it is also an important component of DA, as Matoesian (e.g. 2003, 2010) and Ehrlich (e.g. 2001; 2007) show in their extensive analysis of power, patriarchy, and domination in rape trial discourse. Matoesian (1993) shows how cross-examination of rape victims in court amounts to 'reproducing rape', whereby rape victims are revictimised by their courtroom experience. Ehrlich's (2001: 95) feminist-linguistic analysis of a rape tribunal's questioning of the complainant introduces the notion of 'an ideological frame of utmost resistance', which 'functions as a discursive constraint, restricting the complainants' "talk" about their experiences and producing them as particular kinds of subjects – as ineffectual agents, that is, as agents whose so-called passivity and lack of resistance is considered tantamount to consent'. For example, the complainant is asked by the tribunal chair:

> In your statement, I think, twice, you mention 'he was sounding very angry' and 'I was scared' and I was wondering if you could elaborate on what you mean by that? What was he saying that you found scary?

She replies:

> It was rough. It was mostly ... he just ... it was demanding. I didn't feel like I had any more choice. And whatever he said was no longer a request. It was a demand.

(Ehrlich 2001: 94)

In her analysis, Ehrlich (2001: 95) suggests that 'complainants' representations of themselves as "passive" and "ineffectual" is an institutionally-coerced performance of stereotypical femininity: the complainants are "thrust into" this particular subject position'. Institutional discourse therefore shapes and constructs gendered and sexist representations of subjects.

Discourse transcription

Matoesian and Ehrlich's work also points out the importance of discourse transcription in helping the reader 'see' what is going on in courtroom talk. DA and CA crucially depend on the transcription of professional talk, as Eades (1996) tells us in her article on 'verbatim courtroom transcripts and discourse analysis'. However, transcription is not always straightforward, never neutral and very time-consuming and, even then, transcriptions are always mediations of the talk: 'all transcription involves choices, both in what is written down and what is left out, as well as in how talk is represented' (Eades 2010b: 16). Transcription requires a set of conventions for converting talk into text, such as underlining to indicate a stressed syllable and the use of double brackets to indicate paralinguistic activity in a conversation: ((interviewer consults notes)). Square brackets indicate where talk overlaps between speakers, the equals sign indicates latched utterances (where one speaker latches on to the speech of another with no pause), and the colon indicates lengthening of vowels (e.g. wro:::ng'). Discourse analysis transcription conventions can be found in, for example, Schiffrin (1994), with conversation analysis ones in Jefferson (2004), though many of the conventions are common to both. Where video material is transcribed, additional difficulties present themselves. Matoesian (2010: 541), contributing to the multimodal turn in DA, deals with both the speech and visual signs in a rape victim's narrative to the court in examination-in-chief. He demonstrates how 'both language and embodied conduct mutually contextualize one another in a reciprocal dialectic' (Matoesian 2010: 541), emphasising the need for multimodal transcription (words, intonation and emphasis, and bodily action), and showing how gesture, gaze and posture are 'interwoven into the stream of verbal activity in [a] rape victim's narrative'. In his discussion of the witness's use of the phrase, 'What he did to me was wro:::ng', he points out that the witness moves her gaze to the defendant on 'was'. Also, her production of the word 'wro:::ng' is preceded by 'marked pointing beats', which begin in a pause before the phrase, producing an 'embodied accusation' of the defendant (Matoesian 2010: 548), and then culminate in 'gestural hold toward the defendant during vowel lengthening'.

Through this multimodal structure 'the victim bestows a powerful sense of modal intensity to her verbal conduct' (Matoesian 2010: 552).

Transcription is a painstaking job, but we also have large bodies of written and transcribed discourse available, as a result of electronic communication and digital archives of electronically stored texts in the form of *corpora*. Corpus linguistics has, therefore, become an increasingly essential methodology for forensic linguists to acquire.

Corpus linguistics

Corpus linguistics is essentially a methodology which is useful when there are large bodies of text to analyse. In an always-connected world huge amounts of electronic data are being generated every day and, therefore, tools which can examine this data are important for linguists generally, and forensic linguists, in particular. While DA and CA predominantly use qualitative methods, corpus linguistics combines both quantitative and qualitative methods in a complementary approach, rendering insights potentially more objective and allowing the analyst to identify patterns of use and, therefore, of meaning, across multiple examples. These patterns can easily be seen in the form of concordance lines, using computer programs such as *Wordsmith* (Scott 2012) and *Antconc* (Anthony 2014). Quantification produces 'statistically reliable and generalisable results' and, complemented by qualitative analysis, produces a 'greater richness and precision' (McEnery and Wilson 2001: 77). These advantages mean that corpus linguistics meets the standards of producing rigorous empirical results (See Grant 2013; Solan 2013.), which forensic linguists require for their opinions to be accepted in the courts and in other investigative arenas.

Coulthard (1994) was one of the first to point out the usefulness of corpus approaches to authorship analysis and, more recently, Cotterill (2010) has explained how corpus linguistics can be used in forensic linguistics, drawing on her own corpus-driven study of language use in the O.J. Simpson trial (Cotterill 2003). Corpus-assisted work, such as Heffer's (2005) study of legal-lay language in British jury trials, produces a complex model of trial communication and enables Heffer to demonstrate consistent patterns of language and meaning in a large and representative corpus of trial transcripts. In the applied linguistics field Koester (2010) makes the case for 'small specialized corpora', as does Flowerdew (2004), arguing for the use of 'specialised corpora to understand academic and professional settings'. Kredens and Coulthard (2012) bring this applied work into the forensic field in their discussion of corpus linguistics in authorship identification, and a 2015 special issue of the journal *Corpora* is devoted to corpus approaches to forensic linguistics (Larner 2015).

With large and small corpora to analyse, we need tools that are capable of assisting us. In 'Tools for the trade' (Woolls and Coulthard 1998) and 'Better tools for the trade' (Woolls 2003) Woolls and Coulthard describe some computational tools, not specifically designed for forensic linguistic analysis, but which can and have been used, particularly in authorship attribution cases (See also Woolls 2010;

2015). Among these is *Wordsmith* (Scott 2012) whose features enable us to examine both large and small corpora through wordlists, concordances, collocation patterns, and keywords.

Wordlists allow us to see those words that are used most frequently in a text, and Coulthard shows how *Wordsmith* would have been very useful in his analysis of the Derek Bentley confession. Rather than the many hours of analysis that it took to identify *then* as a significant marker of police authorship, *Wordsmith* can instantly show that this word, out of all the words in the text, is in eighth most frequent position, compared with fifty-eighth in the spoken corpus of The Bank of English (Cobuild's 400 million-word corpus) and eighty-third in The Bank of English overall (Woolls and Coulthard 1998: 35). *Concordances* allow us to see the word we are interested in in its context of use, so in the case of *then*, *Wordsmith* shows the marked post-positioning of *then* (Figure 2.1, in lines 4–9) after the subject, rather than before it.

Collocation is the study of words that frequently co-occur. There have been '50-something years of work on collocations' (Gries 2013), starting with the work of Firth who said, in a now much-quoted phrase: 'you shall know a word by the company it keeps' (Firth 1957: 179). In 1959, Quirk and others began to compile the *Survey of English Usage,* a corpus which now totals 1 million words and which led to the creation of The International Corpus of English usage (ICE), which has a set of 1 million-word corpora covering many of the world's Englishes, including from Canada, India, Jamaica, Sri Lanka, and New Zealand (ICE 2015).

The corpus linguistics field made a great leap forward from the paper-based Survey when computers became ubiquitous, and in the 1980s and 90s Sinclair (e.g. Sinclair 1991), Leech (e.g. Garside, Leech and Sampson *et al.* 1987), and others used computers to kick-start the modern corpus revolution. Through his work on Cobuild's Bank of English corpus, Sinclair developed the idea of the

1	Chris fired again <u>then</u> and this policeman fell down.
2	We got off at West Croydon and <u>then</u> walked down the road
3	We all talked together and <u>then</u> Norman Parsley and Frank Fazey left.
4	Chris <u>then</u> jumped up the drainpipe to the roof
5	Chris <u>then</u> jumped over and I followed.
6	Chris Craig and I <u>then</u> caught a bus to Croydon.
7	told me that they had called and I <u>then</u> ran after them.
8	The policeman and I <u>then</u> went round a corner by a door.
9	The policeman <u>then</u> pushed me down the stairs and I did not see
10	Up to <u>then</u> Chris had not said anything.
11	<u>Then</u> someone in the garden on the opposite side

Figure 2.1 Concordance of all of the occurrences of *then* in Derek Bentley's statement

'idiom principle', an assumption that 'a language user has available to him or her a large number of semi-preconstructed phrases that constitute single choices' (Sinclair 1991: 109). This makes collocation a principle that determines lexical choice, meaning that we do not just select individual words but combinations of one or more words: collocates. Collocations can therefore be described as 'the characteristic co-occurrence patterns of words' (McEnery and Wilson 2001: 85). Coulthard (e.g. 2004; 2013) has shown that the 'co-selection' of words in pairs or lexical strings is what quickly makes individual style unique, allowing forensic linguists to use collocation patterns as markers of authorship in author identification and in plagiarism detection (Johnson and Woolls 2009). For example, Mollin's (2009) study of Prime Minister Tony Blair's language found that *I completely understand* is a 'Blairism'.

Wright (2014) and Johnson and Wright's (2014) work on collocation patterns, or n-grams (two to six-word chunks of language) in the Enron corpus draws on Turell's (2010) notion of 'idiolectal style', which defines this in three parts as:

> a) how this system [of language or dialect], shared by lots of people, is used in a distinctive way by a particular individual; b) the speaker/writer's production, which appears to be 'individual' and 'unique' (Coulthard 2004) and also c) Halliday's (1989) proposal of 'options' and 'selections' from these options.
>
> (Turell 2010: 217)

Wright (2013) found that, even in generically conventional parts of emails – openings and closings – for four authors belonging to the same profession (traders) within Enron – greetings and farewells could be very distinctive, when measured against another 126 authors from the corpus of 176. Their 'consistency' (Grant 2013) in terms of greeting and punctuation (*Hi/Hey/*no greeting; Name+comma/colon/no punctuation) produced distinctive patterns of use, but so did their variation. Each author's range of greetings and farewells contributed to the picture of their idiolect. One of the authors, Zipper, 'was the least variable in terms of his opening greetings [7 different forms over 247 emails], yet he is by far the most variable in his use of farewells [30 different forms]', showing 'that email writers can be more variable in their linguistic selections within one email convention than they may be in others' (Wright 2013: 58). The kinds of variation in greetings and farewells can also contribute to a pattern of distinctiveness. Zipper's seven different greeting forms differ from other authors' forms, making his particular variations distinctive.

Keywords are calculated by *Wordsmith* using log likelihood to list in keyness order those words 'whose frequency is unusually high [in a particular dataset] in comparison with some norm' (Scott 2010: 156). The computer compares all the words used in the study corpus with all the words in a (usually much larger) comparison or reference corpus. So in the case of the Enron study (Wright 2014; Johnson and Wright 2014) the specialised Enron corpus was compared with the 450-million word Corpus of Contemporary American (COCA) (Davies 2012).

Unsurprisingly, perhaps, for a corpus of emails, *please* and *thanks* were both keywords, with *thanks* being top and *please* being second. Keywords therefore tell us what the corpus is about and what its central lexical concerns are. Within the Enron corpus of 176 authors, where almost all the authors use *please* and *thanks* across their emails, you might imagine that it would, therefore, be impossible to use these words as evidence of idiolectal style. Not so. Johnson and Wright (2014: 48) found that in the case of Derrick, Enron's chief lawyer, he consistently used *thank you* rather than *thanks* (the top ranked keyword in the Enron corpus, while *thank* is ranked 444th), making his usage entirely the reverse of the general trend. Indeed his usage of *thank* accounts for 10 per cent of its frequency – and it co-occurs with *you* in all 132 instances; by contrast, '*thanks* is used only ten times and is a negative keyword in his dataset, meaning that he uses it significantly less than all of the other authors in the Enron corpus' (Johnson and Wright 2014: 48). Keywords can evidently be very important in understanding idiolectal style within generic conventions, such as the openings and closings of emails.

Another forensic corpus study, Shapero's (2011) study of 286 suicide notes collected from Birmingham Coroner's Office, found, poignantly and remarkably, that the top lexical keyword for both men and women was *love*. In suicide notes by women the top six keywords (including function words) were: *I, my, you, x, me, love* (2011: 176) and for men they were: *I, you, love, my, me* and *sorry* (2011: 177).

Corpus linguistics, like the other fields we have discussed in this chapter, is important to forensic linguistics because of its methodology (in this case the complementary quantitative and qualitative approach) and the findings that this methodology can uncover, contributing to new linguistic knowledge and theory. It is also important because of its applications in casework and the empirical rigour that its methodology can bring to this work.

Conclusion

The triad of sociolinguistics, pragmatics and discourse analysis is essential to our understanding of the different situations of text and talk in the legal and judicial system. Who is speaking, to whom, where, when and why are all important contextual components of the many different settings and activities involved. The methods and approaches of these disciplines, along with critical discourse analysis and corpus linguistic methodologies, can help us not only to understand the ways in which speakers in legal settings accomplish legal and lay goals, but also to critique and change them.

Students and scholars can equip themselves with these resources to make sense of legal genres, both through studying texts that are the product of legal contexts and through ethnographic research that involves observing language in its contexts of production and use. Although gaining access to many of these domains, such as police interviews or lawyer consultations with clients, is not at all easy, students and researchers can gain insights and understanding through analysing some of the texts that are available on the internet and by vicarious involvement – that is by learning from the experiences of others, by reading ethnographically based research (e.g. Rock 2007; Scheffer 2006), and also by analysing the fictional and real-life examples provided in films and on television. Television frequently gives viewers lengthy opportunities to get inside the mind of the real-life legal professional, whether it be police officer, lawyer or judge. 'Reality TV' shows also provide real situations for analysis, as Linfoot-Ham (2006) demonstrates in her discussion of the American reality TV show 'Cops'. Some suggestions for reading and follow-up activities, related to the extracts, theories and methods explored in this chapter, are provided below.

Further reading

Jaworski, A. and Coupland, N. (eds) (2006) provide a discourse analysis reader featuring important original works by leading analysts. In addition, follow up reading which is referred to in the works cited throughout this chapter. You can find the full bibliographic references at the end of the book.

Research task

1 Examine in more detail and discuss Extract 2.1 and read Hales' (1999) analysis of this and other pragmatic effects of discourse markers in interpreted legal interaction.

3 The language of the law

Counter-Terrorism and Security Act 2015, UK
An Act to make provision in relation to terrorism; to make provision about retention of communications data, about information, authority to carry and security in relation to air, sea and rail transport and about reviews by the Special Immigration Appeals Commission against refusals to issue certificates of naturalisation; and for connected purposes.

Be it enacted by the Queen's Most Excellent Majesty, by and with the advice and consent of the Lords Spiritual and Temporal, and the Commons, in this present Parliament assembled, and by the authority of the same, as follows:—

(www.legislation.gov.uk)

Sir Edward Coke's (1628) definition of murder
Murder is when a man of sound memory and of the age of discretion, unlawfully killeth within any County of the Realm any reasonable creature in *rerum natura* under the Kings [sic] peace, with malice fore-thought, either expressed by the party or implied by law, so as the party wounded or hurt, *et cetera*, die of the wound or hurt, *et cetera*, within a year and a day after the same.

(Coke 1681: 47)

Introduction

Anyone who hears the term 'legal language' thinks immediately of grammatically complex, sparsely punctuated, over-lexicalised, opaque, written text. Is this characterisation accurate and, if so, how did it come to be so?

Tiersma (2001: 75) notes that in Anglo-Saxon times legal language was entirely oral, with written text, when it eventually came to be used, serving at first only as a record of what had already been performed orally:

> What mattered was what was *said* by the participants, not what was *written* by a scribe. The written documents were merely *evidentiary* of the oral ceremony, rather than operative or dispositive legal documents in the modern sense.

Hence the expression 'An Englishman's word is his bond …'. However, over time, the written document, instead of being simply a record of what had already been accomplished orally, that is of the *performative* act, came to constitute the performative act itself, although it took a long time, and in some areas of the law, like the British marriage ceremony for instance, the spoken word still retains its pre-eminence. Tiersma notes a significant change in 1540, when the Statute of Wills made it compulsory to bequeath 'real' property in writing; but, even so, it was another century before the Statute of Frauds in 1677 made it compulsory to bequeath goods and chattels by written will. So Shakespeare, in bequeathing his 'second best bed' to his wife in his will, dated 1616, was obviously being overzealous or over-cautious. Contracts can still, even today, be purely oral, although typically there must also be a written record, or *memorandum*, of the contract. Even so, the memorandum may be nothing more than a sales receipt and legally it is simply the written evidence that there was an oral agreement; it does not constitute the contract itself.

Even in the area of legislation, the written text was originally primarily a report of what had been said. Tiersma notes that Edward the Confessor's eleventh-century laws were prefaced by *we cwaedon*, translatable as 'we have pronounced'. He also observes that, although Parliament started to enact, or at least approve, legislation towards the end of the thirteenth century, it was not until the fifteenth century that written documents finally came to 'constitute the law itself'; in other words the text of the statute rather than the intentions of the law-makers had now become 'authoritative' (2001: 77). The current situation, under what lawyers call the *plain meaning rule*, is that:

> unless there is an ambiguity obvious from the text itself, anything that the legislature said or did outside of the text itself cannot be used to interpret it.
> (Solan 1993 quoted in Tiersma 2001: 77)

Because the crucial period for the textualising of the law was during the period when the king and the nobility standardly spoke French, legal language still displays significant French influences. At first, French was the language of the courts, though from very early on there were concessions to the fact that the language of the majority of the population was English. One surviving lexico-grammatical consequence of the two languages working side by side is the frequent use of *binomials*; that is, pairs of originally synonymous words taken from the two languages like *goods* and *chattels*, *breaking* and *entering*, *acknowledge* and *confess*, with the English member as the first in the pair (see Tiersma 1999: 32). Indeed, binomials are up to five times more frequent in English legal language than in most other prose genres. For centuries the law worked with a strange mixture of the two languages (as well as Latin), nicely exemplified from this extract from a case report written by Mr Justice Hutton Legge in 1631:

> [The prisoner] sudenment throwe ove grand violence un great stone al heade del it Seignior Rychardson quel per le mercy del Dieu did come close to his

hatt et missed him … et le stone hitt the wanescott behind them and gave a great rebound, quel si ceo stone had hitt le dit Seignior Rychardson il voet have killee him.

(Tiersma 1999: 33)

Gradually, the English language drove out the French, and by the sixteenth century the number of French legal terms in active use had shrunk to under a thousand (Tiersma 1999: 32). Melinkoff suggests that 'one reason for the use of French in legal documents was the urge to have a secret language and to preserve a professional monopoly' (Maley 1994: 12). It was not until 1650 that Parliament passed a law requiring that all case reports and law books should be in 'the English Tongue onely' and also that earlier reports of judicial decisions and other law books should be translated into English. However, almost immediately, in 1660, the Act was repealed and the old state of affairs reinstated, with many of the case reports being again written in French and some of the court records even being written in Latin. The use of French and Latin in legal proceedings was only finally and permanently ended in 1731 (Tiersma 1999: 35–36). Its history, therefore, is one of the reasons why legal lexis is complex; the law is also characterised by conservatism, which leads to it holding on to otherwise archaic words.

Legal style and register

Legal language's reputation for archaisms and convoluted syntax, or 'lexical obscurity' and 'syntactic anfractuosity', as Alcaraz-Varó (2008: 100–1) puts it, is well documented, but as Halliday (1973: 34) points out 'language is as it is because of what it has to do'. This is nowhere truer than in legal settings. Ritual openings of encounters, such as the reading of the police caution or the Miranda Warnings at the beginning of an interview, the 'enacting formula', (of the first epigraph) that begins all UK Acts of Parliament and 'endows legislative texts with their formal, imperious quality' (Maley 1994: 20), the reading of the indictment at a court hearing, all use formulaic expressions, which signal the start of a formal legal process. On the one hand, we can argue that such language is difficult to understand and therefore distances and disadvantages the lay participant, particularly speakers with low levels of literacy or for whom English is a foreign or second language (e.g. Stygall 2010), but an alternative functional perspective is that the formulaic formality is part of the way the participants orient to what is going on. It is a signal that a formal 'high stakes' activity is starting and, when it is absent, readers or listeners may not understand the legal nature of the encounter. Davies (2014: 271), for example, notes that *The* [UK] *Highway Code* 'does not immediately invoke the genre of legal language', even though it has to be interpreted as such. Legal language and style, therefore, needs to be acknowledged and understood in order to make sense of legal texts.

As we noted above, one of the comments most frequently made about legal language is that it is impenetrable. As Bhatia (1993: 101) puts it:

legislative writing has acquired a certain degree of notoriety rarely equalled by any other variety of English. It has long been criticized for its obscure expressions and circumlocutions, long-winded involved constructions and tortuous syntax, apparently meaningless repetitions and archaisms.

Extract 3.1, (with instances of archaisms, repetitions, long-winded involved constructions and complex syntax italicised), which is taken from Section 15A of the British Theft (Amendment) Act 1996, demonstrates this very clearly.

Extract 3.1
Theft (Amendment) Act 1996
An Act to amend the Theft Act 1968 and the Theft Act 1978; and for connected purposes. *Be it enacted by* [enactment formula continues …]:–

15A-Obtaining a money transfer by deception.

(1) A person is guilty of an offence if by any deception he dishonestly obtains a money transfer *for himself or another*.
(2) A money transfer occurs when–

   (a) debit is made to one account,
   (b) a credit is made to another, and
   (c) the credit results from the debit or the debit results from the credit.

(3) References to a credit and to a debit are to a credit of an amount of money and to a debit of an amount of money.
(4) *It is immaterial (in particular)-*

   (a) *whether the amount credited is the same as the amount debited;*
   (b) *whether the money transfer is effected on presentment of a cheque or by another method;*
   (c) *whether any delay occurs in the process by which the money transfer is effected;*
   (d) *whether any intermediate credits or debits are made in the course of the money transfer;*
   (e) *whether either of the accounts is overdrawn before or after the money transfer is effected.*

(5) A person guilty of an offence under this section *shall be* liable on conviction on indictment to imprisonment for a term not exceeding ten years.

From the perspective of the legal drafter, that is of the professionals whose job it is to convert legal intentions into unambiguous prose, the constructions in the italicised sections are 'devices which bring precision, clarity, unambiguity and all-inclusiveness', but a critical perspective would argue that they are a 'ploy to promote solidarity between members of the specialist community, and to keep non-specialists at a respectable distance' (Bhatia 1993: 102). These opposing views of legal language show that the legal drafter is in an unenviable position, striving to use language to 'do justice to the intent of Parliament and, at the same time, to facilitate comprehension of the unfolding text for ordinary readership' (Bhatia 1993: 103). Equally importantly, s/he has also to protect the intended interpretation against uncooperative readings by skilful lawyers. Thus we can see that there is a major difference between insider and outsider views of legal language and what we hope to show is that an insider view is one that does give meaning to text that the outsider often thinks is deliberately obscure and at times totally impenetrable.

An analysis of the style of legal statutes reveals consistently used linguistic forms and syntactic features that contribute to characterising the genre. These include the already mentioned binomial expressions (Gustafsson 1984) (*by and with the advice and consent*), complex prepositions (Quirk 1982: 302; Bhatia 1993: 107) (*in the course of*) and long, complex, multi-clause sentences with syntactic matching in the subordinate clauses (such as section 15A (4) of the Act in Extract 3.1). These features make this text instantly identifiable as an example of the genre of a written legal statute. (In the research tasks you are invited to compare similar legal writing – terms and conditions and contracts – with statutes to see how similar they are.)

One of the important characteristics of legal language is the selection of a technical vocabulary or register. This leads us to ask: 'What is meant by a legal register and which words are legal words or, rather, which are found more frequently in legal texts?' Crystal (2003: 374) points to the particular nature of legislative language by noting that it:

> depends a great deal on a fairly small set of grammatical and lexical features. For example, modal verbs (e.g. *must, shall, may*) distinguish between obligation and discretion. Pronouns (e.g. *all, whoever*) and generic nouns (hypernyms, e.g. *vehicle, person*) help foster a law's general applicability. Certainty can be promoted by explicitly listing specific items (hyponyms): if a law concerns a particular category (such as birds), then its provisions may need to say what counts as a member of that category (does *bird* include *ostrich*, which does not fly?).

In looking at the first of Crystal's categories, we saw the presence of the modal *shall* (Extract 3.1, section 5), which is now rare in ordinary British English, and Cao (2010: 86) shows how the omission of the modal verb, *may*, in a translation of an English law into Chinese, in the new bilingual jurisdiction of Hong Kong SAR, (Special Administrative Region) produces a discrepancy that comes to a head in an appeal case. The discrepancy led to the appeal being upheld.

A concern with semantic precision is one of the things that characterises legislation. In the research activities for this chapter, you are invited to investigate the lexical and grammatical nature of laws and statutes in relation to how particular choices are made to ensure inclusiveness, to make rules that are clear and unambiguous, to facilitate the understanding of obligations and responsibilities for action and to clarify what kinds of action transgress the law.

The discussion so far has used the term 'legal language' as though there is 'one homogeneous discourse type', but as Maley (1994: 14) points out, it is not one, 'but a set of related and overlapping discourse types'. Maley (1994: 16), therefore, talks of 'discourse situations and their discourses [such as]: legislation, trial proceedings, and judicial judgments'. We have already taken a brief look at legislative language. In the next two sections we examine the language of legal contracts and, for a fascinating corpus-based study of Supreme Court opinions, go to Finegan (2010). In a corpus of nearly a million words of opinions (COSCO) Finegan finds that judges' attitudinal stance is expressed in a range of grammatical structures, but particularly adverbs and adverbials of stance, or 'attitude and emphasis', such as *correctly, properly, improperly; simply, merely* and *clearly*. He shows how the use of these words in 73 case opinions contributes to a legal style that means that 'justices' words have teeth – and can bite', 'however calm, cool, and collected the logic behind supreme court opinions' is (Finegan 2010: 68).

Grammatical words in legal contracts

In legal contracts the choice and frequency of particular grammatical and lexical items is distinctive. One of the ways in which we can answer the question of which words are legal words, or which words are used differently in legal texts, is to look at frequency lists across collections of texts, or *corpora,* selected from different genres. If we compare the British National Corpus (BNC), which represents a broad range of English genres and text types, with specialist legal corpora, which embody particular genres such as statements, interviews or contracts, we can see how legal language differs from language in general. The corpus of legal contracts, held at Projeto COMET (2007) in Brazil, gives us an opportunity to compare the frequencies of grammatical and lexical words with those in the BNC, obtained from Adam Kilgariff's (24 May 2007) comprehensive summary. A study of the two corpora reveals marked differences.

First, compare the ten most frequent words in the two corpora:

BNC: *the, of, and, a, in, to* (infinitive), *it, is, was, to* (preposition)
COMET contracts: *the, of, or, and, to* (preposition), *in, any, to* (infinitive),
                 shall, be.

Frequency lists always present us with the differences between grammatical words first, since they are the most frequent items in all texts and usually account for nearly half of all the tokens. When we look at a legal text, though, we often pass over the grammatical items, unless they are especially distinctive (for example, complex prepositions), and focus on features of syntax or archaic lexical items in an attempt to isolate what is distinctively legal in character. However, in the ten most frequent grammatical words in contracts above, four: 'or', 'any', 'shall' and 'be' stand out as more frequent and, therefore, distinctive of legal contracts. Also of note is the preposition 'to', which is more frequent than the infinitive 'to' and the preposition 'by' also comes in eleventh place in COMET. By comparison, in the BNC frequency list these words occur well outside the top ten in the following frequency places:

or = 32; *any* = 84; *shall* = not even in top 140; *be* = 15; *by* = 19.

All of these words appear in the Theft Act (Extract 3.1), but you probably did not notice them on first reading. On re-examination they combine with other characteristic syntactic, stylistic and lexically distinctive features. The higher frequency of *by*, for example, is a consequence of the much more frequent passive constructions, particularly in written legal language, such as in 'Be it enacted by' (the 'enactment formula' found in all English Acts) or 'The legal services to be provided by Attorney to Client are as follows' (COMET). In our short Theft Act extract, consisting of a mere 273 words, there are five instances of constructions using 'or':

1   *himself or another; debit or credit; credits or debits*
2   *before or after; presentment of cheque or by other method*

The frequency of 'or' in legal texts is a direct consequence of the communicative task of ensuring the inclusiveness that is necessary to cover all eventualities in relation to actors and entities (line 1 above) and time and activity (line 2 above), although activity is not conveyed by a verb, but expressed instead by a nominalisation: 'presentment'.

   This distinctive and frequent use of *or* is not limited to statutes and contracts, but extends to many other legal sub-genres. For example, when a police officer has taken a statement under caution, s/he asks the suspect: *Do you want to correct, alter or add anything?* The joining of verbs and nouns in lists with an 'or' between the final pair, indicating completion, is extremely common – every possible alternative of action or state is covered. And questions with the alternative or inclusive *or* are also used in interviews and cross-examination. For example, in the police investigative interview with Shipman, questions featuring both alternative and inclusive uses of *or* occur (Extract 3.2).

   Extract 3.2

   Q. 'So just, how many lines are actually on your main line then into your surgery?
        Is it just one telephone *or* does it feed the number?'
   Q. 'Do you use that when you're on your rounds? Is that what the use of it is, *or* is it a general pager for all your business?'
   Q. 'Is it a message paper *or* numeric?'

Q.   'How are *notes* or *records* maintained of what is said and what visits are arranged from them (sic) phone calls.'

Q.   'With regards to the calls that come into the surgery, and you're saying that the receptionist has to assess the urgency, *do they ever* have to come through to yourself and consider whether it is *urgent* or *non-urgent*, or *do you leave* the responsibility to themselves?'

Q.   'So when a patient is seen the person responsible for *administering treatment* or *dealing with that patient* should make a record *as soon as practicable* or *as soon as possible* after seeing the patient?'

(Shipman Trial, Day 24)

By contrast, in the cross-examination of Shipman in court, alternative questions are infrequent but *or* is quite often used inclusively (Extract 3.3).

Extract 3.3

Q.   'Why then, if somewhere between 5 and 7 milligrams was the appropriate dose, were you prescribing 30 milligrams for Lillian Ibottson, **some 4 times or 5 times your dose** for a naïve morphine patient?'

Q.   'Let's try to get one thing straight. When evidence is read out to the jury, do you remember, it will have been **either Mr. Wright or myself** at his Lordship's invitation, saying to the jury that when evidence is read out it is agreed evidence unless they are told to the contrary?'

Q.   'Right. Now that was **on the 3rd September or thereabouts**, was it not?' (Shipman Trial, Day 32)

Distinctive grammatical words are, therefore, not restricted to legal contracts, but found to be distinctive in other legal texts.

Lexical words in legal contracts

We find that it is not just the grammatical vocabulary of legal contracts that displays distinctively different frequencies by comparison with a general corpus – the distribution of lexical items is different too. In the BNC all 56 most frequent items are grammatical – the first lexical item is *said* which occurs in fifty-seventh place; by contrast, and also because it is a smaller corpus, the contract corpus has 15 lexical items in the top 57:

agreement, company, lessee, party, respect, agent, notice, property, time, provided, date, including, parent, guarantor, lessor.

There is one word, though, that needs to be discounted from this list of lexical words – *respect* – because each of its 433 occurrences in the corpus occurs as part of a complex preposition (a function word): *in respect of, with respect to, in respect thereof* and *with respect thereto. Respect* is never used as a lexical noun or verb, but its presence as a high frequency item nevertheless points to its distinctiveness as part of the different grammatical set in the contract corpus. It also highlights the distinctiveness of complex prepositions in the genre and in legal language more generally. The greater number of frequent lexical words implies that contracts are unusually dense lexically and for that reason alone they will necessarily be harder to understand. In addition, there are a great many words that are core in legal texts, which are not core in a general English corpus.

The majority of the words in the above list are nouns (*agent, agreement, company, date, guarantor, lessee, lessor, notice, parent, party, property, time*) and refer to the parties involved in the contract and to the contract itself as an entity (*agreement*) that is transacted by the parties. The two lexical verbs that are present in the list, *provided* and *including*, are important in relation to the function of the contract and the notion of selectivity and inclusiveness already noticed in the use of *or*. The verb *including* is generally used to introduce non-finite subordinate clauses that give provisions and inclusions, which hold important interpretative details. Some examples of the distinctive patterns among the 373 occurrences of *including* (approximately four uses per 1,000 words) in COMET are:

1   *including* preceded by comma or enclosed in brackets:

    –   *and manner of delivery, including the carrier to be used by SUPPLIER.*
    –   *administrative and judicial proceedings (including any informal proceedings) and all orders,*

2   *including* +, *without limitation,* or, *but not limited to*

    –   *(including, without limitation, the Maturity Date)*
    –   *including, but not limited to, the Securities Act of 1933*

3   *including* + list

    –   *including fire, flood, strikes, labor troubles or other*

4   *including* + *all* or *any* + noun or list

    –   *including all common parts, the internal decorations and the fixtures and*
    –   *including any actual loss or expense incurred*

The verb *provided* occurs 389 times (also about four times per 1,000 words) in COMET. It is used just over half the time as a verb in constructions like:

provided + prepositional phrase

    –   *as provided for in the Agreement,*
    –   *as provided in paragraph 10 hereof,*

to be provided herein/under,

noun + *provided* + prepositional phrase

    –   *Investment Banking Services provided to the company*

In the remaining uses it occurs as a 'complex conjunction' derived from the verb (Halliday and Matthiessen 2014: 484), as in: *provided that* (expanded to *provided, however, that* in almost half the cases). The following patterns appear:

preceded by a comma or semi-colon

- *upon confirmation of receipt; provided, however, that any Funding Notice*

followed by a comma and another exclusion clause

- *provided that, subject to the following sentence*

provided that + noun phrase containing a party: *lessor, Company, Landlord, lessee, translator, tenant*

- *provided that the lessee shall have paid*

A final distinctive feature in the use of *provided* in COMET can be seen when we compare its frequency in the BNC. In COMET, verbal use is 16 times and conjunctive use 21 times more frequent than in the BNC. These patterns of inclusive use that surround the verb *including*, and its partner *provided*, underline the dominance of these functions in contracts and show us clearly what contracts are about: everything that is covered, with certain provisos. In addition, the repetition of lexical items (*landlord, lessee, company*), rather than the use of pronoun substitutes (*he, she, we, they*), produces frequency information that underlines the key semantic fields present in contracts.

Other marked features of legal English are Latinisms, like *prima facie, bona fide*; archaic adverbs, *hereinafter, thereunder*; specific prepositional phrases *pursuant to, at the instance of*; a greater use of performative constructions, *X hereby agrees/confers*; a more frequent use of passives, conditionals and hypotheticals; and unusually long sentences. Hiltunen (1984), for example, found that the British Road Traffic Act of 1972 had a mean sentence length of 79 words, with one sentence being 740 words long. And then, of course, there is punctuation, or the lack of it, which can create problems.

Solan (1993) discusses a punctuation-focused case (*Anderson v State Farm Mut. Auto. Ins. Co.* (1969) 270 Cal.App.2d 346) which hinges on the use of a comma, and a similar case also came before the Canadian Radio-television and Telecommunications Commission (CRTC). The story was reported in the Canadian newspaper, *The Globe and Mail*, in both its online (6 August 2006) and print (7 August 2006) editions. The print edition headline, 'The $2-million comma', highlights the cost of the decision to the losers, Rogers Communications. The online report starts:

It could be the most costly piece of punctuation in Canada. A grammatical blunder may force Rogers Communications Inc. to pay an extra $2.13-million to use utility poles in the Maritimes after the placement of a comma in a contract permitted the deal's cancellation.

(Robertson 06.08.06)

The CRTC decision quotes section 8.1 of the contract, the Support Service Agreement (SSA), that was the subject of the dispute.

> Subject to the termination provisions of [the SSA], [the SSA] shall be effective from the date it is made and shall continue in force for a period of five (5) years from the date it is made, and thereafter for successive five (5) year terms, unless and until terminated by one year prior notice in writing by either party.

(para. 16 CRTC Decision 2006-45)

The Commission's decision related to the placement of the second comma (underlined) and, as Robertson states in his article, 'had it not been there, the right to cancel wouldn't have applied to the first five years of the contract'. The Commission's decision was that 'based on the rules of punctuation, the comma placed before the phrase "unless and until terminated by one year prior notice in writing by either party" means that that phrase qualifies both the phrases' (para.27 CRTC Decision 2006-45). This 'controversial comma' shows the vital importance of punctuation.

In answer to our question at the start of this chapter – Is legal language complex and opaque? – we can say that legal style is determined by its history and its function. What is being done has a direct impact on word choice (both lexical words and function words), syntax and punctuation, and this, in turn, produces the distinctive register that can be measured and observed in frequency lists and legal text and talk. These choices are a direct consequence of the communicative purposes of legal language and the activities in which it is used.

Interpreting legal words

It comes as something of a surprise to the layman to discover that 'generally the words "or" and "and" when occurring in statutes may be construed as interchangeable when necessary to effectuate legislative intent' (McKinney's Cons. Laws of New York, Statutes §365, quoted in Solan 1993). Although Solan reassures us that in the vast majority of cases 'and' and 'or' are in fact read in their ordinary language meaning of additive and disjunctive respectively, he reports a case where 'and' was agreed to mean 'or'.

> A Californian man who admitted he had strangled his wife, while visiting her on a day pass from a hospital where he was being treated for paranoia, pleaded insanity. The definition of the defence of insanity the court had to apply was as follows:

> This defense shall be found by the trier of fact only when the accused person proves by a preponderance of the evidence that he or she was incapable of knowing or understanding the nature and quality of his or her act **and** of distinguishing right from wrong at the time of the commission of the offense.
> (Californian Penal Code §25(b)) (emphasis added)
> (Solan 1993: 48–49)

The court found that, although he was unable to distinguish 'right from wrong' at the relevant time, he was capable of understanding 'the nature and quality of his act' and therefore was not legally insane, so he was convicted of second degree murder. On appeal his lawyers argued that the 'and' should in fact be read as 'or' and therefore, as he did satisfy one of the criteria for insanity, he should be acquitted. The appeal court agreed that such a reading was consistent with the traditional insanity defence and therefore chose to 'effectuate legislative intent' by adopting the suggested reading. One wonders what would happen if students who registered for a university degree whose course description was 'Students take six taught modules and write a dissertation of 12,000 words' were to argue for the alternative definition of 'and' and simply submit a dissertation in complete fulfilment of the course requirements.

Potentially ambiguous constructions can cause all kinds of problems in the interpretation of statutes. For this reason, lawyers have interpretive rules, derived from past struggles with texts, which they then apply to new and previously uninterpreted texts. The three 'most basic' are *the literal rule, the golden rule,* and *the mischief rule* (Hutton 2014: 26–27). The literal rule (also known as the plain meaning rule) is quoted above by Solan; the golden rule requires a judge 'to give the words used by the legislature their plain and natural meaning, unless it is manifest from the general scope and intention of the statute injustice and absurdity would result from so construing them'; and the mischief rule requires a judge 'to identify the specific object or target of the legislation and to make such construction as shall suppress the mischief, and advance the remedy' (quoted in Hutton 2014: 26–27). In addition, there is (amongst others) *the last antecedent rule*, which states that the scope of a limiting clause has to be restricted to the immediately preceding antecedent, 'unless the context or evident meaning requires a different construction'. Solan (1993: 29–30) exemplifies from a bizarre case. Here are the basic facts. A Mrs Anderson met a Mr Larson at a county fair and they decided to go off to a restaurant in Mr Larson's car. After spending several hours in the restaurant Mr Larson said he was going to the restroom, but he never came back. After waiting for some considerable time, Mrs Anderson left the restaurant and drove off in what she thought was Mr Larson's car. In fact it was not and what was worse she had an accident. Her insurance company denied liability for the damage she had caused to the 'borrowed' car, and justified this by referring to the following part of her car insurance policy:

> Such insurance as is afforded by this policy … with respect to the owned automobile applies to the use of a non-owned automobile by the named

insured … *and* any other person or organization legally responsible for use by the named insured … of an automobile not owned or hired by such other person or organization *provided such use is with the permission of the owner or person in lawful possession of such automobile.*

(Solan 1993: 30)

At first reading the insurance company's interpretation seems quite clearly correct – Mrs Anderson, 'the named insured', was certainly allowed to drive cars belonging to others, as indeed was 'any other person [for whom she was] legally responsible', but only *provided the owner had given permission* – and in this case there was no dispute that no permission had been given – indeed the owner did not even know her, let alone that she was in his car at the time of the accident. However, Mrs Anderson's lawyers argued for another, more favourable, interpretation of the policy as a result of applying the last antecedent rule. They argued that the correct interpretation of the text was that the requirement *with the permission of the owner* only applied to the immediately preceding *any other person or organization* and not to the *named insured*, who was therefore properly insured to drive the automobile. The court accepted their argument.

Interestingly, Solan cites an apparently similar case involving 'or' where the opposite interpretative decision was taken. A school teacher was threatened with dismissal, after being convicted of the felony of growing one marijuana plant at home. The school board was allowed to dismiss anyone who had a 'conviction of a felony or of any crime involving moral turpitude' (Solan 1993: 34). In this case the court did not apply the last antecedent rule, but found another rule in the case of *Wholesale T. Dealers v National etc. Co* (1938) which read:

When a clause follows several words in a statute and is applicable as much to the first word as to the others in the list, the clause should be applied to all of the words which preceded it.

Using this rule they reasoned that growing marijuana, although a felony, was not a 'felony involving moral turpitude' and therefore argued that the teacher should be allowed to keep his job.

To the lay reader both of these decisions seem strained and the reader might like first to work out how, in both cases, linguistic analysis could support opposite readings to those reached by the court and then study Solan's own analyses (2002: 31–36).

Hutton (2014: 70ff) deals with two UK tax cases which have gained a good deal of public and legal comment and which involve the classification of 'mundane' food items: Jaffa Cakes and Pringles (if you are not familiar with these products, look them up on a search engine). Both were claimed by their manufacturers to be food products that were exempt from value added tax (or VAT), so should be zero-rated. Hutton (2014: 70) explains the relevant tax law that applies to food, showing that food is zero-rated *except* for 'confectionary (defined as chocolates, sweets and biscuits)' which are standard-rated. However, cakes and biscuits are zero-rated, *except* for 'biscuits wholly or partly covered with chocolate or with some product similar in taste and appearance'. In the first case, Jaffa Cakes, which are packaged and eaten like biscuits, were found to have 'have characteristics of cakes, and also characteristics of biscuits or non-cakes' but 'sufficient characteristics of cakes to qualify as cakes ... If it be relevant, I also determine that Jaffa Cakes are not biscuits' (*United Biscuits v Customs and Excise* (1991)). Hutton (2014: 71–72) shows the basis on which this was determined comes down to 11 factors (name, ingredients, texture, size, packaging, marketing, make-up of the sponge part, aging process, presentation, appeal and composition in terms of the cake), six which favoured *cake* and five which favoured *biscuit*. This resulted in United Biscuits, even though it is a biscuit company, successfully claiming their product was eligible for zero-rated VAT. In the second case Customs and Excise argued that Pringles were a kind of potato crisp and therefore subject to VAT under another schedule of UK tax law which defines them as 'savoury snacks' rather than 'other food', while Proctor and Gamble argued that 'Pringles were not similar to the *potato crisp* and therefore should be zero-rated' (Hutton 2014: 73). The decision in this case was different: 'we consider that while in many respects Regular Pringles are different from potato crisps and so they are near the borderline, they are sufficiently similar to satisfy the [reasonable man] test' (*Revenue and Customs v Proctor and Gamble* (2009)). Pringles were effectively found to be crisps, a kind of snack, and therefore liable to standard rate VAT. In both of these cases, therefore, the products were found to be a borderline category of cake/biscuit or crisp/non-crisp, but with different outcomes. As Hutton (2014: 79) observes 'in the Jaffa Cake case, the decision gave priority to the intrinsic qualities, the essential 'cake-like' make-up of the Jaffa Cake, over its more 'biscuit-like' patterns of consumption and social profile, including its shape and size', whereas 'in the Pringles case ... it seems that patterns of consumption and social profile, including the size ... were the decisive factors'. Charnock (2013: 135) attributes the decision in the Jaffa Cakes case to one based on stereotypical features of meaning, although 'whether Jaffa Cakes were really cakes or biscuits, appeared at first sight to be a prototypical question'. Stereotype Theory (Putnam 1970) allows meaning to be determined according to 'a loose knit group of features, known to speakers ... none of which are necessary' (Charnock 2013: 134, summarising Putnam), whereas Prototype Theory organises meaning in terms of instances of a thing (say a bird) which are most representative of the category (Rosch 1975). Rosch's experiments with American students found that the question 'Is a robin a bird?' gained much faster responses than questions with less representative birds such as *penguin* or *ostrich*.

Ordinary and special meanings

With the exceptions noted above, the vocabulary used in a legal text will look very much like that of ordinary English and most of the time the words will have ordinary language meanings. However, a small number of the words in any given legal document will have a *legal definition*, which dictates how an otherwise ordinary language item must be interpreted in the particular contexts to which the document applies. Sometimes the 'defined' word appears in bold, sometimes it is spelled with an initial capital, both conventions being used to indicate that it is, at that point, being used in its defined meaning. For example, one early road traffic act redefined 'carriage' to include 'bicycle', while another had to define 'dusk' in order to be able to forbid people to remain in public parks after dusk. However, a candidate for the most amusing definition, though certainly not the easiest to remember, is quoted in Tiersma (1999: 118). Apparently a Florida ordinance, designed to control the amount of flesh erotic dancers were allowed to expose, required them to 'cover their buttocks'. In order to help these dancers comply with the law (and, of course, to make it easier for the poor law enforcement officers, armed with tape measures, to check that the dancers were indeed observing the law to the letter, or at least to the fraction of an inch), the crucial term 'buttocks' was defined in 328 words, beginning as follows:

> the area at the rear of the human body (sometimes referred to as the gluteus maximus) which lies between two imaginary lines running parallel to the ground when a person is standing, the first or top of such lines being one-half inch below the top of the vertical cleavage of the nates (i.e. the prominence formed by the muscles running from the back of the hip to the back of the leg) and the second or bottom line being one-half inch above the lowest point of the curvature of the fleshy protuberance (sometimes referred to as the gluteal fold), and between two imaginary lines …

Bizarre though this may seem, any officer faced with the practicalities of judging how much flesh needs to be exposed to constitute 'uncovered buttocks' has a difficult task and a definition is therefore a necessary tool for the law enforcer, however complex it may seem. Similarly, where lexical items are homonyms or polysemantic, a more specific legal term is important. One which Johnson remembers from her police days is the word *audible warning instrument* to mean *horn*. In British English *horn* is a homonym: the horn of an animal, as in *the bull had huge horns*; and a car horn, as in *he sounded the horn*. In American English *horn* is not polysemantic, since cars have *hooters*. The offence of sounding the horn after 11p.m. at night, which is a traffic offence in England and Wales, uses the term 'audible warning instrument' which includes a 'horn, bell, gong or siren'. General words or hypernyms like 'audible warning instrument' are clearly more useful as legal terms than taxonomic sisters such as 'horn', 'gong' or 'bell', where using one in a law would signal that warnings using other instruments were acceptable.

In her analysis of two versions of a contract for furniture removal, the second of which was rewritten according to principles of the Plain English Campaign, Davies (2004: 82) sets out to examine 'two different ways of saying the same thing' and to evaluate whether the second text preserves the meaning of the first, as the writers claimed. One of the features she looks at for comparison is 'field-indicative restricted senses of lexical items', or in other words, ordinary words with special legal meanings. She finds that one text uses the word 'parties', whereas the plain English text uses the word 'sides'. Some words occur in both texts: *agreement, cost(s)*, but there is a number of words with special meanings that occur only in the first: *award, difference* (meaning 'dispute'), *question* (meaning 'dispute'), *parties, claim* (legal claim for money or damage), *calling* (in the phrase 'barrister of ten years calling' meaning experience, but coming from the phrasal verb 'called to the Bar'), *discretion, condition, subject of, precedent* (as an adjective). She concludes that this difference leads to 'a more formal tenor', which indicates a restricted field of expertise common to technical varieties of English (Davies 2004: 97). However, although the first 'is not easily comprehensible to the lay readership', she concedes that the second, 'which is much easier for the layman to understand, may not convey exactly the same legal content' (Davies 2004: 98), suggesting that special meanings are a necessary part of the work that legal language does in expressing content.

Specialised lexis can present particular problems, though, for law students in countries such as India, where, because of British colonisation, the laws are written in English, but where English is a second language for the majority of students studying law. Sandhya (2004: 137) discusses the challenges he faces, as a language teacher in an Indian university, with law students who need his help to understand legal English. He observes 'that students had to be sensitized to the dynamic, the problematic and the dialogic aspects of the law-language nexus ... if they were to sincerely deliver justice to the laity' (2004: 137). His investigation with his students into legal language took him into special meanings:

> that if 'detriment' meant 'injury' or 'harm' in common parlance, 'legal detriment' did not necessarily mean harm or injury; that one could not only 'prefer coffee to tea' but could also 'prefer an appeal', that 'damage without injury' and 'injury without damage' had different legal implications and that 'damages' was not the plural form of damage, but 'compensation'.
>
> (Sandhya 2004: 137)

Since English is a world language in former colonies of the British Empire, the legacy of specialised meaning is a worldwide one. However, the Test of Legal English website (http://www.toles.co.uk/) lists test centres in 30 countries around the world in many countries where English was not exported as part of the Empire, including Argentina, Latvia and Thailand. It uses the phrase 'global legal English' in its website, indicating that legal English has a global market and a global set of learners and users.

On applying the law

Texts are the way they are because they are situated in a multidimensional, real-world context that produces complex and dynamic textual and intertextual forces. These forces constrain and determine the nature, meaning and effects of those texts on individuals. We cannot simply interpret laws and statutes as texts, but rather need to consider their use in context. Taking the trial as an example, a defendant faces a charge, such as murder, which is read out by the Clerk of the Court as an indictment. At the heart of this process is the particular law or statute that specifies an offence, but the way that the statute is understood and applied is specific to each case and set of circumstances. The judicial process is influenced by a whole range of prior texts and contexts (police interviews, statement making and taking, meetings with lawyers), both written and spoken, all of which centre on the law.

In the case of murder, in many countries, the US and Australia are two obvious examples, there are written statutes that define the offence, but in England and Wales it is an offence under common law (the law that existed before statutes started to be made by Parliament). Murder is defined by reference to cases, but a definition that is often referred to is that of Sir Edward Coke, as used in the epigraph. This contains a number of conditions, all of which need to be proven in order for someone to be convicted of murder: sound mind, not a child below the age of criminal responsibility (under the age of ten), unlawfully (so not in wartime), any living person (therefore not a fetus), occurring in the counties of England and Wales, and intending serious injury and inflicting a wound or assault that kills the person. Coke's 'year and a day' rule has now been overruled by a law passed in 1996, so that someone can be charged with murder even if the victim dies as a result of an injury sustained more than a year earlier. A trial for murder will therefore concentrate on the evidence that demonstrates that the crime, with which the defendant is charged, meets the above conditions.

In Chapters 4 and 5 we look at linguistic aspects of the collection of evidence to satisfy any charge from the initial call to the emergency services, through the subsequent police interviews to interaction in the courtroom. All of these situations create a 'temporal intertextual chain' (Rock 2007: 36) of talk and texts: interviews, statements, consultations with lawyers, examinations and cross-examinations of witnesses in court and the judicial adjudication. At each stage, the law influences and determines the goals of the talk and the subsequent written record. Where statutes exist, charges are written in accordance with the part of the Act of Parliament that specifies the offence(s), but before anyone is charged with an offence, there needs to be an investigation to establish whether any offence has actually been committed.

It is not just in criminal and civil trials that legislation is important. In the Shipman Inquiry (2001), which followed up Harold Shipman's conviction on 15 counts of murder, and which investigated whether he might have killed any of his other patients who died in similar circumstances, 37 different statutes are referred to as relevant, including the Births and Deaths Registration Act 1953, the Cremation Act 1952 and the Misuse of Drugs Act 1971. These are contained in a section of the inquiry entitled 'Generic Evidence', which 'contains information that provides general background to the matters being investigated by the Inquiry and evidence that may pertain to more than one area being investigated' (The Shipman Inquiry 2001). In addition, 85 different regulations, which have a legal status, are also listed. The extensive nature of this general background is an important part of the generic context and indicates the power of the legal statute as a context for legal encounters.

Conclusion

There is some debate about the need for legal language, which we have not specifically addressed here. On one side of the debate is the argument that legal language has a high degree of precision and inclusivity that is required by the genre. However, The Plain English Campaign (1996a, b) provides a counter argument that this language is 'unnecessary' (1996a: 22–27). Two articles which are written from these two positions (Prakasam 2004; Davies 2004) are suggested in the further reading for this chapter. For the moment, at least, according to Gibbons (2004: 11), we have to 'tak[e] legal language seriously', since there are 'dangers inherent in the editing process [that revises a law into Plain English]' because simpler documents often lose something in translation, which Davies (2004: 98) notes. It is unlikely that major reforms in legal language will take place, since, as Gibbons (2004: 2) points out, 'lawyers exert much effort in finding loopholes and alternative readings of legal documents; so when these documents are produced, a major objective is to avoid leaving them open to hostile or unintended readings' and this produces the need for 'maximal precision'. From time to time, however, changes are made to legal language to make it plainer. For example, in 2007 a legal reform story made the news in the US. Rules governing procedure in federal trial courts had been rewritten according to plain language principles, the authors winning an award for legal achievement: 'Reform in Law' Awarded for First Plain-Language Rewrite of Federal Civil Court Rules in 70 Years (Munro 2007). In addition Clarity-International, an 'organization dedicated to advancing the use of plain language in law and legislation', publishes a journal, has held conferences since 2002, and includes high-profile legal representatives amongst its members (Clarity International 2015). And Tiersma's work on 'redrafting California's jury instructions' (e.g. Tiersma 2010) has 'brought the promise [of the rule of law] closer to reality' (Tiersma 2010: 263) by making jury instructions more accessible to jurors. Judges need to instruct juries on legal principles in cases and, as Tiersma (2010: 263) states 'all parties to a lawsuit, particularly criminal defendants, have a right to have their cases decided by consistent legal principles that are accessible to the public'. Redrafting California's standard instructions, therefore, has been a pioneering endeavour that Tiersma hopes other jurisdictions will follow.

The claim that legal language is incomprehensible can be seen to be partly attributable to a lack of knowledge that leaves non-members of the discourse community without the interpretative resources to make sense of texts. As Crystal (2003: 374) says, legal discourse is in an impossible position, 'pulled in different directions'. Its sentences have to be:

> so phrased that we can see their general applicability, yet be specific enough to apply to individual circumstances. They have to be stable enough to stand

the test of time, so that cases will be treated consistently and fairly, yet flexible enough to adapt to new social situations.

But most important of all, according to Crystal (2003: 374), they 'have to be expressed in such a way that people can be certain about the intention of the law respecting their rights and duties', making legal language carry a heavy 'responsibility' that 'no other variety of language has to carry'.

The words of the law and of legal statutes, whether plain or opaque, clearly produce an important intertextual context for any investigation and for the interactions that take place within it, as we see in Chapters 4 and 5. There is an interdependency between written laws and legal contexts that gives both spoken and written legal language its distinctive features, but it is the work that legal language does that truly characterises it.

Further reading

The Test of Legal English website (http://www.toles.co.uk/ – here you can look at sample exams and answers).
Coulthard, M. and A. Johnson (eds) (2010), chapters by: Bhatia, Cao, Finegan, Stygall, Tiersma, Dumas.

Research tasks

1 Investigate some of the laws and statutes of your own country and compare them with other legal documents such as terms and conditions, contracts (e.g. Projeto COMET, as in task 2) or legal judgments. UK Statutes can be found here: http:// www.legislation.gov.uk/ and Bilingual English/Chinese Statutes of Hong Kong here: http://www.legislation.gov.hk/index.htm. Terms and conditions are documents we encounter every day (even if we tick 'yes' to say we've read them when we haven't), so click on them to read; UK legal judgments are published online (since 2012) at: https://www.judiciary.gov.uk/judgments/ and before that at the National Archives webarchive (http://webarchive.nationalarchives.gov.uk). How do these different legal texts use legal language? How do the lexical and grammatical choices of the legal drafters aim to ensure inclusiveness and produce rules that are clear and unambiguous?
2 Analyse some of the lexical and grammatical features of legal contracts in the COMET corpus, by exploring concordances of some of the distinctive vocabulary of contracts. Take as a starting point some of the lexical and grammatical items discussed in this chapter. Explain the use of the features in relation to the function of contracts and in contrast to a more general corpus or one from a different (legal) field. Legal contracts can be found at: Projeto COMET: http://www.fflch.usp.br/dlm/comet/.
3 A nineteenth-century US statute made it a crime 'in any manner whatsoever, to prepay the transportation of [an] alien ... to perform labor or service of any kind in the United States'. A church was convicted of violating this statute, by having pre-paid the transportation of its rector from England. In an appeal in 1892, *Church of the Holy Trinity v United States*, the Supreme Court was asked to reverse the conviction. What linguistic grounds can you see for them to do this?

4 Before going to the Far East, a Dr Rowland and his wife made identical wills. Both left their property to the other unless the other's death was 'preceding or coinciding', in which case other relatives were to benefit. Both were on a ship which disappeared without trace. The named beneficiary of the wife's will claimed the whole estate, on the grounds that, if their deaths were not coinciding the wife, being the younger, would be deemed by the Law of Property Act 1925 to have survived him. On what grounds would you argue the case that the deaths were not coinciding and how would you expect the husband's family lawyers to respond? You need to consider also how one can tell what the testators meant by 'coinciding' and even if you think this might be different from the literal meaning, how can you argue for this interpretation in this case?

Note: Task 3 is based on Solan (2002) and Task 4 on Zander (1999).

4 Emergency service calls and police interviewing

Collecting evidence in first encounters with witnesses and suspects

1968 in the US – *call to the emergency services that Robert Fw. Kennedy had been shot (CT is call taker and C caller;* ( ) indicates a pause; = indicates a contiguous utterance*)*

```
1   CT.   Police department
2         ( )
3   C.    Yes This is the Ambassador Hotel Em–
4         Ambassador Hotel?
5         ((echo: Hotel))
6   C.    Do you hear me?
7         ( )
8   CT.   Yeah I hear you.
9   C.    Uh they have an emergency= They want thuh
10        police to the kitchen right away.
```

(Zimmerman 1992: 436–37)

1994 in the UK – *arrest interview with Rosemary West (DS is Detective Sergeant Onions and RW is Rosemary West)*

DS You were arrested by myself and other officers on suspicion of the murder of your daughter Heather, who disappeared about 1986/87. You were interviewed, but not about that. Can you just go over the circumstances of when Heather left your house?

RW You ask the questions, I'll try and answer them.

(BBC Crime, 10 August 2006)

Introduction

The first epigraph illustrates the importance of talk in encounters with the emergency services, which can be the first stage in evidence gathering in criminal cases. In this famous case, the shooting of presidential candidate Robert F. Kennedy, the call begins a process that leads to a murder inquiry. Callers and call-takers work towards a shared goal: the provision of appropriate help, though the definition of what is appropriate may not be shared. This is because, as Whalen and Zimmerman (1998: 143) observe, 'an inherent tension exists between callers who regard their circumstances as both stressful and urgent, and call takers who somehow must manage the encounter and mobilize an organizational response', and, while it is 'an extraordinary experience for the caller, ... it is a routine, every-day experience for the professional'. The format of the conversation is one where 'callers act as informants, answering the questions that are designed to elicit the information required for a proper despatch' (Whalen and Zimmerman 1998: 152).

Police interviews with suspects, as in the second epigraph, also make use of questions, to work towards their goals: making a decision about whether the actions and events under investigation constitute a legally defined offence and collecting evidence to be used in any subsequent court case. In court, the role of evaluator falls to a magistrate, judge(s) or a jury, who have to decide whether a case has been proved 'beyond reasonable doubt', if it is a criminal charge, or 'on the balance of probabilities', if it is a civil case. Lay witnesses and juries in court are, like emergency service callers, firmly in the control of the professional, the witnesses talking through a lawyer's questions and juries occupying a recipient role, as talk is performed for them, channelled through the legal experts.

We first examine the nature of talk and the role of listening in calls to the emergency services. We then deal with police interviews with witnesses and suspects, including children and rape victims. Finally, we reflect on the complex context of police interviews and the resulting problems for suspects in the justice system.

First encounters – calls to the emergency services

Drew and Walker (2010: 96) describe the structure of emergency calls as consisting of five phases (opening – request – interrogative series – dispatch response – closing), each of which consists of 'a distinctive task or activity'. These calls are routinely recorded, because they often form part of a subsequent investigation, as in the Kennedy shooting (Extract 4.1, which continues from the extract in the epigraph).

Extract 4.1

```
11   CT.   =What kind of emergency?
12   C.    I don't know honey They hung up I don't know
13         what's happening
14   CT.   Well find out, ( ) We don't send out without=
15   C.    =I beg your pardon?
16         ( )
17   CT.   We have to know what we're sending on,
```

(Zimmerman 1992: 436–37)

Zimmerman (1992: 437) comments that:

while some embarrassment may have attended the subsequent public disclosure of delay in the dispatch of assistance to the scene, it is clear that the caller, a hotel operator relaying information from the hotel's kitchen, is initially not in a position to provide the required information

and that 'the mere characterization of an event as an emergency is, other things being equal, insufficient' to trigger a response. The CTs assessment of the caller's talk (lines 14 and 17) signals that more information is needed to warrant the dispatch of a police officer.

In Whalen and Zimmerman's (1998: 142) study of around 350 emergency service calls in Oregon, they noted that many were 'routine and not especially emotionally charged', whereas others that 'include emotional displays' were characterised by CTs as 'hysterical'. These callers' emotional states impede the management of the call and become a problem for the CT, 'to the extent that they distort callers' speech, affect the coherence of their utterance, or pose further tasks for the [CT] that delay acquisition of necessary information or interfere with the delivery of instructions' (Whalen and Zimmerman 1998: 151). Resources such as 'directives ("Calm down")' or 'reassurances ("Help is on the way")' (1998: 151) are needed to gain control of the call and thereby elicit useful information in order to make appropriate decisions.

Garner and Johnson (2006), in their study of emergency call management in England, also emphasise the role of decision-making and information gathering. They ask: 'Where are the critical decision-points for the handler in the call?' and 'How can critical information elements, such as the location of the incident and the caller's identity and reliability, be established rapidly?' (2006: 57). One call (Extract 4.2), from an elderly female on New Year's Eve, demonstrates how the CT makes an early classification of the situation as 'non-serious' (line 5), but is nevertheless still involved in a long interaction to establish for certain that it is indeed not necessary to dispatch officers.

Extract 4.2

1	C.	I want the police here
2	CT.	This is the police what's happening? (pause) What's happening?

...

3	C.	Well there's a some er er there's some banging going on outside
4		we can't sleep. There (?)
5	**CT.**	**Is it fireworks?**
6	C.	They're not fireworks no they're not fireworks
7	CT.	What is it then?
8	C.	I – will you please send the police?

[Many utterances ensue to establish the caller's name and the precise location and to try to establish the cause of the noise.]

13	CT.	Have you looked out your window?
14	C.	There there's banging going on outside really terrible
15	**CT.**	**Have a look out your window can you see fireworks?**
16	C.	Not fireworks somebody kicking up a row out here
17	CT.	Someone's having an argument?

18   C.   Will you please send the police up to inspect?
      ...
19   CT.   You need to tell me you need to tell me what's happening. If
20   it's just banging then we're not going to come out because it's
      ...
21   CT.   So what's the noise you can hear
22   C.   They're not speaking at all. All they're doing is banging
23   CT.   What sort of banging is it?
24   C.   Just like bombs going off all the time
25   CT.   Okay I expect it's fireworks

(Garner and Johnson 2006: 68–69)

Garner and Johnson note that in calls where the caller is 'argumentative, frightened or upset, it can be hard to reach a decision point' (2006: 70). In this call the decision not to dispatch an officer is made, after three attempts (lines 5, 15 and 19–20). The extract demonstrates what Garner and Johnson (2006: 63) refer to as the 'dynamic tension between natural conversation patterns and a range of overarching constraints ... [such as] aims, operating policies, strategic requirements and organizational culture'. The CT here makes an assessment that the caller needs reassurance rather than an emergency response.

When calls become a crucial part of the evidence in a prosecution case, they can be intertextually invoked. In the following extract from a police interview (Extract 4.3), the suspect (S) identifies himself as the person who made a call to request an ambulance for his girlfriend, after he had stabbed her during an argument.

Extract 4.3

171   S   She said 'I'm bleeding can you get an ambulance'. I said *I can't*
          call an ambulance from here because the phone is out. I'll go and
          get you one.
172   P   Yes.
173   S   I went upstairs, got my jacket, put my jacket on, went out and got in
          my car. And I drove around the block and saw a phone box.
174   P   Yes.
175   S   And made the call from there.
176   P   I think to clarify the position that the gentleman that did phone for
          an ambulance gave his – the same name as yours and I'm prepared
          to accept that it was you that made that phone call.

The police officer (P) converts the suspect's information (*made the call*) into an evidential fact (*clarify the position*) by tying this information to an item in the recorded call (*gave his – the same name as yours*).

Imbens-Bailey and McCabe (2000) report an American 911 call where failure to dispatch an officer may have resulted in a woman's death. In their study of emergency calls they found that callers used three strategies to elicit a response: a *demand* or a *request* for help or a *description* (or narrative) of the emergency, with the third strategy being the most frequent. Like Whalen and Zimmerman (1998) and Garner and Johnson (2006) they note that the dispatcher and the caller can be 'at odds' with each other. Callers want to tell a story to elicit a response, whereas call-handlers need more mundane information first: both a name and a location to respond to their computer prompts.

Drew and Walker (2010: 98) give some statistics to Imbens-Bailey and McCabe's finding that narrative strategies are the most frequent, reporting that 'the majority of "requests" for assistance are of [a] rather implicit or indirect kind', such as: 'somebody has broken into the house'. They cite Drew's (1998) study, conducted for the Metropolitan Police, where he found that this majority, '(a little under 80%) of calls', involved callers who 'only *reported an incident* without overtly requesting police assistance', meaning that the CT needed to respond to 'the request that is embedded in the report' (Drew and Walker 2010: 97). Reporting an incident such as a break-in, therefore, becomes an indirect request. Nevertheless just over 20 per cent of callers in Drew's study use explicit request forms as an initial turn in the call and, in doing so, 'encode speakers' assessments of the *contingencies* that may be involved in granting (acting on) the request, and of their *entitlement* to whatever is being requested' (Drew and Walker 2010: 98). Drew and Walker (2010: 100) show that there is a continuum of request forms from imperatives (that encode high entitlement and low contingency), through 'could you' modal forms to 'I wonder if' conditionals (that encode high contingency and low entitlement). They found that callers to the emergency number use explicit request forms, tending to use the 'could you' requests, signalling high entitlement, whereas, when calling their local police station, they use the conditional forms more, signalling low entitlement, though they also report that there 'can be a mismatch between [the caller's] perception of the seriousness/urgency of the incident, and therefore their request, and the assessment of the CT' (Drew and Walker 2010: 110).

Garner and Johnson (2006: 66) refer to the paradoxical constraints and benefits of technology that, on the one hand, 'can help to give structure to the interaction and useful guidance to the call-handler, but, on the other, the exigencies of filling in the slots can interrupt the flow of the call, or distract the call-handler's attention from the subtle linguistic cues that may be crucial to the interpretation of what is being said'. Call-handling, like police interviewing and courtroom interaction, is characterised by the 'mutual influence of speech and text' (Garner and Johnson 2006: 66), or hybridity, and is therefore a skilled and complex discursive activity, blending features of service encounters with storytelling, interrogation for form-filling, decision-making and assessment. The criteria that determine call-handlers' assessments of the level of emergency are generally known only to the institution and not to the caller. The lay participant can therefore be at a significant disadvantage, since they may not know the rules by which the CT is working, and worse, may not even have all the information required by the institution. Many police force websites give information about what for them constitutes an emergency that requires an immediate response. These include:

- danger to life
- use, or immediate threat of use, of violence
- serious injury to a person and/or
- serious damage to property
- crime, which is, or is likely to be serious, and in progress
- an offender has just been disturbed at the scene
- an offender has been detained and poses, or is likely to pose, a risk to other people

(Home Office 2005: 26)

Research shows (Garner and Johnson 2006; Imbens-Bailey and McCabe 2000) that callers are unlikely to identify many of these criteria for themselves, and therefore it is the success (or otherwise) of the interaction itself that determines whether sufficient, useful information is elicited to allow the CT to make an adequate assessment of the situation.

Active listening in police negotiations when making an arrest

As Royce (2005) shows, in his fascinating case report on 'the role of active listening by a police negotiator in New South Wales, Australia, in the process of serving a "high-risk warrant" on an armed and dangerous man, who was expected to resist' (2005: 5), 'the use of active listening in the early stages of the negotiation was a critical factor in the resolution' of the crisis with the man referred to as 'the bomber'. He 'was allegedly regularly entering a nearby town carrying loaded weapons and wearing a live body-bomb, ostensibly for his own protection against perceived threats' (2005: 6). Active listening was important in this case in establishing rapport, so that the bomber developed trust in the negotiator, and listening is important at all levels of police interaction with the public, as we have seen with call handlers and will see with child complainants and adult witnesses and suspects. Active listening aims to develop a context of trust, although this can be criticised as being synthetic, rather than real. It also involves both 'semantic and verbal skills' (Royce 2005): minimal responses and backchannel signals, paraphrasing and mirroring of the other speaker's turns and the use of pauses. All of these encourage the other to speak. In addition, 'emotion labelling' demonstrates insight into the person's feelings and emotions and '*I* messages' by the negotiator emphasise to the other person that the negotiator is a real person, rather than an amorphous institution.

In Extract 4.4, the negotiator is talking to the bomber via a phone that has been set up at a road block. The bomber was first addressed by means of a megaphone and then directed to the telephone to talk more intimately with the negotiator. The extract is taken from the beginning of the encounter, when the negotiator is trying to get the bomber to divest himself of his body-bomb and lay down his guns. The negotiator, O'Reilly, has already told him that he knows that, although he has been into the local town wearing the body-bomb, he has not hurt anyone.

Extract 4.4

[Mirroring, *I* messages, paraphrases and other active listening features are italicised]

1	Bomber.	No one will be either unless you decide to *declare war on me.*
2	O'Reilly.	No, *we* don't want to *declare war on you*, not at all, not at all, but *I*
3		*do* need you to take off the bomb and to leave the guns on the
4		roadway there.
5	Bomber.	Well, certainly I'm going to keep my weapons: I've had them most
6		of my life.
7	O'Reilly.	*I know* that, *I know* that, but *police* have to make sure that the
8		bomb is disarmed.
9	Bomber.	Yes.
10	O'Reilly.	And *they* can't let you go with the weapons, *they* are going to have
11		to take the weapons from you now. You are under arrest, *O.K?*
12	Bomber.	Now listen, *this is absolutely ridiculous.*
13	O'Reilly.	*I know* from your perspective *it may seem ridiculous* but *the*
14		*people in town* are very worried about it and *the police* are
15		obligated to act, as you can understand.

(Royce 2005: 18–19 and 22)

Royce (2005: 25) suggests that O'Reilly was able to disassociate himself from the 'police' and build a relationship with the bomber, partly through his adaptive use of personal referential pronouns (lines 2, 7, 13). He was also able to create, by using the 'reflective empathizer' *I know* (lines 7 and 13), the impression that he was empathising and this was supported by other active listening techniques such as mirroring (lines 1 and 2; lines 12 and 13) and tag questions (line 11). Interestingly, the bomber makes explicit reference to O'Reilly's listening role, *Now listen* (line 12), indicating that he is coming to see the negotiator as separate from the police and in the role of what Royce describes as 'rescuer' (Royce 2005: 19–20).

Rapport, in the context of a crisis negotiation, or indeed in an abuse interview, means more than simply 'getting on' and is not really about getting to know the other person in the usual social sense. For the professional negotiator it involves the development of an environment for talk, which successfully leads to surrender and arrest. For the interviewer in a child abuse case, it involves the development of a context for disclosure, in which reticence is overcome and honest, open, free and frank talk is achieved.

Leo (1996: 260–61) takes issue with this position, arguing that police interrogation (of suspects) is a 'confidence game' in which the interviewer exploits the powerful relationship, resulting in a 'betrayal of trust'. In this confidence game, Leo argues, 'the suspect's ignorance [is exploited] to create the illusion of a relationship that is symbiotic rather than adversarial' (1996: 284–85). Rock (2001), too, talks of 'simulated concern' by an interviewer when taking a statement from a witness who is struggling to remember details of the event. Thus, a conflicting picture of the professional listener emerges: trust is vital to achieve professional goals, but, at the same time, the activity can be viewed as exploitative, manipulative and an abuse of power. This pretty much sums up a major tension in the criminal justice system as a whole, between, on the one hand, prevention and detection of crime and, on the other, the protection of human rights and social justice.

Police interviews and statements

Police interviews are goal-focused events, the primary aim of which is 'to obtain accurate and reliable accounts from victims, witnesses or suspects about matters under police investigation' (College of Policing 2013) and the collection and synthesis of evidence into a written statement for use in any subsequent court hearing. Statements can be taken from suspects and witnesses, but, whoever they are from, the written statements frequently have more evidential value than the spoken interviews on which they are based. Interviews with suspects are converted into a written text for court cases (known as a ROTI or record of taped interview); this becomes an 'evidential object' in the courtroom, (Johnson 2013: 163; see also Haworth 2010). Statements or interview records can, therefore, literally speak for the witness. Any statements that are undisputed are simply read out in court and accepted as primary evidence, thus sparing the witness(es) from making a personal appearance and also saving the time of the court. So, for example, in the Shipman trial the 'Index of Proceedings' for day 17 shows that more evidence was read out than given in person: ten statements as opposed to only seven witnesses who gave oral evidence and who were cross-examined, (Shipman Trial, Day 17).

Witness statements

As both Rock (2001) and Komter (2006) show, statements are inherently intertextual and dialogic and, although they come to be seen as authoritative versions of the memory of a witness or suspect, they are in fact the result of multiple tellings of the same story in which some details are lost, some transformed and some, it must be admitted, created. The final telling – the statement – is 'moulded through those previous texts' (Rock 2001: 45). Witness testimony moves between spoken and written a number of times on its journey from first telling to presentation in court. Rock (2001 and 2010) identifies four main stages in the 'genesis of a witness statement: (1) witness monologue, (2) questions and answers based on the monologue narrative, (3) note-checking and then (4) the production of a written version (the statement will then be read and signed)'. These result in at least four versions of the story being told, and also, as she acknowledges, the witness will often have told their story several times before they start to tell it to the police officer. Extract 4.5 shows the transitions between the different versions of a witness story as told in monologue, then questioned in two different sequences and, finally, in a written statement.

Extract 4.5
   [IE is interviewee and IR is interviewer]

Monologue

IE   we went to his house anyway and he (.) he invited us in and we was like saw some girls and that and so (.) went up to the house which- (.) the girls (knew) everybody- everybody else there (.) went to the house (.) started having a laugh

(Rock 2010: 136)

Question and answer

175   IR: when you got to the house what happened
176   IE: just talking (.) and laughing and all that and having a little mess about
177   IR: describe the man's house and stuff inside
178   IE: ... ((description of objects in the house)) ...
179   IR: he owns the flat
180   IE: he owns the flat yeah
181   IR: okay um is it a house (.) or is it a like a flat =
182   IE: = it's like it's like a it's a house but it's like put it like two (.) two houses sort of put it as a flat
183   IR: two floors yeah
184   IE: yeah
185   IR: okay and which floor is his house on =
186   IE: = he's he's on the top

(Rock 2010: 135–36)

Checking details in more questions

751   IR: when you get to the top of the stairs where are you
752   IE: urm when you get to the top of the stairs you have to take (.) a right
753   IR: (3.9) yeah
754   IE: and then you have to- when you take a right there's a (.) you got (.) got a door- door on your left door on the right (.) and a door in front of you but we went (.) in the door on the right
755   IR: and what room was that =
756   IE: = that was the living room

(Rock 2010: 135)

Written statement

When we got to the mans [*sic*] house we went in [*sic*] it is a flat on the 1st floor ... To enter the flat you climb up the stairs turn right into the living room.

(Rock 2010: 136)

Rock (2010: 136) describes the steps of moving from monologue to written statement as recontextualisation processes that involve 'transformation', sometimes involving omission of details supplied by the witness. Discrepancies between statements and witness testimonies can be 'highlighted in court, potentially to the great detriment of the witness's testimony' (Rock 2010: 137), making the transformational process not without its dangers.

The statement's story, which is in the voice of the institution, is 'dialogic' in that it bears traces of the underlying dialogue. It is 'another's speech in another language' (Bakhtin 1981: 324) or monologue transformed through dialogue into dialogic monologue. Komter (2006: 196), writing about the Dutch inquisitorial system, defines the talk to text process as 'a chain of events where encounters of spoken interaction are "wedged in" and informed by written documents and where written documents are treated as [the] official basis for decision making on the assumption that they "represent" the spoken interaction'. The interaction of talk and text is therefore a defining and crucial part of the development of a criminal case, from the first oral report, perhaps in a call to the police, through interviews with witnesses and suspects, written statements and notes on file, all the way to a court hearing. What all these genres have in common is a shared orientation, on the part of the institutional participant, to collecting evidential facts for legal decision-making, decisions such as: 'Is a crime taking place?', 'Do the facts constitute an offence?' 'Should the suspect be charged with an offence?' and later: 'Is the defendant guilty of that offence?'

Police/suspect interview structure

Watson's (1976, 1983, 1990) ethnomethodological research into police interviewing practices focuses on the construction of 'reality' through social control in the interview, and, within this context, Atkinson *et al.* (1979) argued for the 'standardization of interrogation procedure' in their report to a Royal Commission. This has largely been achieved with the introduction of the PEACE model in 1992 in Britain and later in other parts of the world, and the Reid technique, in the US and Canada (see Heydon 2012 for a summary of this), though there are continuing strong criticisms of interrogation techiques (e.g. Ainsworth 2010; Berk-Seligson 2009).

The PEACE acronym stands for: Planning and Preparation, Engage and Explain, Account and clarification, Closure, Evaluation. The P and E parts are carried out before and after the interview, giving the interview itself a three-part structure, though part 2 is ideally composed of two phases:

1   *explaining* the legal context and the suspect's rights;
2   (a) getting the suspect to give an *account*, as a freely given uninterrupted monologue;
    (b) probing and *clarifying* it through questioning;
3   *closing* with the legal requirements and explaining what will happen afterwards.

In practice, however, suspects may choose not to give an account, in which case questioning begins to try to elicit an account. See Gibbons (2003: 142) for a more detailed police interview genre.

The Fred and Rosemary West case (the second epigraph for this chapter) is very well-known in the UK. The Wests were convicted of killing their own daughter, Heather, and Fred was convicted of killing 11, and Rosemary nine, other women over a period of 20 years from 1967 to 1987. The police investigation came to the notice of the press in February 1994, when police obtained a warrant to search the garden of the Wests' house. Both Fred and Rosemary were questioned. Detective Sergeant Terence Onions' second interview with Rosemary West begins conventionally (as in the epigraph), with DS Onions' invitation to Mrs West to narrate her own story of how her daughter, Heather, came to leave the family home. Mrs West abruptly declines: *You ask the questions, I'll try and answer them.* Mrs West's decision not to give her own version of events is perhaps unsurprising, since giving the interviewee the initiative can also be seen as an unwelcome freedom. In rejecting the storyteller role, West assigns the role of questioner to the interviewer and puts herself in the role of interviewee. Adopting this role allows West to discover what information and suspicions the police have and her rejection gives her some control of the situation.

After the interview, suspects may give a written statement. Linell and Jönsson (1991: 75) examined the interview and statement stages of eliciting and recording the narrative of a crime in Swedish data. Their interviews were with 'middle-aged or elderly first-time offenders accused of shop-lifting' (1991: 93) and provide clear examples of 'perspectivity conflicts' over the level of detail required. For the suspect:

> the triviality of the legally crucial action – leaving a supermarket without paying for a few articles – may lead [them] to say little about it. Moreover, the majority of them admit the offence, which, from an everyday perspective, may mean that there is no point in wasting more words.
>
> (1991: 93)

However, the police have 'long traditions of professional practice' behind them and much of their institutional role is invested in collecting minute details surrounding the commission of alleged offences. This produces 'an empiricistic, almost behaviouristic, touch to the policemen's concentration on technical details' which 'seem to square well with what is otherwise accepted as legal evidence, such as fingerprints, signatures ... and eye witnesses' testimonies' (Linell and Jönsson 1991: 93–94). The police perspective is the version of events that is written up in the statement or report and the interrogation therefore 'becomes an arena for the authorization of one version of the suspect's alleged criminal conduct' (Linell and Jönsson 1991: 97), although they also note a 'dialogicality underlying the police report' that originates in the two perspectives of the interview. Thus competing narratives are articulated in the course of the interview, but the statement only presents a single, if dialogised, version of events.

Interactional resources in police interviews

Heydon's study of police interviews in Victoria, Australia, builds on the work of Linell and Jönsson and of Auburn *et al.* (1995), who also examine how the police use language to steer the interviewee towards a 'preferred version' of the allegedly criminal events (Heydon 2005: 33). She explores the range of 'discursive practices that construct a police version of events and the role of such interactional resources as accusation-denial/acceptance adjacency pairs, "my side" tellings, topic management tools and formulations' (2005: 117). For example, an accusation-denial structure (Extract 4.6) presents a possible version, which the suspect can accept or deny.

Extract 4.6

Police.   **I put it to you** that you actually went into the kitchen and helped drag in Wayne Gibson one of the bouncers
Suspect.   **no way**

(Heydon 2005: 117)

However, using evidence to challenge a suspect's version of events presents a competing version and attempts to move the suspect towards the police perspective (Extract 4.7).

Extract 4.7

Police.   **all our witnesses say that** you slammed it
           [a shop door, breaking the glass] the second time again
Suspect.   aw well (0.3) **that's what they say**
Police.   you've got nothing to say to that
Suspect.   nup

(Heydon 2005: 130

In terms of topic management she found that suspects introduced fewer new topics than interviewers and that their topics 'were less likely to obligate the recipients to respond to the topic', while interviewers 'initiate new topics disjunctively and even interruptively' in order to construct their version of events (Heydon 2005: 131). Furthermore, the suspect's version was frequently 'formulated' (Garfinkel and Sacks 1970) by the police interviewer in a way that summarised or 'glossed' it, by including some aspects and missing out others, thereby 'fixing' (Heritage 1985) the version in an institutional voice (as in Extract 4.8).

Extract 4.8

Police.	uh **you saw the glass shatter to the ground**
Suspect.	I just kept walking
	I just got in the car
	and Rob me friend said what the hell's going on
	whadcha do
Police.	**so you didn't bother saying anything to them**
	that the glass was broken

(Heydon 2005: 136)

Heritage and Watson (1979: 123) say that in normal conversation a 'formulation enables co-participants to settle on one of many possible interpretations of what they have been saying', but, in police interviews it is overwhelmingly restricted to the interviewer. Heydon draws attention to the suspect's non-confirmation of the first formulation (Extract 4.8 – *you saw the glass shatter to the ground*) leading to the officer repeating the formulation, which provides an evidential gloss on the suspect's action of walking away. Heydon says of the formulation that the investigating officer:

> formulates [the suspect's] prior turns about walking directly to his car after the glass door broke as demonstrating that *he didn't bother saying anything to them*. In this way, [the police officer] constructs a version of events where [the suspect] is remiss, firstly, in evading the suggested course of action by leaving the scene, and secondly, in failing even to consider that such a course of action may have been appropriate.

(Heydon 2005: 137)

Formulating turns – summarising the gist of what has been said before – constitute a micro-narrative, a minimalist reconstruction of the longer narrative detail that the interviewee has contributed, or that the interviewer has inferred from what the interviewee has said. As Heritage and Watson (1980: 247) point out, this activity 'is rarely seen by members as "description for its own sake"'; it 'may be (and very often is) part of some wider conversational activity oriented towards the achievement of an end, e.g., persuading, justifying, making claims'. The police end is to construct an institutionalised, evidential version.

Komter (1998, 2003, 2006), too, looks at formulations in police and courtroom interaction and argues that they are a key resource for the professional in stating 'the record-thus-far' (Komter 2006: 201). Holt and Johnson (2010: 28) show how in formulations the interviewer '*preserves* some information, ... *deletes* other information, … and *transforms* the information' (following Heritage and Watson 1977: 2–3, who describe these as central properties). These powerful police versions of the 'facts' are therefore 'important fact-making moments that distil and encode a version of reality, which will play an important part in any future legal case: an authorized-authoritative version' (Holt and Johnson 2006), if the suspect accepts them. Formulations are often *so*-prefaced (as Extract 4.8 illustrates), a design feature that Drew (1979: 298) finds infrequent in mundane conversations, but frequent, indeed core, activities in a range of institutional settings, as an analysis of police interviews confirms. The detail that is contained in institutional formulations is often intertextually linked with the wording of the law or statute that determines what needs to be proved for the action to constitute an offence. So, for example, the combined acts of choosing goods, passing the till without payment and leaving the store with the goods constitute a theft story rather than a shopping one. This is an issue we return to later.

Topic management is generally controlled by the interviewer, particularly in the interrogation section of the interview and in interviews with children. Johnson (2002) examines the distinctive use of *and*-prefaced and *so*-prefaced questions and the role of these questions in topic connection, topic marking, summarising, development and change. In Extract 4.9, an interview with a child witness, topics are introduced and developed with *and* and *so*.

Extract 4.9
[Child is W; P is police]

1   P.   **Right. So are A and B your brothers?**
2   W.   Yeah.
3   P.   **And** how old are they?
4   W.   A's two and B's eight.
5   P.   That's right. **And** you're the middle one then aren't you at five?
6   W.   (Nods head).
7   P.   Right. **And** can you tell me what your house is like? Can you
8   describe your house to me?
9   W.   Erm.
10   [… Dialogue continues, dealing with W drawing the house and its
          rooms.]
11   **Right. So** can you tell me who sleeps in what bedroom then?
12 W.   My mum and my dad sleep together, and A and B sleep together
13   and I sleep on my own.

So-prefaced questions (lines 1 and 11) indicate topic change and development and *and*-prefaced questions (lines 3, 5 and 7) continue the first topic and connect questions together in a sequence. *So*-prefaced questions, as well as summarising what has been said, can also be used strategically to formulate the 'facts' of the story, as we have already seen.

Reporting prior speech of the suspect, or of other witnesses, can also be an important interviewing resource, as Holt and Johnson (2010) show. In Extract

4.10 the interviewer (IR) reports the indirect speech of the victim – 'she didn't want you to have sex with her' (line 7) – and refers, using reference in 'those words' (line 2) to some prior direct speech attributed by the interviewer to the interviewee (IE): 'X was there and heard you say "If you don't want to shag me I'm gonna get into the bed and shag you anyway"'.

Extract 4.10

```
1  IR:  at that stage she was obviously saying to you she didn't want you to
2       have sex with her otherwise you wouldn't have said those words would you?
3  IE:  No.
4  IR:  D'you see? You're nodding your head.
5  IE:  Yes.
6  IR:  So is it fair to say then that before you had sex with her she was
7       certainly saying to you she didn't want to have sex with you?
8  IE:  She says she don't know I think.
```

Holt and Johnson's (2010: 31) analysis of the turn in lines 6–7 is that the IR 'uses the summarising power of indirect reported speech to persuade the suspect to accept a version of events', a turn that also uses a formulation. In line 8, IE counters this with a weak correction, using indirect reported speech to report his account of the victim's words.

Changes in 'footing' (Goffman 1981) provide another resource which police officers use to switch between acting as a representative of the institution and adopting a more therapeutic tone, as in turns 143, 149 and 163 in Extract 4.11.

Extract 4.11

```
143  We have to find out what's happened to the child. That's our major
     aim as police officers. If you wish to no-reply like your solicitor has
     advised, you can do. If you wish to talk to us and tell us what may have
     happened in reply to the questions that we ask then you have that right
     to do so also.
149  We're here to help you.
163  It's important to you, just for you, to tell us what's happened. You need
     to get it out of your system because at the moment from where we're
     sat you're quite screwed up really about it all.
```

Turns 149 and 163 move away from the institutional voice of turn 143 with its complex subordinated grammar of conditional *if*-clauses and its intertextual reference to the police caution, in the use of the verbs *wish* and *no-reply*, using instead a therapeutic voice that focuses on the interviewee's perceived need to talk, rather than on the institutional need to find out what happened. The institutional *we* (143) seems to change to a more personal *we* (163) and the verb shifts to a more conversational *get it out of your system* from *talk* and *tell*, which is related to institutional aims and rights. The dynamic shift in footing strategically creates a more productive context for disclosure (Johnson 2008).

So far we have looked at interviewer resources, but suspects have interactional resources too. Newbury and Johnson (2006) show in their analysis of one police interview with murder suspect, Shipman, how he appears to be cooperative, but at the same time resists powerful police moves in four ways: through *contest, correction, avoidance* and *refusal*. Contest is when the suspect answers 'no' when the question expects 'yes'; correction occurs in denial and correction sequences like: *No. This happened/is the case.* Avoidance is realised through responses such as *I don't remember, It's a rhetorical question* or *Continue the story* (Extract 4.12) and refusal through *[I have] nothing [to say], There's no answer* or by remaining silent, which is, of course, his right.

Extract 4.12

Police: You see if you examine that record which I'm going to go
           through with you very shortly now to give you the exact time
           that things were altered, it begs the question, did you alter it
           before you left the surgery, which indicates what you've done
           was premeditated and you were planning to murder this lady, or
           as soon as you got back did you cover up your tracks and start
           altering this lady's medical records? Either way it's not a good
           situation for you doctor is it?
Shipman: *Continue the story.*

Although he is asked two questions, (one giving a pair of equally damaging alternatives and the other with a coercive tag), Shipman's resistance strategy avoids information-giving, whilst encouraging the officer to give more information about the construction of the police case or hypothesis. His use of the imperative form, 'Continue the story' 'functions to imply that the interviewer is telling a story and not asking a question and therefore no answer is required' (Newbury and Johnson 2006: 229–30). Since it is in the interviewee's interests to present himself as a cooperative interlocutor, resistance has potentially significant costs, presenting, as it does, a challenge to the consensus of power and control. Shipman attempts to minimise the costs by his skilful manoeuvering. Ehrlich and Sidnell (2006) and Haworth (2006) have also examined resistance strategies, Ehrlich and Sidnell in a Canadian public inquiry, showing similar findings. Haworth (2006: 747), in her analysis of a second police interview with Shipman, shows a further resistance strategy in which he uses 'his professional status [as a doctor] as a shield, shifting the focus of blame onto the institution to which he belongs, instead of on himself as an individual member'.

A final interactional resource is perhaps a surprising one, which can be used by both police and suspects: laughter. According to Carter (2011: 41ff) suspects' use of laughter can 'buttress innocence', 'reject' officer allegations and 'challenge the officer', whereas officer laughter can be used to 'challenge the suspect' and 'break the rules' (Carter 2011: 54ff).

Vulnerable witnesses – on interviewing children and rape victims

Interviewing children requires particularly finely honed skills. In order to answer questions the interviewee needs 'to possess socio-cultural knowledge about question-answer sequences' and needs to 'make assumptions about their interlocutors' intentions, knowledge states and beliefs' (Kremer-Sadlik 2004: 190). It is therefore challenging to pose questions for children, or anyone with communication difficulties, to answer.

One of the first difficulties is the institutional legal voice, which, as we saw in Chapter 3, contains words that have specific meanings not found in everyday conversations. Very young child witnesses have little experience of legal language. Although an adult is capable of responding to a police invitation to tell their story: 'Can you *say in your own words* what *happened*?', a child needs more prompting. In the following example (Extract 4.13), the invitation to a teenage rape victim is long and explanatory, indicating some of the meanings implicit in the italicised words of the shorter: 'Can you *say in your own words* what *happened*?'.

Extract 4.13

Okay you said that you're up here today to **speak** to us about erm this – to catch this person who raped you. Yeah? What I need you to do is **tell me what happened**. I know that you've **told other people what happened**, okay. But **I don't know what's happened**, right. What I want you to do is, **like in a story tell me from say Friday night**, Friday was it four o'clock. **Tell me from Friday four o'clock, all right, evening time. Until Sunday morning. What has happened to you over those – those couple of days. Give me as much detail as you can because obviously I'll go over it again er and– and get as much as I – I need from you, but if you can tell me as much as you can yourself, all right, and I'll just let you talk.** All right, so off you go.

Simply telling what happened is seen as much more: a story with precise start and end points and with details revealed in monologic talk. The invitation is an attempt to elicit 'undialogized' and individual speech (*yourself … let you talk*), newly 'created' and free of the interviewer's 'accented' style and 'given' meanings (Bakhtin 1986: 119–20). The interviewer's presence will determine the storyteller's choices of words and event narration. This 'addressivity' (Bakhtin 1986: 95) is part of the process of story creation.

So-prefaced questions are frequent, as we saw in interviews with adults, as a way of arriving at an institutionally authoritative version of events. In an interview with a teenage rape victim, the complainant introduces the information that the suspect had a knife:

414   *W*   He had a knife and he was slitting down the side of the tarpaulin.

The interviewer questions establish that the witness was quite a distance away from the suspect when she saw this and a challenge comes in turn 435 (*So how far away were you from the lorry?*), signalled by *so*, and made explicit in turn 441 (Extract 4.14) by the metadiscursive verbal group *trying to get at*. The challenge unfolds in the interviewer's turns 443, 445 and 447 and culminates in a reformulation from the officer in 449 where the earlier claim made by the witness (turn 414) is re-presented to the interviewee for agreement.

Extract 4.14

441   Okay. **What I'm trying to get at is if – if you're a distance away, how do you know he had a knife in his hand** and what w–
443   Right. **So you didn't actually see the knife.** You just saw what he'd actually done.
445   Okay. **Did you see the blade at all?**
447   Right. **'Cause I'm talking about from here.** [using map drawn by witness to indicate position]
449   Right, okay then. **So you assumed that he was cutting it with a knife at that time?**

Challenge is necessary to gain accurate and robust facts that will stand up to unfriendly cross-examination in court. In this exchange the officer probes (over 35 turns) the witness's account, accurately identifying a problem and more reliably establishing the point at which the teenager could see the knife. Slightly later (in turn 472) in the complainant's story she says *He put the knife to my throat and says get up* and shortly afterwards the interviewer says *So can you see what kind of knife it is now?* (turn 479), accepting that this is an appropriate point for the witness to describe the knife and inviting her to draw it.

There is therefore a tension in interview interaction, between collecting robust facts and avoiding intimidation. Witnesses are not best placed to evaluate their own talk as evidence, and it is therefore the job of the interviewer to assess the adequacy of the details they are given and to elicit enhanced versions. A further tension is the need for the evidence to be in the witness's own words. In order for intimidation not to occur, the interviewer needs to create a positive and trusting atmosphere and, to this end, in the UK, a whole section of the interview is allocated to establishing rapport, a practice recommended by the Ministry of Justice (2011) in the UK.

Another tension is the need to provide information in questions that children can respond to, but also to avoid leading the witness or putting words into their mouth. This can result in lengthy exchanges in which the interviewer attempts to elicit a narrative in the child's own words. Aldridge and Wood (1998) give an example of one such exchange with a seven-year-old, where the interviewer is trying to elicit her own words for 'vagina' and 'penis' [I is interviewer and C is child].

Extract 4.15

I.   So what part of your body are we talking about?
C.   I don't want to tell you 'coz it'll embarrass me, that's why.
I.   Well I tell you what, say it really quickly.
C.   No.
I.   What about if we do it another way. Do you go swimming?
C.   [Nods]
I.   Right, what do you wear when you go swimming?
C.   A cossie.
I.   Right. On your body, where does your cossie cover? Which parts of you?
C.   All from here.
I.   And what does [name of child's brother] wear when he goes swimming?
     [9 intervening turns]
I.   Right, so you know all about that. All we've got to do now is decide names for those parts of the body isn't it?
     [11 intervening turns]
I.   What's on a boy then?
C.   A long thing.
I.   A long thing. Right, what's that long thing? What do you call it at home?
C.   I don't want to say.
I.   You don't want to say. OK, what does [name of child's brother] call it?
C.   C. Sometimes a jimmy.
     [6 intervening turns]
I   Ok right so what does daddy call it? ...
C.   Well, he calls it a different name.
I   He calls it a different name. What's that?
C.   Which is spelt W.E.L.Y
I.   Is that, if I say it welly?
C.   No.
I.   What is it then?
C.   W.I.L, two Ls, yeah. W.I.L.L.Y.
I.   Right, is that willy? Is that the word you don't want to say?
C.   [Nods]

(Aldridge and Wood 1998: 159–61)

The interviewer and child engage in adaptive strategies to achieve success. It is the child that comes up with the spelling solution w.e.l.y., even though the first attempt is unsuccessful. The child cannot understand fully why the interviewer cannot supply the word, even though she explains that she needs to know the specific name the child has. The child is unable to overcome her embarrassment, so this is something that the interviewer has to try to resolve. The interviewer role needs, therefore, to be patient, persistent and adaptive.

The interviewing of rape victims is an area that has received considerable critical attention. Fairclough (1995: 28–30) discusses an example from an interview between two male officers and a female alleging rape and shows how 'ideologically-based coherence' which is based on ideologies that are seen as 'naturalized' creates conditions in which the woman's story is devalued. The interviewer says *you're female and you've probably got a hell of a temper*, implying that the woman could have done more to signal her lack of consent (1995: 30).

A UK Home Office Report (February 2005) found that there was an increased number of reports of rape and a 'relatively static number of convictions', which they characterised as 'increasing the justice gap' (Kelly *et al.* 2005: x). The authors report that 'all UK studies of attrition in rape cases concur that the highest proportion of cases is lost at the earliest stages, with between a half and two thirds dropping out at the investigative stage' (Kelly *et al.* 2005: x). The report contains a recommendation 'that a shift occurs within the CJS [Criminal Justice System] from a focus on the discreditability of complainants to a concentration on enhanced evidence gathering and case-building' (Kelly *et al.* 2005: x, xii). MacLeod (2010), in her study of interviews with rape complainants describes the ways police interviewers use interactional resources to shape their accounts, pointing to the use of reported speech and formulations, which have a range of effects from supportive ones such as 'cooperative recycling' to, more worryingly, the use of reported speech as 'a threat to authorship' (2010: 131). MacLeod illustrates the latter effect by showing an interviewer's misquoting of the complainant's prior speech, where she reports that some people were taking 'cocaine', the interviewer replacing 'cocaine' with 'coke'. MacLeod (2010: 133) argues that the replacement term 'suggests some higher degree of familiarity with the substance than using its full name' and that 'the possible implications for this in terms of the interviewee's perceived credibility are obvious'. Studies therefore suggest that there are still lessons to be learnt about the investigation of offences in relation to collecting evidence through interviews with children and rape complainants.

Context, intertextuality and audience design

Imagine a bare room containing simply four seated participants and audio-tape recording equipment. This is the environmental context for a standard British police interview. There will normally be two police officers, one an interviewer, the other a note-taker, and a witness or suspect, who may have an accompanying solicitor, parent or social worker. This is what Gibbons (2003: 142) calls the 'primary reality'; there also exist other realities that are equally important and which are illustrated in Extract 4.16 from the early part of a police interview with a male suspected of stabbing his girlfriend during an argument. It begins with the interviewer (I) interrupting the suspect's (S) storytelling.

Extract 4.16

117	I.	Can I can I just perhaps interrupt you there for moment just so I can get a full picture. What sort of a state were both of you in I mean were you drunk, happy?
118	S.	Well I was pretty happy.
119	I.	Drunk I'm talking about.
120	S.	Well it's quite true to say that I had been drinking. I was not paralytic. I was tired. I was wondering why – why she was shouting and screaming and hitting me because I did not understand that. I knew [victim's name] was stoned as well as pissed. I knew that she'd drunk quite a fair amount and I knew that she was stoned.
121	I	You're saying to me that you knew that she was drunk and high on drugs. Is that what you're –
122	S.	– yes.
123	I.	I'm sorry you – everybody must understand exactly what you're saying er ok then. So she's banging your head against the wall did you say?
124	S.	Yeah I kept trying to walk away.

There are three simultaneous realities of context operating in Extract 4.16. Apart from the primary reality of the interview room, there is also 'the secondary reality' (Gibbons 2003: 142), the event that is being talked about, that is the argument and subsequent fight that have resulted in arrest. The transitions between these two realities are indicated by shifts in tense: the interview is in the present tense (*you're saying to me*) and the story in the past: *What sort of state were both of you in?* (interviewer turn 117); *I kept trying to walk away* (suspect turn 124). Sometimes the past is vividly in the present: *she's there shouting* (turn 126) and then moves back to the past. A third reality also exists and is invoked by the interviewer in turn 123, when he makes reference to *everybody*. With only four people present, the referents for this pronoun are unclear, unless we consider the wider future context for the utterance: a judge and jury in a courtroom. The use of *everybody* is thus a 'contextualization cue' (Gumperz 1982, 2003), which signals the institutional meanings of the talk, and draws attention to the virtual presence of the future audience. The relexicalisation of *pissed* and *stoned* as *drunk* and *high on drugs* models the kind of talk that is appropriate for this audience and tells the suspect that future listeners may not understand him. The rewording reshapes the context from the informal and lay to the institutional. The use of *saying* reinvokes the caution with its warning about inferences that may be drawn, if the accused chooses not to reveal some or all of what he knows, and also indexes the legal frame, one that values precision, formality and standardness. The suspect is positioned to view the story recipient (the interviewer) as a representative of the *everybody* who, although absent in the present, will be present in the future. All of these recontextualisations disturb the present and foreground the wider contextual frame of the institutional judicial system that comes into view against the background of the bareness of the interview room.

This future context for interview talk is therefore a very important one, though one which is often only barely recognised by suspects and witnesses, a point also noted by Haworth (2013). The legal field, the present and future participants and their formal relationship with the interviewee, along with the spoken channel that is recorded for future use, all create a complex contextual configuration of *field, tenor* and *mode* (Halliday and Hasan 1989). Haworth (2013) investigates 'the communicative challenges posed by multiple future audiences', using Bell's (1984) 'audience design' model. In her analysis she shows how this contextual configuration is 'discursively counterintuitive to participants' (Haworth 2013: 45), suggesting that some of the effects of this have 'potentially serious consequences' for justice.

The police interview not only looks forward to the future courtroom context, but also refers intertextually to prior texts, including other witness statements and legislation. Johnson (2006: 667) demonstrates the intertextual implications and interactional hybridity of the police interview with an analysis of the closing stages of an interview with a woman suspected of stealing money. The data is represented in Table 4.1. On the left you can see the close of the interview and on the right you can compare it with sections of the Theft Act 1968, which defines the offence and which the interview echoes. The words in bold are those that are intertextually linked.

Comparison of the two columns draws our attention to the hybrid nature of interview talk. On the surface it appears to sum up and close the questioning phase of the interview, but looking beneath the surface it subtly incorporates the legislative genre, a fact which may be at best only partially understood by the interviewee. The effect is to produce a complex and powerful set of communicative actions that create interpretative challenges for the lay participant and implicate her fully in a textbook act of theft, without her uttering any of the words and no more than 'yeah' or 'mhm'. Both of these contextual features, then – the ambiguous future audience and subtle intertextual echoes – are only fully understood by the institution and are therefore problematic for suspects and potential impediments for justice.

Conclusion

In this chapter we have followed the collection of evidence from initial emergency calls to interviews with witnesses and suspects, focusing on some of the common interactional resources used by professionals to support, control and challenge lay speakers and some of the strategies lay speakers use to respond. We have not looked at disputed interviews. That is reserved for Part II. We have also not looked at question types, but rather interactional resources at a more functional level. There are suggestions for further reading (Johnson 2006; Oxburgh, Mycklebust and Grant *et al.* 2010) which deal with question form, also in interpreted police interviews (Nakane 2014), and we develop the understanding of question form and function in Chapter 5 in relation to courtroom questioning. In the further reading you will also encounter a range of approaches, some of which develop the critical stance to interviewing practices we have begun to articulate here.

Table 4.1 Intertextual links between interview talk and legislation

Police interview concerning theft	Theft Act 1968
IR: So is that the amount that you closed the account with – IE: Mhm. I think so. IR: **knowing** for a while that all the **monies** that you've transferred from the date we've just gone through those transactions – IE: Mhm. IR: we're talking from the fourteenth of the second, the transactions I've just done, all the **monies** there, **you knew wasn't your money**? IE: Yeah. IR: And you've actually stolen it from the Skipton Building Society haven't you, that amounts to **theft**. IE: Why do you need –	A person is guilty of **theft** if he **dishonestly [cf. knowing] appropriates [cf. taken] property belonging to another** with the intention of permanently depriving the other of it; and 'thief' and 'steal' shall be construed accordingly (section 1).
IR: You've taken – you've **taken money** which in effect – IE: Yes. IR: – is **property**. IE: Mhm.	**Property** includes **money** and all other property, real or personal including things in action and other intangible property (section 4).
IR: And you've **assumed rights of ownership**.	Any **assumption** by a person of **the rights of an owner** amounts to an appropriation (section 3).
IR: And you've **used that money as your own** IE: Mhm. Yeah. IR: Is that right? IE: Yeah. IR: **Knowing** that that **money is not yours**. IE: Yeah.	A person appropriating **property belonging to another** without meaning the other permanently to lose the thing itself is nevertheless to be regarded as having the intention of permanently depriving the other of it if his intention is **to treat the thing as his own** to dispose of regardless of the other's rights (section 6).

Further reading

Emergency calls: Edwards (2007); Drew and Walker (2010).
Police interviews and statements: Carter (2011); Coulthard and Johnson (eds) (2010) – chapters by Ainsworth, Benneworth, Haworth, Holt and Johnson, Rock, Stokoe and Edwards; Shuy (1998 – Chapters 2, 10 and 11); Oxburgh, Myklebust and Grant (2010); Rock (2001).

Research tasks

1 *Calls to the emergency services.* Explore Nicole Simpson's emergency call available from http://simpson.walraven.org/911-1993.html in relation to the issues raised in the chapter. How does the CT manage the interaction? Then examine how the call is treated in court on 31 January 1995 in the evidence by the CT, Gilbert, at: http://simpson.walraven.org/jan31.html.

2 *Police interviews.* Go to the Harold Shipman or Rose West police interviews referred to in this chapter, or other interviews that you can find. Investigate regular features of interviewing, using features described here and identified in your further reading and compare them with those in guidelines, codes and models, such as the Reid technique (USA) or PEACE model used in England or the law from the Police and Criminal Evidence Act 1984 and its Codes of Practice.

3 Contrast features you have identified in your own study of interviews, or from your reading, with those found in the disputed interviews in Chapters 6, 8 and 9.

4 Follow Rock's (2001) 'Genesis of a witness statement' model and ask: an aquaintance acting as a witness to tell a story of a 'crime' or a true perplexing incident that has happened to them. To replicate similar conditions, your witness should not be a close friend. Make an audio-recording of the whole process, including the writing down of the story at the end and then produce a transcript of the whole event. See if you managed to avoid leading questions and investigate how the story becomes transformed during the retellings, referring to Komter (2003, 2006) and other readings.

5   Trial discourse

Judge: Now, you're going to have the benefit of some very skilful and very, very good lawyers. But let me caution you now. What the lawyers say in the opening statements and the closing arguments is not evidence. And you shall not receive their statements as evidence. The only evidence that you will consider in this case is evidence that you hear from the witnesses who testify before you in open court under oath and any exhibits that are introduced through various witnesses.

(Cited in Harris 2005: 221)

Cross-examination in the William Kennedy Smith rape trial in the United States, 1991 (L is Lawyer; W is Witness)

L: Did you take off your pantyhose at Au Bar? [Pantyhose are tights in British English.]

W: I don't remember doing that.

L: Did you have your pantyhose on when you left the bar?

W: I'm, I think I did.

L: Did you have your pantyhose on when you drove your car from Au Bar [with Smith as her passenger]?

W: Yes.

L: Did you have your pantyhose on when you got to the parking lot at the Kennedy home?

W: Yes.

L: Did you have your pantyhose on when you got out of your car?

W: I'm not sure.

[There follow six more *Did you have your pantyhose on when ...* questions to which the witness replies: *I don't remember.*]

(Conley and O'Barr 1998: 36)

Introduction – into the courtroom

The first thing that strikes any visitor to a courtroom is the strangeness of the setting. Everything about it produces a sense of nervous excitement and hushed voices: the layered, hierarchical, windowless space with the judge(s) or magistrates supreme, ritual conventions of standing to the call of 'All rise!', the professional uniforms of lawyers in wigs and robes (in some countries) and of police officers waiting to give evidence, and witnesses and families looking nervous and dressed up for the occasion. The researcher feels like an intruder in a private space, even though most courtrooms are open, public places, a feeling intensified by the fact that cases often originate in the private domain of domestic matters. The spectator is aware that they are witnessing the lived experiences of their neighbours, though not as they have seen them before.

We also quickly become aware of the power of the legal-linguistic encounter. In the first epigraph we see a judge warning a jury about the force of legal argument and instructing them not to be swayed by it, but to focus their attention instead on the evidence of witnesses, a task that is difficult, particularly when lawyers use questions that imply a legal argument, as we see in the second epigraph. This draws our attention to the power of cross-examination in the adversarial system. During Patricia Bowman's cross examination in the William Kennedy Smith rape trial the defence lawyer uses a highly repetitive questioning technique, producing a perspective of the witness that 'decent people do not lose track of their underwear when in mixed company' (Conley and O'Barr 1998: 37), and controlling the witness's ability to express her perspective: that taking off one's panty-hose is a perfectly ordinary act. 'In an effort to understand the effect' of this distinctive technique, Conley and O'Barr (1998: 37) asked many of their students to analyse the excerpt, reporting that 'the students continually focus on Black's ability to manipulate gender differences in the classification of clothing'. For US men clothing is classified as either *clothes* or *underwear,* with pantyhose classed as underwear, or intimate clothing. For women, however, pantyhose are 'interstitial', somewhere between underwear and clothing. 'Their removal does not always imply intimacy', such as when walking on a sandy beach (as in this case). Nevertheless, the defence lawyer's questions imply: 'How can a man be held responsible for his actions toward such a woman?'. He has 'identified and exploited a topic that has no male counterpart. It is meaningful only because the sexuality of the woman is at issue' (Conley and O'Barr 1998: 37) and his control of the questions prevent the witness from putting forward her perspective, producing a situation 'that may contribute to the process of revictimization' (Conley and O'Barr 1998: 22).

We might be tempted to assume that the asymmetrical courtroom encounter and lawyers' use of power is always perilous for lay people. However, the asymmetrical relationship does not always mean that power is used in a negatively constraining way. In Chapter 6 (Extract 6.9) we use an example from Eades (2002), which shows powerful witness *support*. When a child witness is asked a complex cross-examination question, the prosecuting lawyer steps in and says, 'With respect

Your Worship – there are three elements to that question and I ask my Friend to break them down', at which point the magistrate intervenes and asks the defence lawyer to 'break it up one by one'. In examination-in-chief, too, the lawyer works to support the witness, helping her to present her case in the best way. Adversarial activities of coercion and support, therefore, have to be viewed in sociolinguistic terms: who is speaking, when, and for what purpose, as we pointed out in Chapter 2. As Drew and Heritage (1992: 21) observe, 'the character of institutional inter-action varies widely across different institutional tasks and settings'. As the tasks change from examination to cross-examination, so does the status and identity of the institutional speaker and the witness, and the relationships between the two.

This chapter focuses on trial discourse, first examining its complex structure and developing an understanding of the 'complex genre' (Heffer 2005: 71) that is the adversarial trial. Then, we build on the pragmatic and sociolinguistic issues that we introduced in Chapter 2, extending these into trial discourse and dealing with issues such as narrative, expert witnesses and children in the courtroom. We focus mainly on interaction from the superior courts, (that is not magistrates' courts). Several of the data extracts used here are from the Shipman murder trial transcript (The Shipman Inquiry 2001), available online. Trial transcripts are not readily available to researchers, so this is a valuable resource. Shipman was found guilty in January 2000 of murdering 15 of his patients and forging a will. After the trial an inquiry was established to investigate the deaths of other patients who died in similar circumstances. It concluded that he had killed at least 215 and, thanks to the inquiry, the trial transcript was made available to the public. Other extracts used are from forensic linguistic research, such as the work of Harris and Conley and O'Barr cited in the epigraphs. Some countries provide public access to trial transcripts, such as Brazil or China, so it is worth checking in the country you live in. Generally, though, in English-speaking countries, trial transcripts are not freely available for research, though they can be purchased.

The trial as a complex genre

Heffer's (2005: 71) description of the adversarial jury trial as a 'complex genre' is based on the different sequential activities which structure the trial and the diverse functions which these activities serve (shown in Table 5.1).

Heffer (2005: 67) also identifies three trial phases and principal genres: *procedural* genres of jury selection and the calling and swearing-in of witnesses; *adversarial* genres such as opening statements, witness examinations, and closing argument; *adjudicative* genres such as the judge's summation and sentencing. Cotterill (2003: 94) notes that the trial's highly structured form involves two modes of address: *monologic,* where one speaker is addressing the court, as in opening and closing statements by the lawyers, or the judge instructing the jury and summing-up; and *dialogic,* where two speakers are interacting, such as during the examination and cross-examination of witnesses. In addition, Maley (1994: 16) provides a chart of legal genres, which is expanded by Gibbons (2003: 132–33) to include both pre-trial (e.g. police interview, committal hearing)

Table 5.1 The jury trial sequence, activities, and functions, adapted from Heffer (2005: 71)

Sequence	Activities	Function
1	Jury selection	Decision-making
2	Indictment	Legal construction
3	Opening address	Story construction
4	Prosecution evidence – questioning *Witness 1*	Fact construction – narrative support
	• *examined by prosecution* • *cross-examined by defence* • *(re-examined by prosecution)*	
	Witness 2 – examined etc.	
5	Defence evidence – questioning *Witness 1*	Fact construction – narrative support
	• *examined by defence* • *cross-examined by prosecution* • *(re-examined by defence)*	
	Witness 2 – examined etc.	
6	Closing speeches – prosecution and defence	Story construction
7	Directing the jury and summing-up	Legal construction
8	Jury deliberation and verdict	Decision-making
9	Sentencing	Legal construction

and trial genres, which he describes as *dynamic* genres, which are distinct from *codified* written genres, such as legislation, contracts, and judgments.

The adversarial trial system that exists as a result of colonialism in English-speaking countries around the world, (e.g. USA, Canada, Australia, New Zealand, Kenya, Nigeria, Hong Kong Special Administrative Region (SAR)), does show some small variations in form and structure. For example, in the USA there is no summing-up by the judge, and in Hong Kong SAR juries consist of up to seven members, rather than 12. In England and Wales the defence lawyer only makes one speech to the jury (usually a closing speech), whereas in the USA both prosecution and defence lawyers can make speeches at the opening and closing of the trial.

Speech events involve a large number of participants – judge, jury, clerk, recorder, prosecution and defence barristers (the term used in England and Wales, Australia, Hong Kong SAR) or attorneys (the US term) and their teams, the accused, witnesses, ushers, the press and the public – though the extent to which they speak and listen is different, depending on both their role and the stage of the trial. Witnesses speak when lawyers ask them questions; much of the time the judge listens, though s/he can ask questions too; the jury listen all the time, except when they are sent out of the court during interaction between the judge and lawyers to sort out points of law, until they meet in the private space of the jury room to deliberate. Much of the trial involves the *appearance* of witnesses, as sections 4 and 5 of the table show and as the epigraphs indicate. Irrespective of whether witnesses appear for the prosecution or defence the genre conforms to the following four or five-part structure (Gibbons 2003: 134) – the item in brackets is optional.

1   Opening
    (a) Calling in by *court officer/usher*
    (b) Swearing in with *court officer/usher*
2   Examination-in-chief by *friendly counsel*
3   Cross examination by *opposing counsel*
4   (Re-examination by *friendly counsel*)
5   Dismissal by *judge*

Gibbons (2003: 132) describes the witness appearance as 'the nesting of genres within other structures', since it is contained within the larger structure of the prosecution and defence cases. In Britain, the clerk, who reads the indictment, also invokes an absent participant, the Crown. For all the participants, speaking is strictly controlled by rules and norms which, for everyone except lay witnesses and the defendant, are part of their daily work. Heffer notes that a single question and answer sequence between a defence lawyer and witness:

> involves at least four principal speech participants who remain 'online' during the examination, but with different speaking rights and participant roles. Examining counsel initiates with a question, a right shared by the judge, but not the witness or jury. The witness is obliged to respond. The judge listens and may interrupt at any time. The jury ... listen but may not interrupt, though they are allowed to ask questions indirectly via written notes to the judge. Opposing counsel has the right to interrupt, though this occurs surprisingly infrequently in English courts ... At the same time, non-verbal communication can take place between all four participants in such forms as gaze, gesture, facial expressions, prosodic features and other non-verbal vocalizations.
>
> (Heffer 2005: 47–48)

And, as we saw in Chapter 2, the use of an interpreter in witness examination adds a further complex layer of talk in the otherwise mainly dyadic encounter. At the same time, the judge, clerk and recorder are making notes, and members of the public and the media are listening, but with no right to speak or even whisper audibly. There are many more listeners than speakers in the courtroom, with side conversations constrained and censored. Members of the public will be chastised if they talk and, as Cotterill shows, even lawyers can be censored in their speech by the judge. When the lawyers in the O.J. Simpson trial spoke *sotte voce* close to the jury, they sometimes did not speak quietly enough. Judge Ito disciplined them, as the jury's overhearing could influence their decisions: 'Counsel, if I have to warn you to keep your voice down one more time, it's going to cost you 250 bucks' (in Cotterill 2003: 97).

Trial genres – from jury selection to deliberation and verdict

Since witness examination makes up the largest part of any trial, most of the research that has been carried out has focused on examination and cross-examination. For that reason we make that a major focus of the next section, but, before we do that, it is worth mentioning some of the research that has been done in relation to other trial phases and genres. Cotterill's (2003) investigation of the O.J. Simpson trial deals with all of the phases of the trial including the *voir dire* (the preliminary examination of jurors in the US courts to determine their suitability to serve as jurors), the opening statements, which are described in terms of their ability to frame the narrative through 'strategic lexicalisation', closing statements, where she shows how metaphor is a powerful rhetorical strategy used by lawyers (see also Cotterill 1998), and the deliberation and verdict.

Cotterill's (2003: 65ff) discussion of opening statements examines 'the role of strategic lexical choices in constructing the prosecution and defence narrative frameworks'. She reveals how analysis of the lawyer's lexical selection, which represents actors and actions in positive or negative ways, frames prosecution and defence stories. The prosecution case represented O.J. Simpson as violent to his wife, while the defence represented Nicole Simpson as manipulative and promiscuous. Cotterill suggests that the prosecution's choice of words such as *encounter* and *control* with their negative 'semantic prosodies' (Louw 1993) realised by collocates such as *prejudice, problems, opposition, risks, hazards* is central to the conceptualisation of O.J. Simpson as a violent man capable of murder. The defence, on the other hand, seek to diffuse this image by presenting the violence as 'verbal rather than physical' (Cotterill 2003: 80). This was achieved through lexical choices with much more neutral or positive semantics like *incident, dispute, discussion* and *conversation* as ways of lexicalising talk in the Simpson household, thereby paving the way for a defence narrative that refutes physical violence and the capacity for murder. This framing of the witness evidence to follow is, as Cotterill suggests, a powerful tool in orienting the jury 'towards their side's version of the trial narrative' (2003: 90).

If opening statements frame the evidence of witnesses, the closing statements evaluate the validity, reliability, value, truth and significance of witness stories following examination and cross-examination. This constitutes what Harris (2005 quoting Labov 1972a) calls 'the point' of the story, that is its significance in relation to the defendant's guilt or innocence. Cotterill's treatment of the closing speeches shows how the prosecution use metaphors as 'a structuring device', but the defence use them 'as a dramatic highlighter of particular individuals and events' (Cotterill 1998: 127). The prosecution's use of the jigsaw puzzle metaphor, as a task the jury must perform to make a picture of a guilty killer, is subverted in the defence speech. The defence both attack and extend the metaphor with defence lawyer, Cochran, saying:

when you buy a puzzle ... so you know what the puzzle looks like when it is finished. Well, in this case, the prosecution took a photograph or picture of OJ Simpson first, then they took the pieces apart. ... you don't jump to conclusions at the beginning.

(O.J. Simpson trial online: http://simpson.walraven.org/sep28.html)

Since the defence are allowed the last word, the defence hijacking of the prosecution puzzle metaphor in this case reframes the argument and leaves a different impression on the jury.

Hobbs (2003) also focuses on closing arguments, describing them as 'impression management' and pointing to the ways that lawyers' arguments deal with defendant identities as culpable or innocent. Felton Rosulek (2009, 2015), in her research on the opposing arguments of closing statements, finds that 'silencing, de-emphasizing and emphasizing' are key strategies that lawyers rely on. For example, 'some of the prosecution lawyers emphasized the youth of the victims in the [17] cases by referring to them by their nicknames, while the defence de-emphasized this by referring to them using their full names'; defence lawyers also 'de-emphasized or even silenced the negative (violent, sexual, criminal etc.) aspects of the defendant's alleged or known actions by not mentioning them or using generalizations' (Felton Rosulek 2015: 190).

Heffer (2005) deals with the post-evidence phase of the trial: the judge's summing-up and his directions to the jury, an important pair of trial genres. Summing-up is 'expressly forbidden' in most US states (Marcus 2013: 5), though it is found in most other Common Law systems in Australia, Canada, Hong Kong SAR, New Zealand, and England and Wales. Heffer's corpus exploration of 60 different judicial summations finds that there is 'a range of interconnected strategies' involved in creating 'judicial perspective' (2005: 188). These strategies of 'perspectival modification' range from those that are 'intended to influence' the jury, starting with bald statements such as, *The officer's identification is reliable,* through *intensification, normalisation, hedging, attribution* and *disclamation* (*You may think his identification is reliable. It is a matter for you to decide*). The ones at the end of the range are those 'that are intended to maintain impartiality' (Heffer 2005: 1888–89).

Johnson (2014: 53) examines the many uses of quotation (in Heffer's terms, attribution) in the 11 days of the judge's summing-up in the Shipman trial, focusing on the 'pragmatic effects of the metadiscursive and sensory verbs, *refer, remind, summarise, look, read* and the most frequent and 'key' reporting verbs, *told* and *said*', showing how the judge uses the 'authority of quotation and judicial (re)organization to make the jury question the contrasted material and stimulate meaning-making and decision-making'. In summing-up and through quotation the judge is able to reorganise what was said by Shipman in the defence case, juxtaposing it and making it simultaneous with what witnesses said many days before in the prosecution case. 'This juxtaposition and simultaneity foregrounds difference, making it easy for the jury to make decisions about the opposing facts' (Johnson 2014: 65). While summing-up has been described as monologic, Johnson (2014: 66) demonstrates that it is polyvocal 'as multiple voices, times and contexts occur simultaneously through the one voice and time of the judge's summing up'.

Cotterill's (2003) examination of the jury deliberation in the O.J. Simpson trial focuses on the jurors' post-trial stories and highlights the ways that the differing storytelling abilities of the lawyers in the O.J. Simpson case affected jurors. In that case, jury members were explicitly authorised by the judge to tell their stories after the trial ended. Knox, one of the jurors who applauded the defence lawyers' storytelling abilities, said that 'what both lawyers have in common is their ability to give you a story, an interesting narrative wrapped around their facts'; while the defence 'Dream Team' constituted 'a show' with 'power and charisma', the prosecution 'never knew how to present [their case], they couldn't keep it sharp and simple' (Knox 1995, cited in Cotterill 2003: 222). As Cotterill observes, jury deliberation involves both joint evaluation of narratives and individual use of 'internalised story schemata' (2003: 224).

> In many of the post-trial writings and interviews, jurors spoke of the individual and collective process of *narrative typification* (Jackson 1995: 419) which went on in the jury room, whereby they attempted to 'make sense' of the evidence. Through a process of trying the various stories on for size, the jurors attempted to reach a consensus on the most acceptable 'fit' of the story, given the evidence presented.
>
> (Cotterill 2003: 223)

These story schemata can be linked to 'master narratives' (Bamberg 2004) in the social and cultural world, which are powerful social forces that act on juries as they respond to argument and storytelling within the trial in combination with the master narratives they bring with them as socially constructed and constituted citizens. We deal with narrative in the trial in more depth later in this chapter.

Examination and cross-examination of witnesses

Witnesses are examined, cross-examined, and re-examined entirely through questions. Since questions and their eliciting speech act function are so central to the trial, it is important to understand what we mean by them. Pragmatically speaking, questions are turns that elicit answers as responses. In grammar, questions, or interrogatives, are distinguished from other clause types (statements/declaratives; commands/imperatives) and formally described in terms of five main types:

1   *Wh*-questions (also called polar questions). which 'elicit missing information'
2   *Yes/no* questions, 'to ask whether a proposition is true or false'
3   Alternative questions, 'to ask which of two or more alternatives is the case'
4   Tag questions, which 'seek confirmation of the statement the speaker has just uttered'

5   Declarative questions (Quirk et al. 1985), which typically express statements
    but which serve an eliciting speech-act function.

                                                            (Biber *et al.* 2002: 249)

Thus, the declarative clause – *You are leaving work early today* – can be used as
a declarative question with the addition of rising intonation or made into a *yes/no*
question by inverting the subject and operator (*are* in the verb phrase *are leaving*)
to make: *Are you leaving work early today?* It can also be rendered as a tag question by adding a negative or positive question tag: *You are leaving work early
today, aren't you/are you?*

Stenström (1984: 56) and Archer (2005: 79) extend these five types, Stenström
(1984: 56), for example, making a distinction between the more neutral 'request
for confirmation' (e.g. *Is John in London*) and the conducive 'request for
acknowledgement' (e.g. *This, I think, is perfectly possible, isn't it?*). Archer
(2005: 79) subdivides *wh*-questions into broad and narrow types (*What happened
next? What time did the defendant arrive at the party?*), following Woodbury
(1984) and Luchenbroers (1997).

In addition to the question types outlined above, in legal training, lawyers learn
about leading questions, which are designed to subtly prompt witnesses to produce
a specific answer. They should not be used in examination-in-chief, unless they
are required to develop the witness's testimony, but they are 'positively encouraged during cross-examination' and can be used to 'make an explicit accusation'
or to 'distort the witness's recollection of the events in dispute' (Archer 2005: 79).
Tiersma (1999: 166) uses a particularly effective example from the cross-examination of Detective Fuhrman in the O.J. Simpson trial: *And you say under oath
that you have not addressed any black person as a nigger or spoken about black
people as niggers in the past ten years, Detective Fuhrman?* The positive answer
elicited by this leading question was later found to be false, thereby effectively
undermining the truthfulness and validity of the detective's evidence.

As Gibbons (2003: 98) explains, 'the more information there is in the question,
the less control the answerer has over the information, or the loading in the
language used to describe it'. Loftus and Palmer (1974: 118) carried out an
experiment that found that subtle verb choices in questions affected the way
answerers understood the events they had just viewed in films showing car acci-
dents. The question, *About how fast were the cars going when they X-ed into each
other?* elicited higher estimates of speed when *smashed* was used compared with
collided, bumped, contacted or *hit*.

In effect, though, the five question types above are useful categories which can
be further collapsed into two: *wh*-questions and *yes/no* questions, with types two
to five all being kinds of *yes/no* question. Gibbons (2003: 95) relates these two
main kinds of question to the two objectives of questioning: the 'elicitation of
information' and 'confirmation of a particular version of events', or information-
seeking questions and confirmation-seeking questions. This makes questions
powerful, as, when lawyers ask confirmation-seeking questions (2–5 above),
they are 'hav[ing] someone assent to a particular version of events', thereby

attempting to gain the compliance of the witness 'perhaps in part by not allowing the questioner's version to be denied' (Gibbons 2003: 97). Stygall (1994: 146) notes that lawyers' attention to the form of questions is 'on how to control witnesses' and 'their assumption is that by controlling what the witnesses say, they will also control what jurors think'. Not surprisingly, several researchers have focused on the issue of witness control through questions (Archer 2005; Gibbons 2003: 101–8; Harris 1984; Woodbury 1984). Woodbury (1984: 205) talks of 'a continuum of control' from least controlling questions (broad *wh*) to most controlling (tag questions) and Archer (2005: 79) develops this with a continuum that extends to seven points on the scale:

1   Broad *wh*
2   Narrow *wh*
3   Alternative
4   Grammatical *yes/no*
5   Negative grammatical *yes/no*
6   Declarative
7   Tagged declarative

The more controlling the question (tag questions, for example) the more conducive the question is, Archer argues. Examination-in-chief, conducted by a witness's 'friendly' lawyer would therefore be expected to contain more questions that have a lesser amount of control and conducivity, and cross-examination more of the most controlling questions with the highest levels. In the follow-up activities suggested at the end of this chapter, we invite you to conduct an experiment to test this hypothesis. However, both friendly and unfriendly questioning is designed to control the witness, as neither lawyer wants to leave room for the witness to say too much. In examination-in-chief, allowing open answers too much of the time would perhaps lead to the witness making unplanned and irrelevant responses.

Styles and goals of friendly and unfriendly questioning

A friendly lawyer, that is the one examining his or her own witness, (prosecution or defence), uses their institutional role to produce questioning turns that often simply require confirmation, leading witnesses through straightforward parts of their stories and making use of the exception to leading questions in examination (if they are required to develop the witness testimony). These questions are punctuated with information-seeking turns to elicit more evidentially important detail. This activity is supportive of the witness, providing a routine that co-produces authoritative evidence with minimum effort. Of the first 19 questions put to Shipman by his friendly counsel (Extract 5.1), 15 require confirmation-only responses (bold), although Shipman chooses to amplify two of his responses.

Extract 5.1

Q. What is your full name please?
A. **Full name is Harold Frederick Shipman.**
Q. And what qualifications do you hold?
A. **I hold a Bachelor of Medicine, Bachelor of Surgery degree. I also, sorry, I also have obtained Diploma in Child Health and Diploma in Obstetrics and Gynaecology.**
Q. Dr. Shipman, you were born on the 14th January 1946 in Nottingham?
A. **That's correct.**
Q. You grew up in the area, went to school in the area and thereafter went to Leeds Medical School?
A. **That is also correct.**
Q. From there you studied medicine and qualified, obtaining your primary medical qualifications in 1970?
A. **That's correct.**
Q. Having obtained your primary medical qualification did you thereafter carry out a series of training house jobs in hospitals essentially in the Pontefract area?
A. **Yes.**
Q. And did you there move into the field of general practice certainly in the 1970s, such that by September 1977 did you move into general medical practice in Hyde at Donneybrook House?
A. **I did.**
Q. On a personal level in fact did you marry in 1966 whilst still a student?
A. **I did.**
Q. And your wife, Primrose, is in court today, and of that marriage are there 4 children?
A. **There are.**
Q. By September 1977 you took up your position at the Donneybrook House practice. You were there with a number of other doctors?
A. **I was.**
Q. How many?
A. **6.**
Q. And after one year in practise did you become a partner at that practice?
A. **I did.**
    (7 more questions and answers continue in the same way.)

(Shipman Trial, Day 27)

In Extract 5.1 the straightforward evidence of Shipman's work is dealt with through many *and*-prefaced questions forming a narrative series that emphasises the 'routine elements' of the questioning activity (Heritage and Sorjonen 1994: 5) and which guide his narrative. However, by strategically placing information-seeking questions between those merely requiring confirmation, the lawyer can foreground evidentially important information and facts for the jury and avoid leading questions. For example, in Extract 5.2, where Shipman is giving evidence about his patient, the victim, Mrs Grundy, the questions alternate between those that are straightforward (1, 3, 4, 5, 6, 9), though evidentially important to his general defence of being a caring doctor and not a murderer, and those that are strategically important to his defence (questions 2, 7, 8, 10): that the deceased abused drugs, in particular codeine, which accounts for the fatal overdose. These latter questions and their answers are highlighted in bold.

Extract 5.2

1   Q.   The first 3 entries relate to the year 1993 and then we can pick up an entry there, 12.10.96. In whose hand is that entry?
1   A.   That is in mine.
2   Q.   Could you read it out please?
2   A.   'Irritable bowel syndrome again. Odd. Pupil small. Constipated. Query drug abuse. At her age. Query codeine. Wait and see.'
3   Q.   Now in fact produced for the Court has been the appointment sheet for the 12th October 1996 and it does not appear from that appointment sheet that Mrs. Grundy visited the surgery on the 12th October 1996. Did she so visit?
3   A.   Yes.
4   Q.   Can you help as to why there is no entry on the 12th October 1996 in the appointments book for her visit?
4   A.   As a general practitioner I occasionally saw people who just wanted a word. I would take them into my room. Sometimes it just was word and sometimes it took a long time.
5   Q.   So in respect of this entry for the 12th October 96 you saw Mrs. Grundy on that day?
5   A.   I did.
6   Q.   Can you please tell the Court what occurred at the consultation between the two of you?
6   A.   Once we were in my room she sat down, I sat down. She talked about the problem of IBS.
7   Q.   The irritable bowel syndrome?
7   A.   Irritable bowel syndrome. We had tried every NHS medicine and she had tried a lot of herbal remedies. She gave me the history that she was constipated and I noticed her pupils were very tight, small hole. Codeine can constipate and can make the pupils become smaller. Abuse of drugs in the elderly is becoming recognised. I couldn't offer her any other medication and I let the matter go.
8   Q.   Did you raise with her any question of abuse of drugs as you described it?
8   A.   Not at that time.
9   Q.   Why is the entry in the Lloyd George card as opposed to the computer record?

9 A. Here I was using it for confidentiality but also as an aid memoir [sic]
to think about her when she next attended.
10 Q. And was that as far as you took it on that day?
10 A. Yes.

(Shipman Trial, Day 27)

The questions in bold are designed to *display* Shipman's defence to the jury,
either in the words of the lawyer, through the use of a *yes/no* question that simply
has to be confirmed (question 8), or in the reduced *wh*-question (question 7),
which elicits an explanation from Shipman. Question 2 is what has been described
as a 'requestion' (Danet and Kermish 1978) – a question that is a request for
information – or an 'interrogative request' (Harris 1984).

Friendly counsel's goal is therefore to establish agreement on clear and precise
facts, whereas the cross-examiner seeks to test the reliability of those facts, to
'discredit opposition witnesses and minimize the impact of their testimony'
(Conley and O'Barr 1998: 22). Tiersma (1999: 164) describes cross-examination
as 'not [just] to bolster your own case, but to damage that of the opposition'. In
Extract 5.3 bold face is used to draw attention to cross-examination features
discussed below.

Extract 5.3

Q. Now I am going to now suggest to you that you **created quite
deliberately** 3 **false** written records, the purpose of which was to
suggest that Mrs. Grundy had a **drug habit**. Did you?
A. Did I what, I am sorry?
Q. Create 3 false written records?
A. No.
Q. Let us look at them please. ... 'IBS (irritable bowel syndrome) again.
Odd pupils small. Constipated query. Drug abuse at her age. Query
codeine. Wait and see.' The 12th October 1996 was a Saturday, you
recollect that fact?
A. I am informed that it was a Saturday.
Q. Tell me, was there **some real sign of drug abuse** there to be seen in Mrs.
Grundy, visible?
A. She had episodes of irritable bowel syndrome. She had also got small
pupils and with irritable bowel syndrome you get diarrhoea and
constipation at times.
Q. We have read that. Was there something that **really said** to you, 'Here
is a lady, 81 years of age, with a drug problem?' She would have been
79 then.
A. People don't have small pupils for no reason and her IBS was not
absolutely typical of everybody else's.
Q. Let me **suggest** your **attributing a drug habit** to Mrs. Grundy is **quite
wicked**?

A. If that's what you want to do then that's fine. I tell you that these recordings were made at the time, apart from one, and were accurate.

Q. These 3 entries were made at a time when you contemplated facing trial in relation to one deceased only, Mrs. Grundy, that's right isn't it?

A. What is right, I am sorry?

Q. **You fabricated** these entries at a time when you contemplated being tried in relation to Mrs. Grundy only?

A. No. I didn't.

Q. And if you had been tried in relation Mrs. Grundy only your defence would have been that **she died from drugs she took herself because she had a habit**?

A. I am sorry again, no.

(Shipman Trial, Day 33)

Cross-examining counsel manage to build negative evaluation into their *yes/no* questions to attack the defendant's character and to undermine his story. Note in Extract 5.3 the evaluative items, *quite deliberately, false, the purpose of which, drug abuse/habit, quite wicked, fabricated* and, specifically related to the claim that Mrs Grundy was a drug abuser, *real sign, really said to you.* These linguistic choices mark a 'social attitude that is "wide awake"' and 'discerning' (Hanks 2005: 210), critically pointing to those elements of the defence story that the prosecution wants to attack. Cross-examination of the evidence already given in examination-in-chief results in casting doubt on the veracity and reliability of the defence story: that the deceased woman's alleged drug habit had not been recorded in her patient record because Shipman wanted to protect her confidentiality. It counter-proposes the prosecution version: that records were fabricated as part of a defence against a charge of murder.

In Extract 5.3, along with the evaluative lexis, counsel begins with a question that starts with *I am going to suggest,* and in other questions uses *tell me* and *let me suggest.* As Heffer (2005: 135) notes in relation to negative judgements in cross-examination, at such points 'the counsel's subjectivity begins to appear', reinforced by the use of first-person pronouns (*I* and *me*) and the verb *suggest.* He looks at the '*I*-clusters' produced by cross-examiners (Heffer 2005: 136), noting that the two verbs *suggest* and *going to suggest* are the most distinctive *I*-collocates. Heffer (2005: 137) characterises these clusters as 'spotlights' that 'throw light on the lawyer's subjective intentions', which in Extract 5.3 are to attack and suggest an alternative to the defence account. Heffer argues that, when counsel use *suggest* with the witness, they are also indirectly addressing the jury and offering them this version of events. Deictic markers such as the inclusive second-person pronoun *we/us* (*let us look at them please*; *we have read that*), also explicitly draw the jury into the dialogue and into a jointly produced negative assessment of the evidence. This continually competing and contested evidential perspective epitomises the nature of the adversarial system.

Agreement and lack of contest in examination-in-chief is confirmed by a quantitative analysis of *and*-prefaced questions in Shipman's examination, cross-examination and re-examination, which spanned 11 days. Using *Wordsmith Tools* (Scott 2012) we looked at the number of occurrences of utterance initial *And* (as in the six examples in Extract 5.1 and the one in Extract 5.3). They were almost twice as frequent in friendly examination as in cross-examination (0.63 per cent versus 0.35 per cent). In examination-in-chief these questions were generally followed by agreement tokens such as *yes, that's correct, that's right, yes I did, yes it is, it does, it was, I was, there was* or negative agreement *there is no visit slip*, or a simple *no. And*-prefaced questions are used differently in cross-examination. Coming after disagreement (as in Shipman's penultimate response in Extract 5.3), the *and*-prefaced question (*And if you had been tried in relation Mrs. Grundy only your defence would have been that she died from drugs she took herself because she had a habit?*) signals the lawyer's rejection of Shipman's disagreement and reinforces his continuing goal of pursuing his own side of events: that Shipman had constructed his defence to the presence of morphine in the deceased's body, when he thought he was only going to be tried for one offence of murder, rather than fifteen.

We noticed above that examination questions are intertextually tied to witness statements taken by the police during the criminal investigation. In Extract 5.4 which is from a statement given to the police by one of the witnesses in the Shipman trial, we read his evidence about what he saw, heard and did in Shipman's surgery while witnessing Mrs Grundy's signature.

Extract 5.4

I am a single man and live at the address shown overleaf with my family. I have been a patient of Dr. H.F. Shipman, 21 Market Street, Hyde, throughout my entire life. On the 9th June 1998 (090698) I had an appointment at 4.10 p.m. (16.10 hrs) with Dr. Shipman. I attended the surgery about that time and to the best of my recollection there was only one other woman in the waiting room. Dr. Shipman then came out of his surgery and asked me and the other woman if we wouldn't mind witnessing a signature. The woman and I then followed Dr. Shipman into his surgery. Sat down in the room already was an elderly lady. I did not really see her as she had her back to me. Dr. Shipman then spoke to the elderly lady. I cannot remember what he said, but I recall that whatever it was, it was to suggest to me that the old lady was aware of what was happening. The old lady replied, 'YES'. I was then shown a piece of paper that was folded over so that only the bottom couple of inches were showing. The only thing I saw on the form was K. GRUNDY. I had not seen this being written.

Extract 5.5 comes from the examination of the same witness in court and we notice how closely the prosecution lawyer follows the script of the statement when posing his questions:

Extract 5.5
ANTHONY PAUL SPENCER, sworn
Examined by MR. WRIGHT
(The six opening introductory questions and answers have been omitted)

Q   And on the 9th June 1998 did you have an appointment at Dr. Shipman's surgery?

A.   Yes.

Q.   Ladies and gentlemen, if you turn to page 73 which is in fact 2 pages towards the front of your bundle, you see the surgery appointments diary there. ... did you go to the surgery that day Mr. Spencer?

A.   Yes.

Q.   And did you go into the waiting area?

A.   I did.

Q.   And did you see Dr. Shipman that day?

A.   Yes.

Q.   Did you have any sort of conversation with Dr. Shipman in the waiting room area at any time that day?

A.   In the waiting room area, Dr. Shipman came out of his surgery and asked me if I would not mind witnessing a signature.

Q.   And so what happened then?

A.   I obliged.

Q.   So where did you go?

A.   Into his surgery room.
     [3 questions and answers are omitted here]

Q.   When you got into his room was there anyone else in the room?

A.   Yes.

Q.   First of all, male or female?

A.   Female.

Q.   What sort of age, any idea? Young, middle aged, elderly or what?

A.   Old.

Q.   Pardon?

A.   Elderly.
     [5 questions and answers are omitted here]

Q.   Was she introduced to you at all?

A.   No.

Q.   Did you ever get to discover at that time what she was called, at that time, that afternoon?

A.   Until I saw the signature, no.

Q.   What then happened?

A.   Dr. Shipman folded over a piece of paper with a couple of spare lines on it and asked me if I wouldn't mind writing my name and my address and putting my signature and my occupation on the piece of paper.

Q.   So was the paper handed over to you?

A.   No, it was kept on the desk.

Q.   It was kept on the desk. Did you see anything on the piece of paper?

A.   K. Grundy as a signature.

Q.   Could you see anything else on the paper at all?

A.   Dotted lines.

Q. So far as that name or signature K. Grundy on that piece of paper, had you seen that being entered on to that particular piece of paper?

A. No.

Q. So you had not seen who had written that?

A. No.

(Shipman Trial, Day 6)

Extract 5.6 is from the cross-examination of the same witness about the same events. Note how the defence lawyer summarises and offers simply for agreement those aspects of the story that she takes as unproblematic and then produces information-seeking questions for the parts that she disputes. She also switches from collaborative narration to challenging questioning (indicated in bold). Note also the italicised words, which are discussed below.

Extract 5.6
Cross-examined by MISS DAVIES

Q. Mr. Spencer you were waiting in Dr. Shipman's surgery, he came out and asked if you would witness a signature?

A. Yes.

Q. You went into his consulting room. There was a lady who you described as elderly. She was sitting at the side of his desk and you went in with another lady who was also a patient?

A. Yes.

Q. When you went into the surgery was there a short conversation between Dr. Shipman and the lady sitting at the desk?

A. Yes.

Q. Was it in terms that Dr. Shipman was telling the lady that yourself and in fact Claire Hutchinson as we now know, were going to witness the signature?

A. No.

Q. What was the conversation?

A. Something along the lines of, 'Is this okay,' or, 'Are you sure about this?'

Q. I am sorry?

A. 'Is this okay,' or 'Are you sure about this?'

Q. And she agreed all was well?

A. Yes.

Q. And went ahead?

A. Yes.

Q. On the desk was a document?

A. Yes.

Q. Was a document that was folded?

A. Yes.

Q. Because **it was folded you could not actually see what was on the document itself, could you?**

A. **No.**

Q. **That document was already folded when you went into the surgery, was it not?**
A. **Yes.**
Q. So therefore **when you told the Court that Dr. Shipman folded over the piece of paper that is not correct, it was already folded over. The only bit that was free was where the signature was and where you were to sign?**
A. **Somebody had folded it.**
Q. But **could you not say who?**
A. **No.**
Q. **The position is that when you went into that surgery it was already folded over?**
A. **Yes.**
Q. **And all that you could see was the space where you were to sign and the signature that you have already told us was K. Grundy?**
A. **Yes.**

(Shipman Trial, Day 6)

The switch from collaborative narration to challenging questioning (in bold) signals the point at which the lawyer disputes the evidence the witness has given in examination-in-chief. The shift is marked by moving from straightforward confirmation-seeking *yes/no* questions to highly conducive tag questions, declarative questions and a negative question. The questions also contain lexical choices that mark their challenge: the result adverb, *therefore,* conjunctions of reason (*because, so*) and the adversative *but*. This strategic switch of voice is consistent with her goal of discrediting the witness or at least demonstrating that some of his evidence is unreliable. Nevertheless, she is constrained by the examination-in-chief and the prior statement as to what she can ask the witness – cross-examination can only test evidence that has been adduced in examination and trainee lawyers are warned 'never ask a question to which you don't know the answer'. The witness is also constrained by the ways the questions are put to him. His friendly lawyer (Extract 5.5) has made answering easy by leading him through his statement. In cross-examination, however, story details are selected for confirmation, before being challenged with tag and declarative questions which compel agreement. Gibbons (2003: 101) says that tag questions are 'strengthening devices, which make the demand for compliance greater than that of a simple question' and so the tag form is 'more coercive' than simple polar questions. After extracting the admission that the evidence given in examination-in-chief, *Dr. Shipman folded over a piece of paper*, was incorrect, the lawyer is able to follow-up with declarative confirmation questions that force the witness to agree with the defence story that *when you went into that surgery it was already folded over,* which omits Shipman's agency.

It is clear that in Extract 5.6 the cross-examination makes use of the effective strategy of 'restrict[ing] the opportunity of witnesses under cross-examination to short, direct answers to the specific questions asked' O'Barr (1982: 120–21). The witness occasionally successfully overrides this restriction with one of O'Barr's 'effective witness strategies': 'blurt out relevant facts and opinions ... even though the opposition lawyer may attempt to limit your answer' (1982: 121). So, for example, the witness evades the restrictive design of the *yes/no* question, *So therefore when you told the Court that Dr. Shipman folded over the piece of paper that is not correct, it was already folded over. The only bit that was free was where the signature was and where you were to sign?* with the response: *Somebody had folded it.* Through this 'narrative expansion' (Galatolo and Drew 2006: 661) the witness attempts to limit the damage to his credibility, although the next lawyer question regains control.

As well as being intertextually linked to prior witness statements, examination and cross-examination are also determined by the relevant legislative materials, as Scheffer (2006) demonstrates. He uses an example from a case of Wounding with Intent, an offence contrary to sections 18 and 20 of the Offences against the Person Act 1861. The indictment, which includes wording from the Act, was that the defendant 'unlawfully and maliciously wounded (victim's name) with intent to do him grievous bodily harm [GBH]' (Scheffer 2006: 305). The defence case centres around the issue of impulse versus intent, which is crystallised in a short dialogue, reported by Scheffer, between the prosecution and defence lawyers 'minutes before they appear before the judge' to begin the case; the prosecution lawyer says, 'The only issue between us then is the question of intent' and the defence lawyer replies, 'Yes ... Let's get it done'. (Scheffer 2006: 320). The question of intent is not evaded in the defence lawyer's questions to his client in court either. Scheffer (2006: 329) notes that, at the end of the defendant's friendly examination, the defence lawyer confronts head-on 'the case's most vulnerable point ("I wasn't finished")' which are the words the defendant used to the police in interview, concerning the assault, and which are likely to be exploited by the prosecution, as they imply intent to do GBH. In what Scheffer (2006: 329) describes as 'a forward defence' strategy during friendly defendant examination, the defence view of intent is laid before the jury in advance of the prosecution cross-examination. It is returned to by the defence lawyer in his closing address to the jury, as they are about to decide the case in relation to intent, in the sentence: 'Is it a case in which he [the defendant] did appear to *stop and consider* what he was doing? Or was it a *quick response* to something which *just happened* – perhaps a touching on the shoulder or perhaps, as he suggests, more physical violence? (Scheffer 2006: 334). The jury is therefore invited to consider two possibilities in relation to deciding intent: planning (*stop and consider*) and spon-taneity (*quick response*), with the second of the two rhetorically prominent and underlined by the agentless verb *happened* and the mitigating adverb *just*.

In this brief examination of the roles of questions in witness examination, we have seen that they control and constrain, producing powerful effects. Lawyers are constrained by the genre and prior texts in terms of what and how they can elicit, but they control witnesses, while witnesses are doubly constrained: first, by the lawyers' framing of questions and second, by how the questions are designed to produce particular responses. The styles and goals of the different examination/cross-examination activities also determine the kind of questioning and the question types, and, finally, the pre-trial witness statement(s) determine what the friendly lawyer asks and what the cross-examining lawyer deconstructs.

Questions can, therefore, be used to achieve different goals, depending on the activity in which the speaker is engaged. Though question form (*wh*-question, tag question, declarative question) is important, it is ultimately its function within a particular activity (examination; cross-examination) that determines how a question works in the courtroom.

In this chapter, thus far, we have dealt with the structural elements of the trial genre and what is achieved through monologue and dialogue. In the remaining part we focus on other pragmatic and sociolinguistic aspects of trial discourse, including the role of narrative, the expert witness in the courtroom and children in the courtroom.

Narrative in the courtroom

'Narratives are everywhere', as Toolan (2001: viii) tells us, and a good deal of courtroom interaction is conducted by means of narrative. Therefore research on narratives in courtroom discourse is extensive, since 'the law is awash with storytelling' (Amsterdam and Bruner 2000, cited in Harris 2005: 215). Stories are central to legal cases. Bamberg's (2004) work on master narratives and counter narratives gives narrative an even wider significance in the social and cultural world, as we suggested in relation to jury deliberation in the OJ Simpson trial. Bamberg discusses the 'normalizing' and 'naturalizing' tendencies of master narratives to engulf speakers and subject them to grand récits and meta-narratives, in which cultural expectations are embedded. He points out the tendency of speakers to situate their own narratives within these master narratives, which are therefore socially and culturally constraining (2004: 359–60). Master narratives position social actors, but counter-narratives can create spaces for them to reposition themselves, although articulating a counter narrative is not at all easy and master narratives often remain unchallenged. For Bamberg, master narratives are hegemonic and counter narratives are individual – they orient the individual to who they are, not who society wants them to be.

Prosecution and defence cases work within such master narratives, but also work to counter them. Criminal prosecutions centre around socially-deviant behaviour and the work of the prosecution is to prove that the accused behaved according to individually defined rules and norms which are outside the 'normal' social script. Master narratives can, therefore, provide defence scripts for suspects who seek to appear socially normal. Shipman's defence narrative adhered to the social expectation of a caring doctor, who assiduously attended to his elderly, infirm patients. He resisted the culturally deviant counter narrative, presented by the prosecution, that he was an evil murderer who had cynically abused his position of professional trust. For Shipman, accepting this narrative could only lead to a guilty verdict.

Harris (2001: 72) discusses the wider cultural context of narrative and makes a distinction between 'the over-arching trial narratives of guilt and innocence' and the 'even more wide-ranging social and cultural narratives which are refracted through (and further constructed by) the media' and which trial narratives reflect. On the first day of the Shipman trial, the judge refused a pre-trial submission by the defence that, as widespread media coverage had obviously made a fair trial impossible, the trial should be definitively abandoned. The prosecution counter-argued that media narratives are erased from the minds of the jury by the immediacy of the courtroom experience and the judge appeared to accept this.

Cotterill (2003: 223) refers to some of the 'prejudice triggers', or in our terms master narratives, that are identifiable in the O.J. Simpson trial and that could predispose towards conviction or acquittal verdicts. Successfully triggering the African-American wife-beater script in relation to the defendant might lead to a decision to convict, whereas triggering the young, white, promiscuous woman script in relation to the victim, Nicole Brown Simpson, could produce an acquittal. And overshadowing both scripts was the master narrative of the police as institutionally racist. For this reason it took weeks to select the jury, with the prosecution wanting a majority of women and the defence a majority of black jurors.

In court, the work of lawyers centres on eliciting narratives through asking questions in the adversarial activities of testing and challenging the story. Heffer (2005: xv; see also Heffer 2010) points to 'a strategic tension between two markedly different ways of viewing the trial: as crime narrative or as legal argument', and Harris (2005: 217) notes that trials are hybrid genres with 'the intermingling of narrative and non-narrative modes of discourse'. She makes a distinction between 'narrativity' (2005: 221) and narrative fact and evidence, as in the judge's quote used in the epigraph: *What the lawyers say in the opening statements and the closing arguments is not evidence.* Harris contends that 'opening statements are in the narrative mode, oriented to how speakers tell their stories; and the testimony of witnesses is in the paradigmatic (or non-narrative) mode, oriented to evidence, fact, truth' (2005: 220–21), making the lawyers' statements fictional not factual, a distinction that the judge has to explicitly 'warn' the jury about.

The lawyers' questioning elicits, organises, and embeds facts in a courtroom narrative, which is a powerful determinant of the way jurors 'recognise and analyse the vast amount of information involved in making a legal judgement' (Bennett and Feldman 1981: 5). In some ways jurors are like 'readers of a detective novel or watchers of a mystery movie' (Bennett and Feldman 1981: 4). In opening and closing statements, and the subsequent directions given to the jury by the judge at the close of a trial, these 'narrativised schemas' (Heffer 2005: 206) come significantly into play. In monologue, such as in their opening and closing speeches, lawyers can narrativise the evidence to tell a particular story and create a picture of the defendant, but in examination and cross-examination, their job is to elicit evidential facts from the witness. Nevertheless, as we have seen, it is possible in examination-in-chief to construct, as well as to elicit, narrative responses, and in cross-examination it is possible to powerfully imply meanings that contribute significantly to the narrative picture. However, it is not the narrative of monologue; it is 'fragmented' by 'the question and answer mode of information exchange' (Harris 2001: 71) and disrupted by the sequential activities of examination and cross-examination, as the narrative gets built and then unbuilt. In Extract 5.6 we saw how in cross-examination the defence lawyer moved between storytelling *yes/no* questions and conducive knowledge-questioning moves for strategic effect, in what Harris (2001: 71) describes as a 'shift between "teller" and "knower"'. Narrative disjunction is therefore as much a part of courtroom discourse as is narrative construction and so it is not surprising that jurors report on jury-room deliberations that involve making sense and (re)constructing coherent narratives. Indeed, Hans and Vidmar (1986: 99) report a case 'where the jury *physically* re-enacted a shooting by role-play in the jury room, in order to assess the credibility of the evidence and plausibility of the story' (cited in Cotterill 2003: 224). Such role-play would not have been possible without a filtering of evidence through a story schema that is capable of replay.

The expert witness in the courtroom

Not all witnesses are equal. Most of the evidence will be given by lay witnesses, ordinary people caught up in the crime, as well as the complainant and defendant and police officers, but often experts, such as doctors, scientists, and even, increasingly, linguists, will be called. Expert witnesses present their evidential findings and explain technical aspects of the evidence to the jury, to enable them to evaluate its importance. We look at this in more detail in Chapter 10 and you are invited to explore expert witness testimony in one of the research tasks.

Expert witnesses can be forensic scientists with scientific expertise in testing material evidence, academic or trade experts with specialist knowledge, or doctors who can assess the extent of illness or harm (Heffer 2005: 43), whereas lay witnesses' evidence centres around their memory of what they saw, heard, said, and experienced. Heffer investigated extended turns in lay and expert evidence and found that 'expert witnesses have by far the highest proportion of extended turns', and that these were non-narrative in content, explaining rather than storytelling. He also found that expert witnesses produced more 'expanded confirmation' (more than *yes* or *no*) to *yes/no* questions than other witness types (complainants, defendants, police), which 'suggests that they … appear to interpret polar questions as requests for explanation rather than confirmation', whereas 'defendants and female witnesses seem to provide restricted confirmation [*yes, I did/That's correct*] more frequently' (Heffer 2005: 117).

When prosecution or defence lawyers call expert witnesses whose role is to explain complex science for the jury, they have to achieve a difficult 'balance between credibility and comprehensibility' (Cotterill 2003: 196). A juror in the O.J. Simpson trial recalled her exasperation with one expert, who got the level of accommodation wrong, and the consequent oversimplification made the jurors feel that she was talking down to them.

Unfortunately, there's no way to let people know that you got it. You can't just raise your hand and say 'Dr Cotton, I understand what you're talking about. Move on.'

(Second juror in Cooley *et al.* 1995: 115, cited in Cotterill 2003: 197)

Since jurors are silent receivers of evidence, one of the most important ways of managing what jurors hear is through questioning. We will now look at how difficult questions posed to children can influence what the jury hears.

Children in the courtroom

Children, who attend court as witnesses or victims of physical or sexual abuse or in sexual crimes, also have to endure cross-examination. Lawyer practices have been severely criticised, particularly for over-aggressiveness and unfair use of complex questioning (Brennan 1994a, 1994b; Drew 1992; Ehrlich 2001; Levi and Graffam Walker 1990, Graffam Walker 1993). Brennan and Brennan's (1988) and Brennan's (1994a, 1994b) research into children's experience in Australian courtrooms suggests that children giving evidence in abuse cases are 'doubly abused' and revictimised by hostile questioning. Brennan describes some of the effects and explains how questions in cross-examination are deliberately 'aimed at not admitting the experience of the child'. He demonstrates (Extract 5.7) how questions can be designed to be unanswerable and to elicit *I don't know* answers from the child, and then points out that 'the response "I don't know" can stand for a variety of states of knowledge, but the purpose of the cross-examination is well served as the response reduces the credibility of the witness' (1994b: 207).

Extract 5.7

Q. And where was your mother?
A. I don't know.
Q. You do not know, but she was in the house when you went to bed was she not?
A. I think so.
Q. Yes. Sorry, you think so.
A. Yes.
Q. Can you not remember?
A. Yes.
Q. Where would she have been if she was not in the house?
A. I don't know.

(Brennan 1994b: 206–7)

Brennan (1994a) suggests that the 'strange language' used in courts, particularly in cross-examination, adds up to 'a discourse of denial' of the child's world. He identifies 15 problematic constructions that have the effect of constraining, limiting and confusing the child. These range from negative rhetorical questions

(*Now you had a bruise, did you not?*) to the lack of grammatical or semantic connection between questions and the use of the passive voice. Gibbons (2003) and Maley (2000) both report on the manipulative in-built constraints in professionals' questions. These are coercive for adults, but for children this experience can put them at an even greater disadvantage. Eades (2002) reports on a case in the Australian courts where Aboriginal children are witnesses and shows how multi-faceted questions are inappropriate; children are unable to respond adequately and presented with questions that are not interrogative and frequently also multiple, children can only fail.

Although the lawyer obviously needs to maintain control of such things as topic and event structure, and cross-examination is by its very nature unfriendly, limiting the opportunities for children to give their evidence adequately is contrary to the spirit of the criminal justice system. Trials are places where the witness's story is exposed to public and hostile legal scrutiny, and children are particularly vulnerable in adversarial systems, since cross-examination is so probing and critical. The rape victim in Extract 5.8 experiences destructive cross-examination.

Extract 5.8

1	Q.	Your aim that evening then was to go to the discotheque?
2	A.	Yes.
3	Q.	Presumably you had dressed up for that, had you?
4	A.	Yes.
5	Q.	And you were wearing make-up?
6	A.	Yes.
7	Q.	Eye-shadow?
8	A.	Yes.
9	Q.	Lipstick?
10	A.	No I was not wearing lipstick.
11	Q.	You weren't wearing lipstick?
12	A.	No.
13	Q.	Just eye-shadow, eye make-up?
14	A.	Yes.
15	Q.	And powder presumably?
16	A.	Foundation cream, yes.
17	Q.	You had had bronchitis had you not?
18	A.	Yes.
19	Q.	You have mentioned in the course of your evidence about wearing a
20		coat.
21	A.	Yes.
22	Q.	It was not really a coat at all, was it?
23	A.	Well, it is sort of a coat-dress and I bought it with trousers, as a
24		trouser suit.
25	Q.	That is it down there isn't it, the red one?
26	A.	Yes.
27	Q.	If we call that a dress, if we call that a dress you had no coat on at all

28   had you?
29   A.   No.
30   Q.   And this is January. It was quite a cold night?
31   A.   Yes it was cold actually.

(Levinson 1992: 82–83)

Consider the effect of these questions. What picture is being built? This episode is followed by questioning about her previous sexual experiences (Extract 5.9).

Extract 5.9

 1   Q.   ... you have had sexual intercourse on a previous occasion haven't
           you?
 2   A.   Yes.
 3   Q.   On many previous occasions?
 4   A.   Not many.
 5   Q.   Several?
 6   A.   Yes.
 7   Q.   With several men?
 8   A.   No.
 9   Q.   Just one.
10   A.   Two.
11   Q.   Two. And you are seventeen and a half?
12   A.   Yes.

(Levinson 1992: 83)

Levinson comments that 'careful juxtaposition [with what has gone before] does the job of suggesting that a girl of seventeen who has already slept with two men is not a woman of good repute'. Over the course of the cross-examination, the questions:

> build up to form a 'natural' argument for the jury ... that goes something like this: the victim was dressed to go dancing, she was heavily made up – something of a painted lady, in fact – and, despite the fact that she had been ill, she was wearing no coat on the cold winter's night. The implicit conclusion is that the girl was seeking sexual adventures.

(Levinson 1992: 84)

Cross-examination, as we have seen, constrains the witness through the use of questions; an argument is, thereby, built up over time, which produces inferences for the jury. Levinson argues that our understanding of what is going on in the questions 'rests on our knowledge of the kind of activity that the talk occurs within' (Levinson 1992: 85). Within a rape trial and within the cross-examination genre, the cleverly phrased and sequenced questions can organise a rape complainant narrative to be interpretable as implying consent rather than resistance, producing a narrative that undermines the prosecution story. Cross-examination's power lies in the lawyer's skill in assigning blame and responsibility to the victim and presenting this as 'natural' (Fairclough 1989). Two particular sequences from Extracts 5.8 (lines 27–30) and 5.9 (lines 7–11) can be analysed in terms of how the lawyer uses conjunctions to present unrelated events as 'naturally' connected. In Extract 5.8 (lines 27–30) a connection is made between the witness having *no coat* and the month being *January* and in Extract 5.9 the connection is between the number of sexual partners (*two*) and her age (*seventeen and a half*). These connections have inferential value. The implication in Extract 5.8 is that the woman was dressed for display rather than comfort and in Extract 5.9 that she had loose morals. What is clear is that cultural and gender ideologies are at work in the courtroom. Ideologies are beliefs, myths and assumptions about gender, age, language, *etcetera* that circulate in society and which are taken for granted and seen as common sense. As Eades (2008), Ehrlich (2001) and Matoesian (2001) show, cultural and linguistic ideologies – folk beliefs about the ways that language works (Matoesian 2001: 49) – can be dangerous phenomena that produce and reproduce power, dominance and control in courtrooms around the world. A critical discourse analysis view of this cross examination extract, therefore, reveals 'how power and discriminatory value are inscribed in and mediated through the linguistic system' (Caldas-Coulthard and Coulthard 1996: xi). The master narrative of a promiscuous young female looking for adventure produces a context of blame, rather than a narrative of victimhood.

Conclusion

In this chapter we have seen how the competitive and competing goals of interaction that characterise trial discourse produce distinctive patterns of lexis, syntax and generic structure. Lexical selection creates semantic contrast between prosecution and defence accounts of the same events and narrative accounts are juxtaposed through challenging questioning that produces inferential meaning. As we saw here, and in Chapter 2, the courtroom produces a complex context for interaction, with the silent and overhearing audience of the jury having a major impact on turn design. Listeners are indexed in the talk through deictic reference (*you*), and particular modes of elicitation indicate the presence of audience design in conscious attempts to accommodate the jury as addressees, particularly in cross-examination. The highly ordered, yet fragmented nature of talk makes the courtroom a rich linguistic domain for study.

Courtroom research produces some of the most critical writing on linguistic issues in the justice system: Eades' (2008) account of power and ideology in the Australian courts, Ehrlich's (2001) examination of the representation of rape in Canada, and Atkinson and Drew's (1979) and Drew's (1990, 1992) focus on the strategies used by American lawyers to undermine witnesses and discredit testimony. O'Barr (1982: 120–21), looking at lawyer strategies, focuses on what witnesses can do to resist the powerful control of lawyers' constraining questions, and Matoesian (2010) shows that witnesses can and do take control of their testimony, producing powerful meanings through gestures accompanying their talk.

Kurzon (2001) examines another of the participants in the courtroom in his study of the linguistic behaviour of judges. The ways that interpreters' interventions are not always beneficial to the witnesses' testimony they are interpreting has also been widely critiqued (e.g. Berk-Seligson 1999; Hale 1999) and Ng (2015: 203) points to the effects that judge's interventions in witness questioning have on interpreting, leading to omissions in a way that 'potentially compromises the administration of justice' in Hong Kong's bilingual courtroom. The language of all of these courtroom participants is extensively researched, but in this chapter we have recognised the central importance of juries and it is perhaps surprising, given their importance, though not given the secrecy that necessarily surrounds much of their talk, that juries are the least researched group. They have a largely silent and invisible role, despite the fact that they are the primary addressees for the vast majority of the linguistic work done in the courtroom.

In this first part of the book we have examined legal language in a wide range of contexts, from the texts that constitute the law to the way that the language and discourse processes of the law are played out in real settings. We have considered how professional and lay speakers interact in institutional settings from initial calls to the emergency services to interview and court. In Part II we move from the language that characterises the legal process to look at language which is used as evidence in cases where institutional practice is disputed and where discourse analysis is employed in expert reports and evidence to uncover what might have happened.

Further reading

Coulthard and Johnson (eds) (2010), chapters by: Aldridge, Archer, Ehrlich, Rosulek, Hale, Heffer, Matoesian, Schweda Nicholson, Tiersma, Tkačuková.

Research tasks

1 Compare the question forms in examination and cross-examination activities with a single witness appearance or across witnesses in the same trial. Are the question types similar or different? What cross-examination strategies are used and what are their pragmatic effects? Use the Shipman trial (http://webarchive.nationalarchives.gov. uk/20090808154959/, http://www.the-shipman-inquiry.org.uk/trialtrans.asp), where prosecution witness examination begins on Day 4, or the O.J. Simpson criminal trial (http://simpson.walraven.org/) where the witness examination begins on 31 January 1995.

2 Compare the start of the prosecution opening speech (on Day 40 of the Shipman trial) and the defence speech (on Day 41), looking at the first 1,000 or so words (both speeches are over 30,000 words each). Examine how the prosecution lawyer's vocabulary emphasises the contrast between the trust expected by the patient and the actual breach of trust, resulting in murder, in words such as: *entrust, trust, trusted* (3), *entrusted, honesty, integrity* versus *breached that trust, killed, duped, falsified, save his own skin, cover his tracks, misled, deliberate misstatements*. And examine how the defence lawyer creates a different picture of the defendant through words such as

doctor, patient, and *care.* If you are more adventurous, carry out a contrastive analysis of both speeches using corpus methods.

3 Look at the evidence given by two expert witnesses (e.g. Days 19–22 of the Shipman trial). How are questions posed and responded to? How does the lawyer's examination enable the expert to make his or her expertise comprehensible to the jury? Cotterill (2003: 180) examines lawyer turns that use the phrase *When you say* as simplification questions. Are there other questions like this and if so what do they do? Can you find any occasions when the lawyer lays claim to as much expertise as the expert? A number of expert witnesses are called by the prosecution in the Shipman trial on Days 20–22.

Part II
Language as Evidence

6   The work of the forensic linguist

Have you any impairments? … Loss of sight or hearing? … Loss of arm or leg? … Are you crippled or deformed? … If so explain …

(from insurance proposal form)

Introduction

Over the past 30 years there has been a rapid growth in the frequency with which courts in a number of countries have called upon the expertise of linguists. In this chapter we will give examples drawn from a large number of cases to illustrate the kinds of problems they have been asked to address and the wide range of tools and techniques they have used in their work. All cases require a different selection from the linguist's toolkit – phonetic and phonological, morphological, syntactic, lexical, discoursal, textual and pragmatic – and in what follows we have tried to group them according to linguistic criteria.

Morphological meaning and phonetic similarity

Shuy (2002b: 95–109) reports his contribution to the case of *McDonald's Corporation v Quality Inns International, Inc.,* which revolved around whether McDonald's could claim ownership not simply of the name McDonald's, but also of the initial morpheme 'Mc' and thereby prevent its use in other trademarks. The case began in 1987 when Quality Inns announced they were going to create a chain of basic hotels and call them McSleep, claiming, when challenged, that they hoped the 'Mc' prefix would evoke a Scottish link and with it the Scots' well-known reputation for frugality. McDonald's, who had previously success-fully prevented the use of the name McBagel's, when a judge had decided that the prefix could not be used in conjunction with a generic food product, decided to challenge the McSleep mark, claiming it was a deliberate attempt to draw on the goodwill and reputation of the McDonald's brand.

In supporting their case, McDonald's pointed out that they had deliberately set out, in one advertising campaign, to create a 'McLanguage' with Ronald McDonald teaching children how to 'Mc-ize' the standard vocabulary of generic words to create 'McFries', McFish', 'McShakes' and even 'McBest'. Fanciful as this linguistic imperialism might seem to be to ordinary users of the language, particularly to those of Scottish or Irish descent, who would seem to be in danger of losing their right to use their own names as trademarks, the lawyers took the claim very seriously. Quality Inns' lawyers asked Shuy to help with two linguistic arguments: first, that the morpheme 'Mc' was in common use productively, in contexts where it was not seen to be linked in any way to McDonald's and second, that such examples showed that the prefix, originally a patronymic and equivalent in meaning to the morpheme *son* in John*son*, had become generic and thus now had a meaning of its own, which was recognisably distinct from both of the other major meanings, 'son of' and 'associated with the McDonald's company'.

Shuy chose to use a corpus linguistics approach and searched to find real text instances of what one might call 'McMorphemes'. Among the 56 examples he found were general terms like 'McArt', 'McCinema', 'McSurgery' and 'McPrisons', as well as items already being used commercially such as the 'McThrift Motor Inn', a budget motel with a Scottish motif, and 'McTek', a computer discount store which specialised in Apple Mac computer products. On the basis of such examples, Shuy argued that the prefix had become, in the language at large, an independent lexical item with its own meaning of 'basic, convenient, inexpensive and standardized' (2002b: 99). Rather than resort to linguistic evidence themselves, McDonald's hired market researchers to access the public's perception of the prefix directly and to do so through interview and questionnaire. Their experts reported that their tests confirmed that consumers did indeed associate the prefix with McDonald's, as well as with reliability, speed, convenience and cheapness. Faced with this conflicting evidence, the judge ruled in favour of McDonald's, thereby giving them massive control over the use of the morpheme.

Of course, the successful defence of a trademark may occasionally have unwanted consequences. In March 2007, McDonald's went to war against the Oxford English Dictionary after it described a 'McJob' as 'an unstimulating, low-paid job with few prospects, [especially] one created by the expansion of the service sector', with a first example taken from *The Washington Post* in August 1986: 'The fast-food factories: McJobs are bad for kids'. The company's 'chief people officer' (sic) for Northern Europe suggested that Oxford should ignore such corpus evidence of general usage and change the definition to '... a job that is stimulating, rewarding and offers genuine opportunities for career progression and skills that last a lifetime'. In fact, this is just one further skirmish in the constant battle to maintain the mark, because it is insisting that the word 'mcjob' can only have one meaning – 'a job at McDonald's – which is patently not what it is taken to mean by the general population (Stern and Wiggins 2007).

Trademark owners sometimes feel the need to defend their mark against other marks which are thought to be phonetically confusable. Tiersma and Solan (2002) list several pairs that have been found to be confusingly similar, including Beck's Beer and Ex Bier; Listerine and Listogen; Smirnoff and Sarnoff, while Gibbons (2003: 285–87) discusses in some detail an Australian case about the names of two drugs, Alkeran and Arclan, which at first sight seem quite distinct. However, he explains why some possible pronunciations of the words could be confused, in a country where 'a substantial proportion of the ... population speak English as a second language'.

In one of the earliest trademark cases involving phonetic similarity, *Pathfinder Communications Corp. v Midwest Communications Co.* in 1984, the dispute was over the names of two radio stations – WMEE and WMCZ (those who do not have North American accents may need to be reminded that the letter 'z' is pronounced 'zee'). Dinnsen (ms, quoted in Levi 1994b) reports that he gave evidence in court that the typical pronunciations of the two sets of letters were 'overwhelmingly similar ... and moreover likely to be confused' and he adds that the judge granted an injunction.

In a recent case in Brazil, Unilever, the owners of the international beauty products brand Dove, (the first vowel pronounced in Portuguese like the first vowel in the English word Dover) successfully forced a local producer, Davene, to withdraw their toiletries brand Dave (with vowels as in the English word Danny). As neither 'word' has any meaning in Portuguese the case was simply a question of phonetic similarity and therefore confusability

Shuy (2002b) reports a case fought over the names of two versions of a 'gooey tactile substance' which had been developed as an activity toy for young children and labelled GUK and GAK respectively. Shuy argued that the names were sufficiently dissimilar so as not to be in conflict. However, you might like to pause at this moment and consider whether you actually agree with Shuy that the two words are indeed sufficiently distinct phonetically so as not to cause confusion. What counter-arguments could you advance if you were asked to write a report for the other side, arguing that the marks are indeed confusingly similar? Then you can read Shuy's own detailed analysis and reasoning in his *Linguistic Battles in Trademark Disputes* (2002:118–19).

Japan is one of the world's major markets for whisky and there are many local and imported brands. In 1983, the makers of the Scottish whisky *White Horse* sued the Japanese producers of a recently introduced whisky labelled *Golden Horse* for trademark infringement. To the outsider the case seems convincing: gold as a colour has more prestige for credit cards and airline frequent flyer programmes and for whisky as well – Johnny Walker has an 18-year-old Gold version priced above its Red and Black. Also whisky drinkers assume that an older whisky is better and *Golden Horse* was matured for 12 years as opposed to the seven years for *White Horse*. So the implication is that *Golden Horse* is the premium version of *White Horse*. However, *White Horse* lost the case and for a purely linguistic reason. Although both brand names are in English, the judges chose to work with translations into Japanese. They argued that in Japanese (and therefore by implication in the minds of Japanese-speaking consumers), there is no possible confusion because whereas 'golden horse' consists, as in English, of an adjective plus noun, there is a single unrelated word that means 'white horse', so lexical matching is not facilitated by the language, the judges concluded, and so confusion is unlikely. (See Okawara 2006: 83ff for further details.)

Syntactic complexity

Levi (1993) reports a case in which she acted as an expert witness, testifying on syntactic complexity. The plaintiffs argued that a letter sent to them with information about how to claim benefits was so badly written that it had actually failed to inform them of their rights. In supporting their claim Levi identified a series of syntactic features which, she argued, were likely to interfere with understanding; for example, 'multiple negatives, complex embeddings, nominalizations ... passive verbs without subjects and difficult combinations of logical operators like *and, or, if* and *unless*'. She quotes the following extract from the letter as an example of the kind of syntactic problems encountered:

> If your AFDC financial assistance benefits are continued at the present level and the fair hearing decides your AFDC financial assistance reduction was correct, the amount of AFDC assistance received to which you were not entitled will be recouped from future AFDC payments or must be paid back if your AFDC is cancelled. (Levy 1995: 7)

This 'translates' into, or rather can be reduced to the following structural analysis:

> If X happens and then Y happens then either Z will happen [expressed in very complex terms including a negative with a relative clause] or – if R has also happened – then Q must happen. (p. 8)

Levi then characterises the syntactic complexity as consisting of 'a complex internal structure built out of seven clauses, six passive verbs without subjects' ... and several complex compound and abstract nouns (for example, 'financial assistance reduction'), which themselves contain nominalised verbs without expressed subjects (pp. 8–9).

Sadly she does not report the outcome of the case, nor give any indication of what the judge thought of her evidence, but at least she was admitted as a witness on syntactic meaning, which is by no means always the case – indeed one judge in the US explicitly refused to admit the linguist Ellen Prince as an expert on the grounds that it is the function of the court to decide on meaning. Certainly, it is more difficult when the texts involved are legal texts, because lawyers and judges usually see themselves as the guardians of and adjudicators on such meaning. Stubbs (1996) reports an English Appeal Court case where he wrote an expert opinion arguing that the language of the judge's summing-up in the original trial could have pre-disposed the jury to convict. The Lord Chief Justice refused to consider his evidence arguing that:

> what the meaning is of the language used by a learned judge in the course of his directions to the jury is a matter for this Court and is not a matter for any linguistic expert.
>
> (Stubbs 1996: 239)

However, even in this area, linguists are occasionally allowed to express a professional opinion, although it does help if they are lawyer-linguists and/or have a lawyer as co-author, as happened in the next case.

Lexico-grammatical ambiguity

Kaplan *et al.* (1995) report on an appeal which went to the Supreme Court in 1994. The facts are as follows: a certain Mr Granderson pleaded guilty to a charge of destroying mail, for which the maximum custodial sentence was six months in prison, although there was the option for the judge of fining the person and placing him on probation. The judge chose the latter; he fined Mr Granderson and put him on probation for five years; that is 60 months. Subsequently Mr Granderson violated his probation when he was caught in possession of cocaine. In such cases the law instructs the court to 'revoke the sentence of probation and sentence the defendant to not less than one third of the original sentence'. This presented the court with a problem because, if it took the 'original sentence' to refer to 'probation', imposing a sentence of 'not less than one third' that is 20 months probation, could in fact reduce the penalty, as he had not yet served 40 months of his probation. In the end it was decided to sentence him to 20 *months* in *jail*; that is a prison sentence which, rather than being 'not less than one third', was more than three times greater than the original maximum prison sentence.

Kaplan *et al.* (1995) argued that this particular interpretation of the crucial clauses was inadmissible on linguistic grounds, because one cannot allow an admittedly ambiguous item to have both of its meanings simultaneously – they pointed out that the court had interpreted the phrase 'original sentence' as referring to 'imprisonment' for the purpose of determining the *type* of punishment, but to 'the initial imposition of five years' (of probation) for the purpose of determining the *length* of the sentence. One of the authors observed that what the court had done was the linguistic equivalent of a Frenchman taking the phrase 'Pierre a fait tomber l'avocat' to mean, 'Pierre did something to the lawyer [l'avocat$_1$] and caused the avocado [l'avocat$_2$] to fall'.

This case was methodologically interesting because Kaplan *et al.* had not even been invited to write an expert opinion. What they did was to write an academic article, about linguistic aspects of not only the Granderson appeal, but also three other appeals to be considered by the Supreme Court, published it in the *Yale Law Review*, and then sent copies of the article to the Supreme Court judges. The judges not only read the article, but took note of the linguistic arguments and then in their judgment 'cited, and to an extent [even] tracked, the team's analysis' (Kaplan *et al.* 1995: 87). The judges decided to change the interpretation to 'a sentence of not less than two months in prison' and, as the accused had by this time already been in prison for 11 months, almost double the original maximum sentence, he was released immediately.

Lexical meaning

In some cases the linguist's contribution may be restricted to the meaning of a single word. Eades (1994) reports a case in which the expert testified that the verb 'killem', as used by a Torres Strait Islander, has a much wider semantic range than the Standard English word 'kill', which the uninformed might think was an equivalent. In fact, apparently the range of meanings for 'killem' can include 'hit' and thus the use of this word by the accused, when he was describing a fight with a man who subsequently died, could not be used to claim that he had necessarily confessed to manslaughter.

The accused may be even more vulnerable when the incriminating word(s) are in an unrelated language. In 2004, an Iraqi Kurdish refugee in the US was arrested after a sting operation and accused of having been willing to launder money in order to buy a shoulder-fired missile that was to be used to assassinate the Pakistani ambassador to the UN. It was said that the accused had links with an Islamist terrorist group, because his name was listed in an address book found in a terrorist training camp in northern Iraq, in which, according to the Defense Department, he was referred to with an Arabic word meaning 'commander'. Late in the day translators at the FBI got to see the relevant page and announced that the word, although written in Arabic script, was in reality Kurdish and was a common honorific 'kak', with a completely innocuous meaning, which, depending on the level of formality of the surrounding text, ranged from 'Mr' to 'brother'.

In another case, Sinclair (ms) was asked to give an opinion on the ordinary man's understanding of the word 'visa'. Apparently in law a visa is not in fact an 'entry permit' as most people think, but rather 'a permit to *request* leave to enter'; in other words, even with a visa, a traveller can legitimately be refused entry to a country. Sinclair was asked to provide evidence that this is not the commonly understood use and meaning of the word. In such cases judges traditionally turn to dictionaries, but Sinclair, who had revolutionised the making of dictionaries in the 1980s by creating vast databases, or corpora, of 'real language' from which to derive evidence about how words are actually used, chose to use corpus data. He based his evidence mainly on a five-million word corpus of *The Times* newspaper, although he supplemented this data by reference to the whole of his Bank of English corpus, totalling at that time some 28 million words – it now contains 4.5 billion words and has been renamed The Collins Corpus: http://www.collins. co.uk/page/The+Collins+Corpus.

The Times corpus included 74 instances of the words *visa* and *visas* in the sense under consideration, of which over 50 co-occurred or, to use the technical corpus linguistics word, *collocated,* with common verbs like *grant, issue, refuse, apply for, need* and *require,* Sinclair noted that, although the commonest modifier of *visa* is *exit,* it also co-occurs with *entry* and *re-entry* as in the following examples:

- you cannot *enter* an Arab country with an Israeli visa stamped in your passport …

- British passport holders *do not require* visas …
- non-Commonwealth students who *require* an *entry* visa will *need* a *re-entry* visa, even if you only *leave* the country for a couple of days …

On the basis of evidence like this he concluded that:

> the average visitor, encountering everyday English of the type recorded in the corpus, would deduce that a visa was a kind of permit to enter a country.… There is nothing … in these examples to suggest that a person who is in possession of a valid visa, or who does not require a visa, will be refused entry. The implication is very strong that a visa either ensures entry, or is not needed for entry. The circumstances of someone requiring *leave to enter*, in addition to having correct visa provision, does not arise in any of the examples, and the word *leave* does not occur in proximity to *visa(s)* except in the meaning *depart*.
>
> (Sinclair ms)

This is an example of what can be achieved with a fairly common word and a reasonably small corpus and demonstrates very clearly the usefulness of a corpus-based approach. Indeed some judges have recently begun to search legal data-bases to discover for themselves 'meaning in use' rather than simply relying, as before, on dictionary definitions. Also, corpora are now integral to much forensic linguistics work as can be seen in much more detail in Chapter 8.

There are times when linguists are asked to give evidence on special vocabulary, perhaps coded drug words, occurring in otherwise non-incriminating utterances, but Gibbons (2003: 294–95) reports a much stranger case in which he was faced with apparently incomprehensible phrases embedded in otherwise normal language in a tape-recorded conversation – for example, 'I'm just so nervous of gepoeping epinsepide'. What the speakers were doing in fact was using a disguise well-known to many school children and often called 'pig latin', where an encoding nonsense syllable is inserted between every syllable of the word(s) to be disguised. In this case the nonsense syllable used was 'ep' and once the expert had explained how the code worked, the jury were in a position to decode the message for themselves and hear 'gepoeping epinsepide' as 'going inside'.

Sometimes the lexical problem may involve the meaning of a series of key terms. McMenamin (1993) reports a case which hinged on the meaning of the words *accident, disease* and *syndrome*. A child was certified to have died from Sudden Infant Death Syndrome (SIDS) and his parents subsequently made a claim against an accident and life insurance policy. Their claim was refused, however, on the grounds that the policy did not cover deaths from illness or disease. McMenamin successfully demonstrated, using medical dictionaries and publications, that a *syndrome* is not regarded by professionals as a disease. Apparently a disease is 'a temporally bounded state between health and death' and those who have a disease either recover or die, whereas a syndrome is something a healthy child has or does not have and a child who does have it is either healthy or dead – there is no in-between 'diseased' state, so it was irrelevant for the insurance company to point out that the policy did not cover 'deaths from illness or disease'. In addition, McMenamin demonstrated that SIDS is treated linguistically and collocationally like an accident; so, for instance, the expression 'near miss' co-occurs regularly, and, of course, the parents were claiming against an *accident* and life insurance policy. The insurance company eventually paid out.

Levi (1993) reports on a lexical analysis of a set of jury instructions concerned with imposing the death penalty, which she undertook as part of an expert report in the case of *US ex rel. James P Free Jr v Kenneth McGinnis et al.* She was asked to express an opinion on the question 'How well could [the language of the jury instructions] have served its purpose in communicating clearly to the jury those legal concepts they needed to understand for sentencing in a capital case?' (p. 10). The instructions in question were (italics added):

> If you unanimously find from your consideration of all the evidence that there are no mitigating factors *sufficient* to *preclude* the imposition of a sentence of death then you should return a verdict imposing a sentence of death.
>
> If, on the other hand, you do not unanimously find that there are no mitigating factors *sufficient* to *preclude* the imposition of a sentence of death then you should return a verdict that the sentence of death should not be imposed.

In considering 'sufficient', Levi focused on the inherent vagueness of the word. She pointed out that 'sufficient' has only a contextually derivable meaning and that the instructions themselves did not give an individual juror any help on how to decide what would count as a sufficient mitigating factor in the particular situation of sentencing someone to death. In addition, there was real doubt as to whether a single factor that was perceived to be 'sufficient to preclude', but only so perceived by one juror, would in itself be 'sufficient' for the whole jury to be able to 'preclude'. According to the law, it would, but would it according to the text?

In considering 'preclude' Levi chose a different approach; she pointed out that, while this word did have a context-independent meaning, most of the jurors were unlikely to have known the meaning. She supported this assertion by testing some 50 undergraduate students, who happened to be attending one of her courses; only three of these students were able to provide the correct definition. Her conclusion was that there were grave doubts about the comprehensibility of the instructions. Unfortunately, she does not report how the court evaluated her evidence.

Pragmatic meaning

Some cases require reference to the pragmatic rules which govern the production of coherent interaction. Grice (1975), in his seminal article entitled 'Logic and conversation', observed that one of the controls on speakers' contributions is the *quantity maxim*, which he summarised as:

1 make your contribution as informative as is required
2 do not make your contribution more informative than is required.

What Grice is concerned with here is the fact that all utterances are shaped for a specific addressee on the basis of the speaker's assumptions about shared knowledge and opinions and in the light of what has already been said, not only in the ongoing interaction, but also in relevant previous interactions. This appeal to what Brazil (1985) called 'common ground' makes conversations frequently opaque and at times incomprehensible to an overhearer, as we can see in this question/answer sequence from a police interview:

> *Policeman:* Why did you do it?
> *Accused:* Well he told me if I didn't do it it would be even worse for me.

It is for this reason that it is impossible to present truly 'authentic' conversation on the stage, because the real addressee of any stage utterance is, in fact, the overhearing/audience, who needs supplementary background information. Thus, there has arisen the dramatic convention of over-explicitness, which allows characters to break the quantity maxim and to say to each other things they already 'know', even things that are strictly irrelevant, in order to transmit essential information economically to the audience. This is a convention which the dramatist Tom Stoppard parodies at the beginning of *The Real Inspector Hound*:

> Mrs Drudge (into phone) Hello the drawing room of Lady Muldoon's country residence one morning in early spring … for they had no children. (To appreciate the humour and see the full extract, go to: http://www.crescent-theatre.co.uk/Y2014/audition/hound-pages-6-9-mrs-drudge-simon-gascoyne.pdf (accessed 4 January 2016))

When we think about someone who sets out to fabricate a text in a legal context, we can see that s/he is in a situation directly analogous to that of the dramatist – s/he is creating a text with the overhearer, such as a policeman or a jury, in mind, and for this very reason is anxious to make the incriminating information as unambiguous as possible. Thus, at times, the fabricator, just like the dramatist, will break the maxim of quantity, although rarely as extremely as in utterances B3 and A4 in Extract 6.1 below, which is taken from the beginning of a fabricated telephone conversation, sent to the police after his trial, by a convicted defendant, who is here Mr B. The purpose of the fabrication is to discredit one of the witnesses, Mr A, who had given evidence against him.

Extract 6.1

A1. Hello.
B1. Hello, can I speak to Mr A please?

A2.   Speaking.

B2.   Are you surprised I've phoned you instead of coming down and seeing you as you asked in your message over the phone yesterday?

A3.   No, I'm not surprised. Why are you phoning me here for? Why don't you come in to see me if you want to see outside?

B3.   Well you've dragged me through a nightmare and I don't intend to give you an opportunity to set me up again for something else or beat me up again and abandon me miles away as you did outside Newtown prison with the two detectives; and for your information, as you may know, I've filed an official complaint against you and the two CID detectives.

A4.   The detectives and I beat you up and the CID they denied, they didn't beat you up but you can't do anything because you got no proof.

The over-explicitness in this case is comical, and it would have been comparatively easy to demonstrate that in court, but sadly there was no need for a linguist to explain Gricean maxims to the court, because there were audible clicks at the end of each utterance, where the tape recorder had obviously been switched on and off between speakers.

Over-explicitness can also occur in the choice of small linguistic units, like noun groups. In a disputed confession attributed to William Power, one of six Irishmen who later came to be referred to collectively as the Birmingham Six, who were accused and later convicted of carrying out a series of pub bombings in Birmingham in 1975, (see Coulthard 1994a), there was frequent reference to 'white plastic (carrier) bags':

> Walker was carrying *two white plastic carrier bags* ...
> Hunter was carrying *three white plastic carrier bags* ...
> Richard was carrying *one white plastic carrier bag* ...
> Walker gave me *one of the white plastic bags* ...
> Hughie gave J. Walker his *white plastic bag* ...

Our knowledge of the rules of conversational composition tells us that it is unlikely that Power would have used the combination, *numeral + white + plastic + carrier + bag(s)* even once, let alone three times. First, it is a noted feature of speech that speakers do not normally produce long noun phrases of this kind; rather they assemble complex information into two or three bits or bites. Second, this phrase represents a degree of detail that does not occur elsewhere in his statement. Finally, these particular details do not seem to have any importance in the story as *he* tells it and it is very unusual for narrators to provide details which have no relevance to *their* story. Let us compare the way similar information was conveyed over two utterances and three clauses in Power's interview with the police, which has a ring of authenticity:

> *Power:*   He'd got a holdall and *two bags.*
> *Watson:*   What *kind of bags*?
> *Power:*   They were *white,* I think they were *carrier bags.*

It takes three clauses to convey the information and even then there was no mention of 'plastic'. Extract 6.2 taken from his cross-examination during the trial, confirms clearly that, once a full form of a referring expression has been used, a speaker's normal habit is to employ a shortened version on subsequent occasions:

Extract 6.2

Barrister: And did you say '*two white plastic carrier bags?*'
Power: Yes sir.
Barrister: Whose idea was it that Walker was carrying *two white carrier bags*? Were those your words or the Police Officers' words?
Power: They were the Police Officers'. They kept insisting that I had told them that they carried *plastic bags* into the station.
Barrister: But was it your idea?
Power: No. They kept saying that I had already told them that they were carrying *plastic bags* into the station. When I said that, they said 'who was carrying *them*? who was carrying *them*?' They threatened me. I said 'They were all carrying *them*.' They asked me how *many* were they carrying and I just said *one, two, three, one and one.*

Thus the conclusion must be that, at the very least, the police officers expanded what Power said to make it fully transparent to another audience.

Tiersma (2002) uses similar concepts to shape a general discussion of the linguistic features of product warnings, on which the legal requirement is that they be 'adequate' and he then uses Gricean maxims to evaluate the adequacy of some warnings. He reports a case, *American Optical Co. v Weidenhamer,* where safety glasses, despite being marketed under the labels *Sure-Guard* and *Super Armorplate,* came with a warning 'lenses are impact resistant, but not unbreakable'. The manufacturers were sued on the grounds that this warning was not adequate. The jury sided with the plaintiff and deemed the warning to be inadequate on the grounds that it was written in small letters. Tiersma explains the decision saying that, given the nature of the warning, the labels were breaking the maxim of *relation,* because it is natural for a user, when faced with an apparently conflicting message, that is:

the contradiction between the name of the product in larger print – [*Super Armorplate*] – and a warning in much smaller letters that the product is not unbreakable ... to try to treat each as relevant [and] therefore conclude that [the] glasses will guard the eyes under all normal circumstances.

(Tiersma 2002: 58)

While this might be a natural and justifiable Gricean-based conclusion, in this case it was not a true conclusion in the real world and hence the manufacturer lost the case.

Tiersma (2002) looks at the applicability of other Gricean maxims. In discussing one of Dumas's (1992) cigarette packet examples – 'Cigarette Smoke Contains Carbon Monoxide' – taken from a case where smokers were suing tobacco companies for not warning them adequately about the dangers of smoking, Tiersma suggests that this warning can be seen to be breaking the maxim of *quantity*. By not providing sufficient information to the smoker/reader, it not only presupposes that the reader knows that carbon monoxide is dangerous in small quantities, but also that the reader has the ability to work through an inferential chain to reach the 'real' warning, which is now expressed explicitly on many cigarette packets worldwide and often supplemented by shocking photographs – 'Smoking kills'.

Most products, from medicines and household cleaners to televisions and portable barbecues, come with instructions and, if necessary, warnings, although as Hagemeyer points out many warnings in medicine leaflets appear to be designed more to protect the producer from prosecution than the consumer from unwanted side-effects, (Hagemeyer and Coulthard 2015: 63). Coulthard (2014) reports a case where a Canadian sued the manufacturer of a gas-fired barbecue designed for outdoor use, but he had actually installed indoors. The barbecue had exploded and his son had suffered third degree burns.

The case involved the interpretation of a set of warning labels and the book of instructions that accompanied the barbecue and whether one legitimate interpretation of these texts did in fact allow installation inside. The crucial label, affixed to the barbecue itself, began:

... CERTIFIED UNDER ANSI Z21.58A-1998
OUTDOOR COOKING APPLIANCE FOR OUTDOOR USE ONLY.

which seems unambiguous. However, immediately following was the sentence:

IF INSTALLED INDOOR (sic) DETACH AND LEAVE CYLINDER OUTDOORS

Despite the preceding observation, this sentence seemed to contemplate indoor use provided the gas cylinder, indicated elsewhere to be the dangerous part of the barbecue, remained outside, as indeed it had done, being linked to the barbecue by metal tubing through the outside wall. Other parts of the documentation proved also to be interpretable as supporting indoor installation and eventually the manufacturer settled out of court. The whole problem derived from the fact that not only was the barbecue manufactured in China, but so was the accompanying documentation and the crucial word 'installed' was a linguistic mistake – it should have read 'stored'. Surprisingly, a prosecution expert went so far as to suggest in his report that it was not the documentation, but the consumer who was to blame; he argued that any competent reader should have realised not only that 'installed' was a mistake, but also that the intended word/meaning was 'stored'. *Caveat Emptor* indeed.

Prince (1981) reports possibly the earliest forensic application of a pragmatic analysis. It is a case where a 58-year-old cement worker sued an insurance company. The company was refusing to pay his disability pension, because they asserted that he had lied when he responded to four of a long series of questions on the original insurance proposal form. One of the questions read as follows:

> Have you any impairments? ... Loss of sight or hearing? ... Loss of arm or leg? ... Are you crippled or deformed? ... If so explain ...

The insurance company argued that the man had lied when he wrote 'no' in answer to this multiple question, because 'he was overweight, had a high cholesterol level and occasional backaches', even though they did not dispute his counter-assertion that none of these conditions had ever caused him to take time off work (Prince 1981: 2). In her report, Prince approached the document from the point of view of an imagined co-operative reader, who was genuinely trying to make sense of the meaning of the document. For the question quoted above, she focused on the vagueness of the word *impairment*, and argued that any 'co-operative reader' would reasonably infer, given the content of the three phrases which follow the word 'impairment' and which in fact constitute the only textual clues in the proposal to the intended meaning of 'impairment', that the word was being used by the company, in that particular specialised context, to mean a relatively severe and incapacitating physical condition. The typical reader, faced with an unknown or unclear word, does not go straight to a dictionary, but tries to work out the meaning from the context. Given that 'impairment' was not specifically defined and that the examples helpfully provided in later parts of the question suggest a meaning of 'major physical problem', the examples are at best unhelpful, if not downright misleading, when one is made aware of the meaning the insurance company insisted the word was intended to have. Therefore, Prince argued, the man had indeed answered 'no' 'appropriately and in good conscience' to the question he legitimately understood them to be asking (Prince 1981: 4). The judge ruled in favour of the plaintiff.

The recording of interaction in written form – police interview notes

Some cases revolve around disputes about the accuracy of the written record of an interaction between the police and the accused. Converting the spoken to the written, as anyone who has attempted it is well aware, is not an unproblematic task, but, even so, police forces in most countries have no explicit guidelines about the procedures to use and what could or should legitimately be omitted, even when the aim is to produce a verbatim record in the interviewee's own words. In this context it is useful to consider Slembrouck's (1992) observations about the production of *Hansard* versions of proceedings in the British Parliament, where transcribers, who are similarly linguistically untrained, are charged with the creation of highly important verbatim records of what was said. Slembrouck (1992: 104) notes that:

there is filtering out of 'disfluency' and other obvious properties of spoken-ness (e.g. intonation, stress). Repetitions, (even when strategically used ...), half-pronounced words, incomplete utterances, (un)filled pauses, false starts, reformulations, grammatical slips, etc. are equally absent.

In the typical police handwritten record the same rules seem to apply. For this reason the appeal of Robert Burton, *R v Robert Burton*, in the English Court of Appeal in 2002 was fascinating. Burton was captured red-handed with several companions, trying to steal from trailers loaded with £250,000 worth of whisky from an overnight trailer park. Until he was arrested he did not realise that all his companions were in fact undercover police officers. Burton's defence was that he had tried to call off the operation on several occasions, but the undercover police officers, who he had thought were real criminals to whom he owed a lot of money for drugs, forced him to go through with the robbery. Thus, his defence was that the undercover police officers had been involved in an illegal action, 'incitement to commit a crime'.

When the case went to court, the police submitted, as part of their evidence, several records of telephone calls, which they claimed an undercover officer, using the codename Charlie, had written down from memory immediately after each of the conversations with Burton had ended. Paradoxically, part of Burton's defence was not that these records were inaccurate and therefore unreliable, as one would expect them to be, if someone had written down what had been said from memory; rather Burton claimed that the records were too accurate and there-fore could not have been produced from memory. This would have to mean that the conversations had been transcribed directly from audio-recordings. He claimed that the police had denied the existence of such recordings because they did not want to submit them in evidence, as the recordings would have revealed that the transcriptions were partial and that in omitted sections of these same conversations police officer 'Charlie' was indeed pressurising Burton to commit a crime.

A linguistic analysis confirmed that either the police officer had an amazing ability to recall conversations verbatim or there had indeed been audio-recordings. This opinion was based on the occurrence of two sets of features. First, the appearance in the records of a set of spoken discourse items which are regularly produced by speakers, although they carry little or no significant content and which are therefore typically forgotten or at least not reported by those producing remembered accounts of what was said. For example:

1   discourse markers – items which typically occur at the beginnings of utterances – *well, right, so*;
2   acknowledgements of replies to questions – what some call *third parts* of *exchanges* – realised by *yeah, okay, alright* and repetitions of whole phrases from the preceding utterance;
3   other kinds of cross-utterance repetition and reformulation;
4   fillers such as *like* and *you know what I mean*;

5 adverbial modifiers like *just*, *really*, *actually* and *fucking*;
6 slang items and non-standard grammatical forms like *gonna*.

Second, and even more surprisingly, Burton had a marked stammer, which he had learned to partially control by the use of what speech therapists call a 'step word', a word which the speaker learns to produce automatically to disguise the fact that s/he is experiencing difficulty with the articulation of other words. In the case of Burton the step word was 'like' and this too had not simply been reproduced in the 'remembered' records, but reproduced in the kinds of linguistic contexts in which Burton typically used it. Many of these discourse features are exemplified and highlighted in bold in Extract 6.3 from one of Charlie's records:

Extract 6.3

I said,	'You **gonna** take something heavy, do **you know what I mean**, to make things easier in there.'
Bob said,	'No, **fuck off, like** that's too much, I'll **just** have a blade, that'll do.'
I said,	'**Yeah okay**.'
Bob said,	'I'm **just** a bit jittery **like** as its getting close **like**.'
I said,	'**Yeah, okay** but keep in touch.'
Bob said,	'**Yeah**, sorry about that Charlie, there's no problems honest, I'll chase that **bloke** up and find out what's happening whether there's 2, 3 or 4 there.'
I said,	'**Okay** we may have to do it on two to get it done by Christmas.'
Bob said,	'**Yeah okay**.'
I said,	'**Alright**, see you later Bob.'
Bob said,	'**Yeah** later Charlie **mate**.'

In order to test the ability of a group of lay people to remember conversations, Burton and Coulthard conducted a short, three-minute conversation about aspects of the case in the presence of ten 'subjects', all of whom knew that their task was to produce, immediately afterwards, a verbatim record of what had been said. In order to give the 'subjects' at least the same advantage as 'Charlie' would have had, they were allowed to make notes, in any form they wished. One of the ten subjects was a trained shorthand typist and she was asked to write down contemporaneously as much as she was able to using shorthand and was then allowed to go back and make any alterations and additions to her record that she thought necessary. The conversation was also audio-recorded.

The subjects in the experiment varied considerably in their accuracy. As one would expect, none of them could match the shorthand typist in terms of accuracy of wording and most had significant problems with the gist as well – they all omitted and/or mis-remembered crucial information. Extract 6.4 is from a verbatim transcription of the audio-recording of the conversation, followed by the secretary's shorthand version (Extract 6.5) and then by the version produced by one of the subjects (Extract 6.6). I have indicated what they omitted in strike-through form contained inside square brackets in order to assist comparison:

Extract 6.4: Actual

M.   where were the meetings
B.   there was a meeting at Kings Cross
M.   yep
B.   and there was a meeting at Chesterfield
M.   were these night meetings or day
B.   no they was during the day

Extract 6.5: Secretary's version

M.   Where were the meetings
B.   There was a meeting at Kings Cross, [yep and there was] a meeting at
     Chesterfield
M.   Were they night meetings
B.   No [they was] during the day

Extract 6.6: Subject 1's version

M.   where were the meetings
B.   [there was a meeting at Kings Cross]
M.   [yep]
B.   [and there was a meeting at] Chesterfield
M.   were these night meetings [or day]
B.   [no they was during the day] mainly at night, yeah

As is evident Subject 1 misses out the Kings Cross meeting altogether and wrongly reports the Chesterfield one as being at night. These findings robustly confirmed that it is impossible to remember verbatim what was said, even immediately afterwards, even when, as noted above, the task for the subjects in the experiment was much less demanding than that facing Charlie, because they had much less to remember, and consequently a much shorter time over which to remember it, before starting to write it down.

The linguistic evidence supporting the claim that some of the telephone records were too accurate to be a record of a remembered interaction was accepted unchallenged, but the appeal failed on other grounds.

Narrative analysis of a disputed statement

There are times when the linguist's knowledge of the rules for producing spoken narratives is relevant. It is not uncommon for an accused to claim that a mono-logue confession attributed to him was in fact the product of a question and answer session during which the police officer provided much of the information. The 2001 appeal of Iain Hay Gordon against his 1953 conviction for murder involved such a claim:

> The whole statement was his entirely, in thought and wording … To give just
> one instance of what is typical of the whole statement, when he said 'Would

you offer to escort her home?' and I said 'Probably', that went down as 'I offered to escort her home'.

(tape-recorded interview, 2001)

Gordon makes a similar claim about the statement that was taken on the previous day, 'all this statement was in reply to questioning'. It was certainly not unknown for police officers at times to do exactly what Gordon claimed had happened on this occasion. Chief Inspector Hannam, in another murder case, that of Alfred Charles Whiteway in 1953, explained to the court how he had elicited a statement from the accused in this way:

> I would say 'Do you say on that Sunday you wore your shoes?' and he would say 'Yes' and it would go down as 'On that Sunday I wore my shoes'.

(Court Transcript, p. 156)

It had been put to Gordon that he probably did not remember much about the murder as he must have had some kind of a blackout at the time and Gordon said he was persuaded by this. If Gordon's claims are true, one would expect to find in his statement not only traces of the language used by the interviewing officers and their structuring of the content, but also an unusual number of expressions of uncertainty about the facts. In Extract 6.7 Gordon apparently confesses to the murder and disposal of the murder weapon, with items indicating uncertainty highlighted in bold:

Extract 6.7

I am **a bit hazy** about what happened next but I **probably** pulled the body of Patricia through the bushes to hide it. I dragged her by her arms or hands, but I **cannot remember**.

Even before this happened I do **not think** I was capable of knowing what I was doing. I was confused at the time and **believe** I stabbed her once or twice with my service knife. I had been carrying this in my trouser pocket. I am **not quite sure** what kind of knife it was.

I **may** have caught her by the throat to stop her from shouting. I **may** have pushed her scarves against her mouth to stop her shouting.

It is all **very hazy** to me but **I think** I was disturbed **either** by seeing a light **or** hearing footsteps in the drive. I **must have** remained hidden and later walked out of the Glen at the Gate Lodge on to the main road.

As far as I know I crossed the main road and threw the knife into the sea.

As we can see, the majority of the reported facts have an associated overt marker of the potential unreliability of the assertion. This is very odd for a single-author narrative, but of course quite natural for a narrative which has been constructed piece by piece out of a sequence of questions to which the required answer is simply an indication of the truth, probability, possibility or falseness of the proposition – i.e. such answers would be versions of 'yes', 'probably', 'possibly', 'no' – or alternatively expressing an inability to give a firm opinion – 'I don't know', 'I can't remember'.

The Appeal Court judges accepted that these linguistic observations cast 'a substantial degree of doubt upon the correctness of the officers' averments (sic)'. As a consequence they felt that the confession could not be used as evidence and that without it the conviction, which had stood for 48 years, was 'unsafe'.

The challenges for non-native speakers

Language comprehension

There are many cases when defendants claim that their competence in the language in which they were arrested and/or interviewed was inadequate. These claims can range from whether, on being arrested, they understood the caution or Miranda warnings sufficiently well, to whether, on being interviewed, they should have been offered the services of an interpreter. Although Applied Linguists have a great deal of experience in assessing the linguistic performance of non-natives, most of their tests are predicated on the assumption that the testee is trying to do their best, whereas in many court cases it may actually be in the interest of the accused to under-perform. One solution to this problem is to use naturally occurring interaction, rather than specially elicited samples, for assessment purposes.

In evidence presented in the trial of *R v Javid Khan*, Cotterill (personal communication) used an analysis of 21 minutes of police station CCTV footage of Mr Khan being interviewed on the night of the offence, in order to support her opinion that Mr Khan's level of English, 'both in receptive and productive terms ... would cause him serious communicative difficulty'. She cites examples such as those in Extract 6.8:

Extract 6.8

Officer.	And your occupation please?
Mr Khan.	Er (?) Market Rasen (place)
Officer.	How tall are you Javid?
Mr Khan.	Sorry?
Officer.	How tall are you?
Mr Khan.	Sorry?
Officer.	*(Gesturing)* How tall are you?
Mr Khan.	How tall, I don't know. Maybe er 5 something *(gesturing '5' with hand)*, 5 3, 5 4, I don't know
Officer.	Did you say you suffer from a weak heart? *(Mr Khan looks at the two arresting officers for clarification)* Officers 2/3. *(gesturing at heart)* Heart problem?
Officer.	Have you got a heart problem?
Mr Khan.	Yeah I said somebody [unintelligible]
Officer.	You haven't got a heart problem then?
Mr Khan.	No, no, I don't have a heart problem

She notes that, despite the evident struggle to understand and despite Mr Khan explicitly confirming his communication difficulties:

Officer. Do you understand English properly?
Mr Khan. *(Mr Khan shakes his head)* Not properly

he was not offered the services of an interpreter at any point. All too often though, the linguist does not have access to such relevant data and has to argue from a present measured competence level to an estimated earlier incompetence. Following a series of cases in which confession evidence elicited from non-native speakers was subsequently rejected in court, it is now official policy in Australia and the UK to insist that any suspect with evident communication problems is interviewed using an interpreter, even when suspects consider themselves linguistically competent.

Language production

There are times when the defence wants to challenge a police record on the grounds that some of the language in it could not have been produced by their client. Evidence submitted by two linguists in the case of *R v Lapointe and Sicotte* (see Canale *et al.* 1982) highlighted significant linguistic differences between the level of English produced by two French-speaking defendants in tape-recorded interviews and that attributed to them in typed versions of confession statements. However, as we have noted elsewhere, police officers are not trained transcribers and even trained transcribers make notable mistakes when making a written record in real time, so the weight given to such evidence can vary from court to court. In this particular case the court, while accepting the observations of the linguists, concluded that the changes were not deliberate attempts by the police to alter the content of what was said.

McMenamin (2002) reports the case of a contested will of a woman who died at the age of 85 in Alaska, having been born in Japan and grown up in Hawaii. Her will apparently left everything to a couple of neighbours and was supported by photocopies of five letters on the topic of the will. These letters had supposedly been dictated by the deceased to a friend called Kim and were later discovered in the boot of a car. Kim was untraceable, as were the originals of the letters.

The 'Kim' letters had a series of typical creolised English features such as the deletion of articles, subjects, objects and some auxiliary and copular verbs, as well as the omission of plural and tense morphemes. However, by contrast, the known writings of the deceased, although they 'evidenced some features of Hawaiian Creole English' (McMenamin 2002: 132), were much closer to Standard English.

In addition, some of the creolisations found in the letters did not occur at all in the known writings. More worryingly, all the creole features in the suspect letters were deletions of grammatical elements, like articles and auxiliaries, whereas McMenamin notes that there is 'no variety of English known to be defined by a single process of variation like deletion' (McMenamin 2002: 132). To add further doubt, the known writings of the deceased did include other creole features that were not simply deletions, such as mismatch between verb and complementiser and mass nouns used as count nouns. The reported linguistic facts and the derived opinions convinced the judge, who found that:

> the ... 'Kim' papers were prepared by the [neighbors] or at their direction ... [and that] the language usage ... is concocted and a fraud.
>
> (McMenamin 2002: 135–36)

Cross-cultural differences in rules of interaction

One problem in native/non-native interaction is that the native speaker will assume that the non-native is using the same rules as s/he is and therefore linguists may need to explain to the court the basis of the consequent potential misinterpretations. Eades (2002) reports some of the problems that Aboriginal witnesses face in English speaking courts. First, silence following a question has a totally different significance for the two speech communities. An Aboriginal, she says, will typically pause before answering a question in order to indicate that s/he is giving proper weight and consideration to it, whereas for an English audience, silence, particularly following a question in court, raises doubts about the veracity of the answer.

Eades borrows the term 'gratuitous concurrence' from Liberman (1985) to label another intercultural communication problem, 'the tendency of Aboriginal people to say "yes" in answer to a question ... regardless of whether the speaker agrees with the proposition and [even] at times [when] the speaker actually does not understand the question' (p. 166). (Those who, like myself, have struggled to communicate in a language in which they have low competence, will recognise this strategy.)

Eades demonstrates how *gratuitous concurrence* functioned to greatly disadvantage three teenage Aboriginal witnesses in a crucial trial where police officers were accused of unlawfully depriving them of their liberty. Six police officers picked up three adolescents aged 12, 13 and 14 in a shopping mall after midnight, drove them 14 kilometers out of town to an industrial wasteland and then left them to find their own way back. The defence was that 'the boys voluntarily [gave] up their liberty, while the police took them for a ride' (2002: 162). Eades exemplifies, using an extract from the cross-examination of one of them, (extract 6.9 below), how the boys were frequently asked multiple questions, with the answer being assumed to apply to all components.

Extract 6.9
[L = Lawyer; D = David]

L1   David – let me just try to summarize if I can – what you – what you've told us. (3.1) You told us yesterday that the real problem wasn't anything that happened getting into the car or in the car but the fact that you were left at Pinkenba – that right?

D1   (1.5) Mm.
L2   Mm – that's the truth, isn't it?
D2   Mm.
     (4.3)
L3   You see – you weren't deprived of your liberty at all – uh in going out
     there – it was the fact that you were left there that you thought was wrong?
D3   (1.2) Yeah.
L4   Eh?
D4   Yeah.
     (3.5)
L5   you got in the car (2.1) without being forced – you went out there with-
     out being forced – the problem began when you were left there?
D5   (1.5) Mm.

Fortunately, at this point the prosecution lawyer made one of his all too rare inter-
ruptions, which caused a surprising and highly significant change in the boy's
responses:

[PL = Prosecuting Lawyer; Mag = Magistrate]
PL   With respect Your Worship – there are three elements to that question
       and I ask my Friend to break them down.
Mag   Yes – just break it up one by one Mr Humphrey.
L6   You got into the car without being forced David – didn't you?
D6   (1.5) No.
L7   You told us – you've told us a (laughs) number of times today you
       did.
D7   (1.3) They forced me.

This and similar examples cited by Eades provide a powerful tool for linguists to
contest 'confession' interviews in which the interviewee only confesses by concurring. Her observations and explanation were subsequently supported by Gibbons
(1996) who reports a case of an audio-recorded confession interview in which an
Aboriginal suspect had concurred with proposals of his guilt offered by the interviewing police officer. In this case, however, the suspect also gratuitously concurred
with the final question in the interview, 'Has any threat, promise or inducement been
held out to you to give the answers as recorded in this interview'. In this case this
concurring 'yes' negated the evidentiary value of all the previous concurrences.

   Eades (1994) reports another case in which she contested the accuracy of a
police record of a confession to murder by an Aboriginal, on the grounds that it
contained 'an alarming number of precise answers with quantifiable specification', for example:

Q.   When did you do this?
A.   Quarter past four
Q.   How long has she been your woman?
A.   Three weeks
       (Eades 1994: 122)

She successfully argued that such replies were 'most uncharacteristic of Aboriginal English ways of being specific' – these, she noted, are typically 'relational, using social, geographical or climatic comparisons', for example '"When did that happen?" "Not long before the sun went down"' (Eades 1994: 122). In other words, although the two exchanges may have seemed unremarkable to a native speaker of Australian English, the responses are abnormal for Aboriginal interaction. Further than this the expert cannot go; it is up to the court to decide whether it is more likely that the evident unnaturalness is a product of very inaccurate and unreliable note taking or of deliberate fabrication.

Different language communities also have different conventions for the form of responses to polar questions. For instance, whereas in standard English the typical response to what is labelled, for this very reason, a yes/no question, for example 'Was she bleeding?' would be 'Yes' with the optional addition of 'she was', for a Portuguese native speaker carrying over into English the Portuguese response rules, the natural response form would be 'she was bleeding', with no 'yes' at all. Eades (1994: 123) notes that there are also different conventions in Aboriginal English. In the same suspect interview referred to above, a third of the replies to yes/no questions were in the form 'Yes' + auxiliary phrase, whereas this form actually occurred in only 1 per cent of the responses in an authenticated interview, which again suggested at best mis-transcription by the recording officer.

Language Analysis in the Determination of Origin (LADO)

One of the newest areas in which forensic linguists have been asked to express opinions is LADO, the use of language testing to help the process of determining the nationality of people who are claiming refugee status. Currently there is perceived to be a major problem of people applying for political asylum and falsely claiming to be citizens of countries where the political situation makes such applications legitimate under the 1951 Geneva Convention. Several countries have chosen to make language testing part of the process of investigating asylum claims, but linguists in many countries have questioned the reliability of the current procedures and the professional competence of many of the testers.

Much criticism has been levelled against the Swedish Immigration Authority, which delegated the work to two private companies, Eqvator and Sprakab, companies which have also done work for the Australian and several European governments – by 2015 Sprakab had undertaken some 45,000 assessments in 15 years and at the time of writing the number of cases handled annually is still rising. The qualifications and identities of the assessors are not disclosed, but Eades *et al.* (2003), focusing on assessments made by Eqvator of Afghani applicants applying for asylum in Australia, concluded that the staff lacked the expertise necessary to construct an informed assessment, because apparently their main qualification was an ability to speak the language, not any training in (socio-) linguistics. Thus, the central question raised earlier needs to be reformulated: if carried out by someone trained in linguistics, is 'linguistic' analysis a viable way of determining a person's nationality?

Singler (2004) argues that 'in some cases at least ... with reformulation of the notion "nationality" to "country of socialization," it is possible to carry out [reliable] "linguistic" analysis', a contention supported by Maryns (2004). However, both express the caveat that this is only possible when there is sufficient linguistic knowledge of a sociolinguistic and dialectal nature about the country of socialisation and they warn that for some populations such data simply do not exist. For this reason, Singler (2004: 232) criticised Eqvator's work on Afghan claimants because it claimed to be able to distinguish speakers of Hazaragi who came from Afghanistan, from those who came from Pakistan, whereas Eades *et al.* (2003) noted that, 'The border between Afghanistan and Pakistan has had very little linguistic study' (p. 191). Singler goes on to warn that:

> So long as the fundamental linguistic work has not been done, it is not possible to determine whether Hazaragi in Afghanistan can be reliably distinguished from Hazaragi in Pakistan or in Iran, where it is also spoken.

Thus LADO is an area where developing the linguistic methodology and resources is in its infancy and for this reason it is vitally important that those charged with determining origin are aware of the problems. Eades (2010a) gives a detailed presentation of the current situation and linguists' attempts to improve it. She refers to the game-changing 2,000 word set of *Guidelines* produced in 2004 by an international group of linguists, the Language and National Origin Group, which was:

> intended to provide some elementary understanding for governments, lawyers and refugee advocates on linguistic issues relevant to LADO, particularly 'in deciding whether and to what degree language analysis is reliable in particular cases'.

> (Eades 2010a: 414)

In particular, the *Guidelines* stress that linguistic analysis cannot be used to determine national origin, but only to draw conclusions about a speaker's country of socialisation and then only sometimes. Sadly, many governments are still not taking sufficient notice of the warnings; see https://journals.equinoxpub.com/index.php/IJSLL/article/viewFile/555/13860, for the full Guidelines.

Conclusion

We have tried in the space available to give an idea of the diversity of the problems tackled and the techniques used by forensic linguists. The field is expanding rapidly as more lawyers become aware of the potential of linguistic analysis and readers are urged to consult the latest volumes of the two journals *Language and Law – Linguagem e Direito* and *The International Journal of Speech, Language and the Law*. Details of many other cases not specifically referred to above can be found in the Further Reading section.

Further reading

Cotterill (ed.) (2002), particularly chapters by Berk-Seligson, Coulthard, Solan, Stygall and Tiersma; Coulthard and Johnson (eds) (2010), particularly chapters by Butters, Dumas, Eades and McMenamin; Shuy (2002), particularly chapters 3, 7, 8 and 14.

Research tasks

1   Brazil is the largest market in the world for Johnny Walker Red Label whisky. Diageo, owners of the brand claimed 'trademark infringement by translation' against a Brazilian company that had marketed a sugar cane spirit, called locally *cachaça*, with the name *Joao Andante*, which translates literally as 'John [the] Walker'. Search for the images of the two products online and then decide how you would have advised the producers to defend themselves against the charge? In fact, the *cachaça* producers obviously received bad advice, as they lost the case and had to change the name; it is now known as *O Andante – the Walker –* a walker who on the label now whimsically has no legs. However, there was a happy ending – the remaining bottles with the original name and label now sell at a premium.

2   Below is the text of the will of a wealthy semi-literate unmarried Californian real estate developer. There was a dispute between his long-time partner, Ms Carolyn Davis, and his relatives over the interpretation of the text – the question is whether the will assigns the whole of his estate, or just $2 million plus the house, to Ms Davis. What linguistic evidence and arguments can you adduce to resolve the problem? When you have reached your own argued conclusion you may like to read Kaplan (1998).

side one	side two
THis is my will	in case I die
incase something	this is my will +
Happens if I am	I leave her $2,000,00
disabeled that I can	2 million dollars AND
not speake or am	my Home as 51 Monte
unable to do my	MAR Dr SUALito CALIF
ability to speke or	This will is made out
Parilized Carolyn Davis	on THis DAY FEB 18 1995
shall Have the full	unless superseded
wrights as my wife	By a future will AFRE THIS DAY IT STANDS AS A LEGAL will

3   Collect a set of warnings from 'over the counter' medicines and household cleaning products. How clear are they and how much inferencing is required of the reader? What changes would you propose to ensure that the average customer fully understands the warnings and what changes would you suggest to the manufacturer in order to make the warnings proof against claims for damages? (You may find it useful to read Hagemeyer and Coulthard 2015.)

7   Forensic phonetics

Police and security services are trying to identify a suspected British jihadist who appeared in footage of the killing of a US journalist. [...] Unconfirmed reports suggest the man in the video [...] is from London or south-east England and may have guarded Islamic State captives.

(BBC News, 21 August 2014)

The screams are clearly coming from a distraught male, whose repeated cries for help end abruptly with a gunshot. What is not clear from a recording of a 911 call [...] is the identity of the screamer: George Zimmerman, the volunteer community watchman, or Trayvon Martin, the unarmed 17-year-old he killed...

(New York Times, 22 June 2013)

The work of the forensic phonetician

The forensic phonetician is concerned with all aspects of speech as evidence. This can involve deriving information about a speaker's social and regional background on the basis of their voice. This is what was asked of linguists by the media when videos emerged online of a member of Islamic State beheading a man who had been held hostage, as reported by the BBC in the first epigraph. Forensic phoneticians are also asked by police or legal teams to offer an opinion on whether the speaker in two or more separate recordings is the same, such as in the Zimmerman case, in the second epigraph, in which an unidentified scream was heard in the background of a telephone call and a phonetician was asked whether it was possible to classify that scream as belonging to either George Zimmerman or Trayvon Martin. Both of these cases are discussed in more detail in this chapter. In addition, forensic speech scientists can help police forces with the transcription and interpretation of disputed recordings, and offer advice in the design of 'voice line-ups', also known as 'voice parades'. These are similar to identity parades, but involve victims and witnesses who have heard, but not seen, the perpetrator of a crime. When the police arrest someone as a suspect in such a crime, recordings of the suspect's voice, along with a set of similar voices, are played to the witness, and the witness is asked whether they can identify the voice that they heard at the scene of the crime.

Transcription and disputed utterances

Many court cases involve the provision and presentation of transcriptions of tape- or video-recorded evidence. The recording(s) concerned may be of people talking about future or past criminal activity, or of them actually committing a crime, as in the case of bomb threats, ransom demands, hoax emergency calls or negotiating the buying or selling of drugs. Very few of the transcriptions presented in court have been made by someone with a qualification in phonetics, although occasionally a forensic phonetician is called in, typically when there is a dispute over a small number of specific items, which could be single words or even a single phoneme. Such recordings can come from a variety of sources, including recorded face-to-face interactions, recorded telephone and emergency service calls, like in the Zimmerman case, or 'covert' undercover recordings made without the knowledge of the speaker(s), all of which can include voices of native and non-native speakers. The expert is tasked by either prosecution or defence to provide an accurate and reliable account of what was said in the recordings. However, any researcher or student who has transcribed recordings of any kind will know that this is not a straightforward task, but one that demands considerable time and effort, and one that presents many challenges, even to the trained ear of the professional linguist. Unlike with writing, the sounds produced in speech are continuous and non-discrete, often difficult to distinguish when uttered at speed and with particular stress and rhythm, even in the clearest of recordings. Furthermore, Fraser (2003: 204–5) highlights the challenges posed by human perception when we hear sounds in recordings. She argues that:

> Although we generally don't notice our own contribution to perception, speech perception is an active, rather than a passive, process, with the hearer actively constructing, rather than passively picking up, the speaker's message.

In other words, the listener does not necessarily hear what was said, but rather hears their *construction* of what they *think* was said; they subconsciously combine the speech signal (the sounds) with prior knowledge of speech, language and context in their own heads (Fraser 2003: 206). This is exemplified by Fraser (2014: 13–14) as she describes an earlier study by Bruce (1958), in which participants listened to a number of sentences, partially 'masked' with a hissing noise, after being given a key word as to the content of the recording, such as 'sport' or 'weather'. Listeners' heard the same masked sentences, but with different key words. What was found was that their perceptions of what they heard changed in response to the key words, despite the fact that they had listened to the same sentences. Such difficulties are compounded when the recordings are unclear or of a low quality, most commonly a result of poor recording equipment or extensive background noise (Fraser 2014: 9).

Fraser *et al.* (2011) exemplify the challenges posed by listener perceptions of unclear recordings with experimental results using a recording from a real forensic case in New Zealand. The case itself is that of David Bain, who was convicted of five counts of murder after the deaths of his parents and siblings at the family home in 1994. In one of the appeals against the verdict, a detective listening to the crisis call Bain made to the police claimed to hear Bain utter the words 'I shot the prick' under his breath, and it was alleged by the prosecution that this barely audible utterance constituted a previously unheard confession. The defence, meanwhile, argued that the speech was uninterpretable, and perhaps not even an utterance at all, but actually Bain gasping for breath. After lengthy legal disputes, a re-trial was granted, but it was decided that that the emergency call was to be played to the jury with the disputed utterance removed. Innes (2011) provides a detailed account of the case itself. Although it is impossible to know how the jury in the trial would have interpreted the utterance, Fraser and her colleagues investigated what their participants 'heard' in the recording after they had received additional information about the case, which they were given at various 'evidence points' throughout the experiment (Fraser *et al.* 2011: 266). At the first evidence point (of six), after the listeners had already heard the call and been asked about their immediate impression of the caller, they were told that the speaker (Bain) had returned home to find his family shot dead, and were asked whether this 'evidence' changed their initial impression of the call and caller. At this first stage, the most frequent responses from the 200 participants were that the disputed utterance was either 'I can't breathe' or was not speech at all (Fraser *et al.* 2011: 274), and nobody perceived the utterance to be 'I shot the prick' (though 'shot' and 'prick' were actually heard by some participants as isolated words). At the third evidence point, the participants were randomly assigned to one of two groups and were given systematically different information in order to observe whether the information affected what they heard. Group A was given a story in which suspicion fell on the caller, while Group B were told that the police suspected the caller's father had killed his family and then shot himself. Notably, the groups were also given different possible interpretations of the disputed section of the call. Group A was told it was alleged to contain the words 'I shot the prick', while Group B was told it was 'he shot them all'. At this point, 'I shot the prick' became by far the most common interpretation response in Group A participants, while Group B's interpretations were relatively unaffected by the possibility of the utterance being 'he shot them all'. While there was an increase in responses that included the words 'shot' and 'killed', some of which also heard the pronoun 'he', nobody heard the alleged phrase (Fraser *et al.* 2011: 276). Findings such as these provide strong support for the argument that listeners construct speakers' messages through a combination of the sound signals themselves and their own contextual knowledge of the talk. That is, if the sounds alone are not enough to extract meaning, as in the David Bain case and many others, listeners use other background contextual information to interpret utterances. In turn, we are 'primed' to interpret unclear utterances in a particular way; different contextual knowledge provides different primings for listeners' perceptions.

Such findings pose obvious challenges for those expected to produce accurate and reliable transcriptions for the court, particularly of unclear and questionable utterances. Therefore, transcribers must be aware of the ways in which these influences can produce errors in their perceptions of what is said, and their subsequent transcriptions. Fraser (2003: 221) argues that such skills and knowledge are 'only gained through considerable study of linguistics, phonetics and psycholinguistics'. In cases where forensic evidence is central to a judicial decision, and where such decisions are made by judges or juries on the basis of spoken linguistic evidence, accuracy and reliability is paramount, as mis-transcriptions can have serious legal consequences. For example, in one case in which Coulthard was involved, an indistinct word, in a clandestine recording of a man later accused of manufacturing the designer drug Ecstasy, was mis-heard by a police transcriber as 'hallucinogenic':

> … but if it's as you say it's hallucinogenic, it's in the Sigma catalogue

whereas, what he actually said was 'German':

> … but if it's as you say it's German, it's in the Sigma catalogue.

In another case, a murder suspect with a very strong West Indian accent, was transcribed as saying, in a police interview, that he 'got on a train' and then 'shot a man to kill'; in fact what he said was the completely innocuous and contextually much more plausible 'show[ed] a man ticket' (Peter French, personal communication).

French (in Baldwin and French 1990) reports a much more difficult case, which appeared to turn on the presence or absence of a single phoneme, the one that distinguishes *can* from *can't*. Most readers, if they record themselves reading these two words aloud, will notice not one but two phonemic differences between their pronunciations of the words – the absence/presence of a /t/ and a different vowel phoneme. Using a Received Pronunciation (RP) or near-RP British accent, at least when the words are produced as citation forms, the vowel in *can't* is also longer. This contrasts with many North American accents of English in which the vowels in *can* and *can't* are more similar. However, in an ordinary speech context, as in the phrase 'I can't refuse', the /t/ often disappears and the vowel is shortened, so that the phonetic difference between the two words is very significantly reduced. In French's case a doctor, who spoke English with a strong Greek accent, had been surreptitiously tape-recorded apparently saying, whilst prescribing tablets to someone he thought was a drug addict, 'you can inject those things'. He was prosecuted for irresponsibly suggesting that the patient could grind up the pills and then inject them. His defence was that he had actually said just the opposite, 'you can't inject those things'. An auditory examination of the tape-recording showed that there was certainly no hint of a /t/ at the end of the 'can' word and thus confirmed the phonetic accuracy of the police transcription. However, the question remained, was the transcription morphologically incorrect; that is, was the doctor intending to say and actually producing his version of *can't*? Auditory analysis of a taped sample of the doctor's speech showed that there was usually an absence of final /t/ in his production of *can't*. Also, even a trained phonetician found it virtually impossible to distinguish the doctor's /a/ vowels, when they were produced in words which, it was possible to deduce from the context, were unambiguously intended as either *can* or *can't*. So, whichever the doctor's intended meaning on any particular occasion, it had to be determined by the untrained listener from the context and not auditorily. There would, therefore, be occasions when there was genuine ambiguity.

Forensic phoneticians transcribing recordings for court are not simply asked *what was said?* As well as questions of content, they can also be asked *who said that?* A difficulty facing anyone attempting to transcribe spoken language in which there are overlapping voices is to ensure that they correctly attribute utterances to speakers. As Bartle and Dellwo (2015: 230) note, when transcribing recordings for use in police investigations, utterances may be attributed to named individuals or 'Speaker 1, Speaker 2, etc.', and this may in turn constitute incriminating evidence. In such cases, the transcriber must be able to differentiate between the voices on recordings in order to reliably attribute any speech to a speaker. If this cannot be done reliably, then 'the validity of any attribution is clearly compromised' (Bartle and Dellwo 2015: 230). Bartle and Dellwo (2015: 230) give details of a case in which the UK Court of Appeal overturned a conviction after police officers' attributions of utterances to speakers in covert audio recordings were ruled as inadmissible after phoneticians argued that it was impossible to reliably distinguish between the different voices in the recording.

Analysing the human voice

Acoustically, speech is a very complex and constantly changing combination of multiple and simultaneously produced noises and resonances or *frequencies* ranging across much of the audible spectrum. These sounds are produced by restricting and sometimes momentarily stopping the stream of exhaled air as it passes from the lungs, through the vocal tract to exit through the mouth or nose.

At this point a brief consideration of the physiology of speech might help. As we breathe normally, air passes freely to and from the lungs through the *glottis*, which is a gap between two small muscular folds in the *larynx*, which are popularly called the *vocal cords* but which phoneticians call the *vocal folds*. When we start to speak, the position of the vocal folds is altered to narrow the gap between them and the pressure of the escaping air now causes them to vibrate and in so doing creates sound.

Any vibrating object emits a sound, or note, whose perceived pitch is directly related to the *frequency* of the vibrations – thus anything, be it vocal folds, piano or guitar strings, vibrating 262 times or *cycles* a second will produce the sound we have learned, at least in the English speaking world, to call middle C. Cycles per second, or 'cps', is now universally referred to as Hertz (Hz). The frequency at which an object vibrates, and therefore the perceived pitch of the sound it emits, is a function of both its physical composition and its length, and thus an alteration in either or both of these will affect the vibration rate and therefore the perceived pitch. If one were to take a piano wire and cut it in half it would vibrate exactly twice as fast and produce a note exactly an *octave* higher; cut it in half again and it would vibrate four times as fast and produce a note two octaves higher. However, whereas each note on the piano has its own wire, speakers have only one set of vocal folds, and so variations in the pitch of the voice have to be achieved by tightening and slackening the muscles and thereby altering both the length and the thickness of the folds and therefore the frequency at which they vibrate.

What we call vowels are literally multi-note chords, that is, combinations of several separate pitches, which are produced simultaneously by modifications of the vocal tract, which thereby allow separate sections of the vocal tract to amplify multiples, or *harmonics*, of the underlying base frequency vibration of the vocal folds. These notes or pitches are called *formants*. Formants can be detected by acoustic analysis using electronic equipment. These are only one in a range of features that forensic phoneticians can focus on when analysing speech recordings. These can be classified as being either 'segmental' features, which means they manifest in individual phonemes, or 'suprasegmental' features which extend over more than one phoneme. These features are summarised in Table 7.1 opposite.

These phonetic features are often supplemented by relevant lexico-grammatical choices which may provide useful information about a speaker. Some of the features in Table 7.1 are related to an individual's anatomical and physiological characteristics. Pitch and voice quality, and the production of vowels and consonants, are determined by the length, thickness and movement of the vocal chords, and the composition of and interaction between articulators such as lips, teeth and the hard and soft palates. At the same time, regional and social factors influence a person's speech, resulting in the acquisition of particular accent features.

Such features can be used by forensic phoneticians to distinguish between groups of speakers. An obvious example is that people living in the same dialect area share similar vowel and consonant pronunciations. Similarly, pitch can be used to distinguish between sexes. Whereas boys and girls have similarly pitched voices, the male vocal folds thicken and lengthen at puberty and thus adult male voices have, on average, a significantly lower pitch than female voices. However, even within groups there is still considerable individual variation. For example, some female voices are naturally lower in pitch than some male voices. Indeed, the power of individual variation in human voices has been revealed in studies of twins. As Watt (2010: 79) notes, it has been found that identical twins who have very similar vocal tracts, who have lived in the same region and have received the same education and parental input, still exhibit differences in speech production. For example, speakers have been found who have consistently more fronted vowels than their twins, (Loakes 2008) and have different pronunciations of sibilant and stop consonants (Weirich 2011).

Experts exploit group and individual variation within the parameters of speech in Table 7.1 when they are addressing two main types of forensic phonetic problem: *speaker profiling* and *speaker comparison*.

Table 7.1 Features used by forensic phoneticians in the analysis of speech

Parameter	Description
Pitch	Caused by the vibration of the vocal folds. The faster the vibration, the higher the pitch (e.g. 124 Hz).
Voice quality	A general set of characteristics which are a product of the configuration of the speaker's vocal chords and vocal tract (e.g. *breathy, nasal, creaky, shimmer* or *vocal fry*) (Jessen 2010: 391).
Articulatory setting	The medium- to long-term setting of all the articulators (e.g. tongue, hard/soft palate, teeth, lips) in relation to one another, which results in different pronunciations of sounds across speakers (O'Grady 2013: 13).
Intonation and prosody	Patterns or melody of pitch changes or stress across stretches of connected speech (e.g. rising rather than falling intonation at the end of declarative sentences).
Rhythm	Relates to the timing and length of stress and syllables in speech.
Speaking rate/tempo	The speed with which someone talks, measured by words per minute or syllables per second.
Vowels	Distinctive realisations of sounds in which there is unimpeded airflow (e.g. the pronunciation of [aɪ] in <time>).
Consonants	Distinctive realisations of sounds which involve restriction or closure of the vocal tract (e.g. the pronunciation of [ɫ] in <milk>).
Connected speech processes	Presence or absence of phonological processes across word boundaries (e.g. assimilation, linking, elision) (Knight 2012: 197).
Pathological features	Medical conditions which have long-term effects on speech production, such as stuttering and sigmatism (Jessen 2010: 382)

Speaker profiling

There are times when the police have a recording of a criminal's voice, either committing or confessing to a crime, but have no suspect, and are thus anxious to glean any information at all that might enable them to narrow down the group of potential suspects. Examples might include an obscene phone call, a ransom demand, a bomb threat, extortion, or an audio recording of an attack or murder. In such cases, the forensic phonetician may be asked to undertake 'speaker profiling'. We have already mentioned in the Introduction one of the earliest high-profile cases, dating from 1979, that of the Yorkshire Ripper where the forensic phonetician was amazingly successful in placing the speaker regionally, but such cases are not uncommon.

The first quotation in the epigraph of this chapter is a BBC News report of a video that emerged online and through mainstream news networks of the beheading of journalist James Foley at the hands of an Islamic State terrorist. After this video, a series of others were released apparently showing the same man murdering British and American journalists and aid workers. Upon the emergence of these videos, media coverage focused on the killer's British accent, and their reporting included quotations from renowned linguists. On the basis of his British accent the killer became widely known as 'Jihadi John'. In August 2014, phonetician Professor Paul Kerswill from the University of York, was quoted in *The Guardian* as identifying the man's accent as Multicultural London English, probably with a foreign language background (Chulov and Halliday 2014). A few months later in February 2015, *The Washington Post* identified the man as Mohammed Emwazi, who was born in Kuwait, but grew up in West London (Mekhennet and Goldman 2015), a profile which corresponds to the linguistic background offered by Kerswill.

In forensic cases, phoneticians work hard to derive as much information as possible about the speaker from the sample(s) of speech made available to them, using both their expertise in phonetics and specialist software. The characteristics of a speaker that forensic phoneticians may be able to make a judgement on range from biological features such as age and sex, to socio-cultural factors such as ethnicity, geographical region and first language. The identification of some of these is more straightforward and reliable than that of others.

One of the most addressable questions relates to where a person is from, as was the case with the Yorkshire Ripper hoax. In these cases, the expert closely examines the recording for identifiable features of accent, namely vowel and consonant realisations, but also for lexico-grammatical features of dialect. Once they have identified a pool of variables that may give an indication that the person is speaking with a particular accent or in a particular dialect, the expert can then compare, verify and confirm their findings with those in authoritative descriptions of language varieties, and the research literature in language variation and sociolinguistics. Ultimately, the forensic phonetician is then able to offer a geographical profile of the speaker, localising them to where they are from and where they may have lived. This is not always straightforward, however, and Schilling and Marsters (2015) describe a fascinating case in which forensic phoneticians were asked to create a speaker profile for a woman who claimed to be a girl who had been missing for 20 years. In this case, the 'unusual' combination (and lack) of accent and dialect features in the woman was such that locating her geographically was very difficult. Schilling and Marsters' discussion highlights the implications that dialect acquisition, contact and mixing have for regional profiling of individuals through voice. That said, research by Köster *et al.* (2012) found that German experts could accurately identify a speaker's region on the basis of their voice with a success rate of 85 per cent, with the majority of errors occurring as experts selected accents which were neighbours of the one in question. Therefore, forensic speaker profiling can provide useful evidence for tracking down criminals or suspects in police investigations.

As well as region, other social characteristics forensic phoneticians can include in their profiles include the age and gender of the speaker. Both of these can be estimated through an analysis of the pitch of the voice. As Jessen (2010: 383) points out, under normal circumstances the decision as to whether a speaker is a male or female is straightforward for experts and laypeople alike. This is because women generally have a much higher average pitch level than men due to physiological differences in vocal fold length, and can be identified either by ear or by quantitative fundamental frequency (f0) analysis, measuring the average rate of vibration in the vocal folds.

Age, however, is less straightforward. Jessen (2010: 383) points out that most of the changes in speech patterns occur in childhood, puberty and old age, and so these age groups have been the focus of research. However, he states that criminal offenders tend to be between 20 and 40, for whom there is less research. French and Stevens (2013: 186) comment that speaker age 'lies only marginally within the range of addressable profiling questions' because features such as pitch can only be used in determining age if they are compared with the pitch in earlier speech from the same speaker. This is rarely the case in forensic contexts. Kelly and Harte (2015), however, show that in experimental conditions for which there are recordings of the same speakers over time, lay listeners can correctly detect 'vocal ageing' in a speaker. Participants in their experiments were asked to decide whether the same speaker was older or younger in two sets of recordings. Listeners were able to answer correctly 64 per cent of the time when the difference in age was ten years, and 86 per cent when the difference was 30 years. Furthermore, ageing was found to be more easily detectable in female speakers than male speakers (Kelly and Harte 2015: 175). Speaker profiling can also be undertaken in collaboration with clinical linguists to help identify whether speakers have any medical conditions and speech disorders that have long-term effects on speech, such as stammering, cleft palate and dysphonia, which are impairments in the ability to produce sounds (Jessen 2010; French and Stevens 2013; Schilling and Marsters 2015: 199). Such information can be helpful in police investigations if the speaker has been subject to clinical attention and their condition traceable through medical records (French and Stevens 2013: 186). Some argue that a speaker's body size (height and weight) can also be discernible through measurement of their vowel formants (Jessen 2010: 382), while others argue that such physical characteristics 'cannot be realistically addressed' by forensic speaker profiling (French and Stevens 2013: 186).

Finally, speaker profiling is also central in cases where linguists, sometimes in combination with native speakers, perform language analysis for the determination of origin (LADO) to draw reasonable conclusions about the nationality – or more specifically the language of socialisation – of asylum seekers. LADO is becoming its own specialist sub-field of speaker profiling, and has a substantial and growing literature surrounding the practice, methods and cases involved (e.g. Eades and Arends 2004; Patrick 2010, 2012; Cambier-Langeveld 2010, 2014; Fraser 2009, 2011); see Chapter 6 for more details.

Ultimately, forensic speaker profiling can help narrow down the number of potential perpetrators responsible for committing a crime when the police do not have any suspects. Such cases are rare, however, in comparison with those in which the police have an incriminating speech sample and *do* have a suspect in mind. In such cases, the role of the forensic phonetician is one of speaker *comparison*.

Speaker comparison

The vast majority of the cases undertaken by forensic phoneticians involve speaker comparison. These are cases where there is a voice recording of a person committing a crime, and the police have identified one or more suspects, and the phonetician is asked to express an opinion as to whether any of the suspect voices is consistent with, or shares close similarities with, that of the criminal. A basic problem to overcome is that there will always be differences between any two speech samples, even when they come from the same speaker and are recorded on the same machine and on the same occasion. So, the task for the forensic phonetician involves being able to tell whether the inevitable differences between samples are more likely to be within-speaker differences or between-speaker differences (Rose 2002: 10). They measure the similarity and difference between the samples, and estimate the relative likelihood of obtaining these measures in the context of two competing hypotheses: that the samples were produced by the same speaker, versus two different speakers. Or, in other words, the expert considers the extent to which the evidence supports the prosecution (same-speaker) versus defence (different-speaker) hypotheses (see also Chapter 10).

The criminal, 'disputed' or 'questioned' speech samples may be recordings of telephone calls, or covert recordings made by police or witnesses. These criminal recordings are then compared against known recordings of the suspect's speech, which most often consists of recorded police interviews. In comparing speech samples and attempting to identify speakers, forensic phoneticians can draw upon any and all of the speech parameters listed in Table 7.1 above, from voice quality and pitch to vowel and consonant production. As Gold and French (2011: 302–3) emphasise, rather than one individual feature of speech being sufficient to distinguish between voices, it is the overall combination of features that is crucial in discriminating speakers.

Auditory and acoustic approaches

There are two major traditions for analysing and comparing speech samples, the *auditory* and the *acoustic*. *Auditory* techniques consist of the forensic phonetician listening to the speech samples and producing a narrow phonetic transcription using the International Phonetic Alphabet (IPA). In doing so, they identify features of speech that appear to be consistent in the voice of the offender in question. Such analysis focuses predominantly on segmental features such as vowel and consonant realisations and connected speech processes, but notes on intonation, prosody, rhythm and voice quality may also be made from auditory analysis. Foulkes and French (2012) detail a case in which a criminal recording comprised a mere four seconds of speech transmitted across a building's intercom system, which was to be compared against known non-criminal recordings of a suspect in the case. The transcription of the disputed sample is:

> Text: *I've come to see the lady at number two [operator's turn removed] (I'm fro)m the Home Care I've come to collect her sheet(s).*

IPA: av ˈkʰʊm tsiː? ˈlɛɪdjə? nʊmbə ˈ↑\tʰəɐuː [...] (...)m? ˈʌʊm kʰɛːɹ av ˈkʰʊm tʰə ˈkʰlɛktʰ ə ˈʃiiː?

(Foulkes and French 2012: 564)

Despite being only four seconds in length, an IPA transcription of the disputed recording identified as many as 12 pronunciation features characteristic of the perpetrator's voice. These included vowel realisations such as the reduction of the diphthong /aɪ/ to a monophthong /a/ in the word *I've,* and the northern English vowel /ʊ/ in the words *number* and *come* among others. Observable consonant pronunciations included glottalised /t/ in *at* and *sheet* and /h/-dropping in *home* and *her.* As well as vowels and consonants, the experts also used the IPA transcription to identify patterns in the speaker's intonation (as in *two*), and found that she used word-final linking /r/ between *care* and *I've.* Even though it was short, the criminal recording proved to be a rich source of data. Furthermore, every one of the potentially useful features identified in it was also found in the police recordings of the suspect's voice, providing evidence in support of the assertion that the known and disputed samples were spoken by the same person.

In contrast to auditory analysis, where the expert's focus is primarily on their aural perception of segmental vowel and consonant production, *acoustic* analysis involves the use of specialised computer software to quantify and measure elements of speech. One such parameter which is commonly analysed using acoustic methods is voice pitch. Such analyses can be presented visually, in *spectrograms* such as those in Figure 7.1, (see overleaf) which is a visualisation of two separate utterings of *'what time's the train?'* The spectrogram has the words written in ordinary orthography, but the actual pronunciation can be better represented using the International Phonetic Alphabet and removing word spaces which are obviously not articulated, so the first one may sound like /wɒttaɪmzðətreɪn / while the second seem to be a less formal pronunciation without the first 't' pronounced, at the end of 'what', /wɒ?/, an assimilation of the first consonant of *the* to the end of *times* resulting in an initial /z/ /taɪmz zə/ giving a compete version of /wɒ?taɪmzzətreɪn/. Readers will note a thin line below the pitch printout, which indicates the carrying pressure of the air expelled from the lungs to create the individual sounds.

In the image, one can see all the different component pitches on the vertical axis and how they change over time along the horizontal axis. *Intensity,* or perceived loudness, is represented by a darkness scale – the darker the print, the louder the sound. The average pitch of someone's voice, their fundamental frequency (abbreviated f0), can also be expressed as a numerical value in cycles per second, as for instance in the observation that, say, the average f0 of a given voice over time is 124 Hz. This number can then be compared with population data to identify whether the person in question has a higher or lower pitched voice than average. Vowel formants are also frequently measured in acoustic analysis, correlating with how the vowels are articulated, and similar analysis can be conducted to measure the duration and articulation of consonants. The results produced by such computational methods are then subjected to human

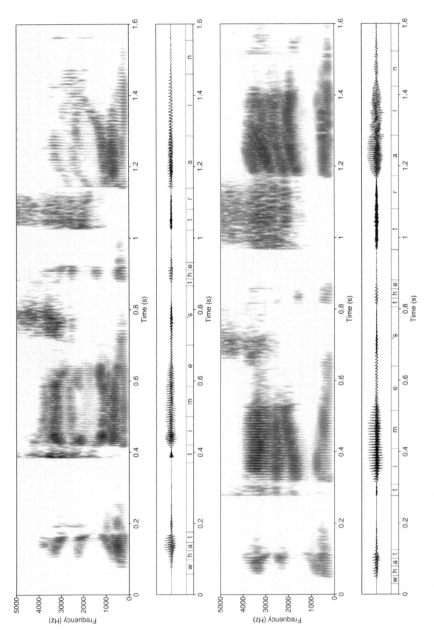

Figure 7.1 Comparison of spectrograms of two utterings of 'What time's the train?'

examination and evaluation by the phonetician when comparing those of the known and disputed speech samples.

Some practitioners (e.g. Hollien *et al.* 2014) argue that auditory analyses, which they refer to as 'aural-perceptual', performed by humans are the most accurate of all available methods. At the same time, even in the early stages of technological developments, others observed that 'in principle ... the ear may be inherently ill-equipped to pick up some differences between speakers, which show up clearly in an acoustic analysis' (Nolan 1994: 341). Indeed there is a consensus, supported by the majority of the members of the International Association for Forensic Phonetics and Acoustics (IAFPA), that forensic phoneticians should use a *mixed* method, with the detailed type of auditory analysis and a rigorous instrumental acoustic analysis reinforcing each other. The procedure and process of such mixed methods are explained in Watt (2010), Foulkes and French (2012), Eriksson (2012), French and Stevens (2013). In their survey of international forensic speaker comparison practices, in which they consulted 36 experts from 13 countries, Gold and French (2011) found that the mixed 'Auditory Phonetic cum Acoustic Phonetic analysis' is the one most routinely employed by practitioners, and is used in Australia, Austria, Brazil, China, Germany, Netherlands, Spain, Turkey, UK and USA, as well as in universities, research institutes, and government/agency laboratories. Similar results were found in a survey of speaker identification practices used by global law enforcement agencies (Morrison *et al.* 2016).

'Voiceprints'

At this point, a discussion of *voiceprints* is necessary. 'Voiceprinting' essentially involves the visual matching of pairs of spectrograms, such as those in Figure 7.1, showing the known and suspect speakers uttering the same word(s). In the USA in the 1960s the dominant tradition was the 'voiceprint', a label deliberately formed to echo and thereby borrow prestige from 'fingerprint':

> closely analogous to fingerprint identification, which uses the unique features found in people's fingerprints, voiceprint identification uses the unique features found in their utterances.
>
> (Kersta 1962: 1253, as quoted in Rose 2002)

However, this method never achieved the same level of reliability as finger printing. The attraction of the spectrogram for this kind of 'voiceprint analysis' is that it gives a 'picture' of the sounds spoken, but the fatal flaw of the voiceprinting method was that it involved checking the degree of similarity between two spectrograms by eye. A major problem with this approach is that, as observed above, there is always significant within-speaker variation. For example, if a speaker uttered 'the train' one-hundred times in quick succession, no two utterings would be identical. You might like to spend a few moments trying to decide visually whether these two prints of utterings of 'What time's the train?' are from the same or from different speakers. You will of course quickly realise that you don't know which bits to focus on, nor what weight to give to dissimilarities. Both were in fact produced by the same speaker, but using different accents. However, neither of them is a disguise in the accepted sense, because both fall within the speaker's 'active natural repertoire, [that is] he may shift quite unconsciously between the two [accents] in response to perceived differences in the communicative situation' (French 1994: 172). Nevertheless, the two prints do look very different.

Critics of the voiceprint approach note that its practitioners failed to publish an explanation of the methodology (even when they later added an auditory comparison as an integral component of the analysis), and asserted that this was because there was no firm scientific basis to either of the components. They further observed that for the auditory part of the comparison there was no evidence that the analysts were performing any better than an experienced layperson – they certainly didn't have any professional training in descriptive or acoustic phonetics.

Despite this, Koenig (1986), after reviewing 2,000 FBI cases stretching over a 15-year period, where voiceprints had been analysed, found that there was an error rate of less than 1 per cent. Hollien, by contrast, claimed error rates of between 20 per cent and 78 per cent in voiceprint analyses and reports that he has testified in court that voiceprint evidence is 'a fraud being perpetrated on the American public and the Courts' (1990: 210). In 1985, a Californian court enquiry into voiceprint analysis concluded that 'there exists no foundation for its admissibility into evidence …' (Rose 2002: 121). Despite this, voiceprint evidence is still admissible in some American States and indeed it was presented, although its admissibility was contested, during the 2013 Trayvon Martin case, when George Zimmerman, a member of the local Community Watch, was charged with shooting and murdering the unarmed black teenager, Trayvon Martin (this case is discussed in some detail on p. 143). Interestingly, the FBI, has a dedicated voiceprinting unit and uses voiceprints for investigative purposes, but does not permit the use of voiceprint evidence in court.

A distinction should be drawn between this 'voiceprint' analysis and the acoustic analysis used in combined auditory cum acoustic methods regularly used today. 'Mixed' does not mean simply adding voiceprints to narrow phonetic transcriptions, but rather using tools such as spectrograms in a very different way, to focus not on the overall pattern, but on the acoustic make-up of (parts of) individual sounds and the transitions between them. The auditory analysis identifies possibly evidential linguistic features and these can then be probed quantitatively by acoustic analysis. For example, particular realisations of vowels and consonants may be revealed in an auditory analysis, such as that described with the four-second intercom clip above, and then an acoustic analysis can be used to systematically examine the specific way in which these sounds are articulated, for example, by measuring and comparing vowel formants across samples. French (1994: 177) exemplifies the use of spectrograms in such a way in a case involving a stammerer. He notes that there are two kinds of stammer, one called *prolongation*, typically co-occurring with fricatives, when the consonant is lengthened and the other called *block,* typically associated with plosives, when the consonant is arrested. Spectrograms allow the length of individual sounds to be measured easily and so are ideal for such purposes. In French's case the suspect and the known sample not only shared the same two stammer phenomena, associated with two particular fricatives, /s/ and /f/ and two particular plosives, /t/ and /d/, but also shared the same average stammer durations.

Potential difficulties in forensic speech comparison

A number of factors can complicate forensic speaker comparison. The quality of criminal recordings available might be very poor due to low quality recording equipment or considerable background noise. In such cases, there are procedures in place to clean or 'enhance' the recording before subjecting it to analysis (Hollien 2002: 8). If the speaker was originally disguising their voice in some way, either simply by using a different accent or by temporarily changing the pitch of their voice, this can have 'considerable detrimental effect on speaker identification' (Eriksson 2010: 87). Other potentially problematic factors include when a suspect's speech was affected by alcohol in the criminal recording (Schiel and Heinrich 2015; Hollien *et al.* 2014), when the voice was originally transmitted over the telephone (Yarmey 2003; Byrne and Foulkes 2004; Nolan *et al.* 2013) and when the suspect was shouting (Blatchford and Foulkes 2006) or whispering (Bartle and Dellwo 2015). All these factors influence a speaker's voice, or at least the recording of their voice, in such a way as to complicate the comparison of disputed with known interview recordings.

The trial of George Zimmerman, who was charged with, but acquitted of, second-degree murder for shooting 17-year-old Trayvon Martin in Florida, USA in February 2012, involved a particularly difficult and controversial case of forensic voice identification. The evidence in the trial included an emergency 911 call made by a local resident who observed the fatal encounter between Zimmerman and Martin. In the background to the call a scream is clearly heard, and forensic phoneticians were asked to determine whether the scream was that of Zimmerman, who argued he was acting in self-defence, or Martin. In a pre-trial hearing, prosecution evidence was submitted from forensic audio consultants who compared the scream with recordings of ordinary speech of both Zimmerman and Martin and judged that the screaming voice was Martin's, not Zimmerman's. This speech evidence, therefore, would have been damaging to Zimmerman's case of self-defence. Zimmerman's defence lawyers called four expert witnesses to comment on the evidence forwarded by the prosecution. The experts contested the methods used by the prosecution experts, arguing they were not reliable and that the evidence should not be admitted. One of the defence experts, Peter French, emphasised the difficulty (or impossibility) of comparing screaming with recordings of normal speech, given that screams do not include any of the speech parameters required for voice comparison. Therefore, he argued that the recorded evidence in this case was not 'remotely suitable for speaker comparison purposes'. At the conclusion of the pre-trial hearing the judge excluded the testimonies of the prosecution expert witnesses.

Automatic Speaker Recognition (ASR)

The desire to automate forensic speaker comparison is growing ever stronger, and Automatic Speaker Recognition (ASR) systems are becoming increasingly popular with practitioners in Europe and the US (Gold and French 2011: 296). As the name suggests, these methods rely on automated computational approaches in comparing voice samples. ASR systems work by:

> taking a known (suspect) recording, performing complex mathematical transformations on it and reducing it to a statistical model [...]. The recording of the questioned voice (the criminal recording) is similarly processed and a set of features is extracted. The system then compares the extracted features with the statistical model of the suspect's voice and produces a measure of similarity/difference (distance) between the two.
>
> (French and Stevens 2013: 188)

The main way in which these automated methods differ from the combined auditory and acoustic techniques is the amount of human input in the comparison of voices. Although there are still decisions to be made regarding the excerpts of a recording that are to be analysed automatically, the human interpretation of features and judgements about degrees of similarity and difference between samples is removed. This objectivity and replicability is attractive to courts, and as French and Stevens (2013: 188) note, ASR can perform in seconds a comparison that would take many hours using the combined auditory-acoustic approach. In addition, it is well established that automated techniques are very accurate in comparing and recognising voices when operating under ideal conditions (Rose 2002: 95). However, forensic speech evidence is rarely ideal. The influence of such issues as poor quality recordings and speaker disguise on the ability to identify voices is exacerbated when relying solely on automatic systems (e.g. Eriksson 2010). Similarly, as pointed out by Foulkes and French (2012: 565), the four-second intercom recording analysed above would be far too short for any automated analysis, despite being a rich source of features of the suspect's speech. The features extracted and considered in ASR systems are related to the acoustic signal produced by 'vocal tract resonances arising from the geometry of individual cavities' (French and Stevens 2013: 189) and are not easily translatable into the segmental and suprasegmental features that phoneticians are well trained in analysing and interpreting. As a result automated methods are unable to draw on the distinctive speech features of individuals which are central to auditory-acoustic methods. It is for this reason that it is generally agreed that ASR approaches used alone cannot replace the valuable evidence obtained through close phonetic analysis performed by humans (e.g. Eriksson 2012: 46). However, while the use of ASR approaches alone is generally rejected by forensic speech scientists, it is now considered a valuable part of the expert's analytical toolkit when approaching a forensic speaker comparison problem, and can be, (and most commonly is), used in combination with auditory and/or acoustic approaches (e.g. Cambier-Langeveld 2007: 240; Gold and French 2011: 296; Eriksson 2012: 49; French and Stevens 2013: 191; Morrison *et al.* 2016).

Naïve speaker recognition, earwitnesses and voice parades

In 1933, the baby son of the American aviator Charles Lindbergh, famous as the first man to fly solo across the Atlantic, was kidnapped and later found murdered, but not before a ransom had been demanded and paid. Eventually the police arrested and charged a suspect. Lindbergh had talked to the kidnapper twice, once on the telephone, which in those days would not have provided a very good reproduction, and once in person, briefly and at night, while handing over the ransom money. Almost three years later, when the case came to trial, Lindbergh testified that he recognised the voice of the accused as being that of the man he had talked to. The defence set out to challenge his testimony and employed a psychologist to discover what was and what was not possible in terms of memory for voices.

This Lindbergh case is an example of what we now call 'Naïve Speaker Recognition' which involves laypeople, untrained in forensic speech science techniques, making judgements about voices in legal cases. There is now a vast literature on how to evaluate such judgements. In the process of collecting and preparing evidence, the largest role played by naïve speakers is in 'voice line-ups' or 'voice parades', where people act as 'earwitnesses' to a crime. Hollien *et al.* (2014: 174) define earwitness line-ups or voice parades as:

> a process where a person who has heard, but not seen, a perpetrator attempts to pick his or her voice from a group of voices. [...] the witness listens to the suspect's exemplar embedded in a group of four to six similar samples produced by other people.

Nolan (2003) reports an earwitness case in which a voice parade and naïve speaker recognition contributed significantly. In November 2001, a woman died in a house fire in London, which police suspected to have been an arson attack by a man who had previously had a relationship with the woman. After the fire, a lodger in the man's house told police that he had overheard his landlord commissioning a young man to carry out the arson attack on the evening it happened (Nolan 2003: 277). The lodger claimed to recognise the voice of the unidentified young man from previous visits. Shortly afterwards, the lodger's landlord and the young man became defendants in a murder investigation. A voice parade was carried out using voice samples of the suspect taken from police interviews and samples from police interviews with other young men from the same London Asian community as 'foils' (non-suspects used for comparison purposes). The witness not only identified the suspect correctly from the voice parade, but also from an identity parade. Both men were eventually convicted of murder.

Voice line-ups should be fair to both sides of a case and should only be used if they are likely to produce reliable results. However, Nolan (2003: 187) warns that 'it is very difficult to achieve a voice parade whose fairness cannot be called into question for one reason or another'. Early work on voice parades produced promising results. For example, Künzel (1994: 55) noted that '[Speaker Identification] by non-experts may attain a high degree of reliability under favourable circumstances'. Two years later, Nolan and Grabe (1996) drawing on earlier work by Broeders and Rietveld (1995) concluded that 'a carefully carried out voice parade should ... be capable of contributing usefully to the balance of evidence'. Recent commentary has focused on what constitutes a 'carefully carried out voice parade', and has examined the accuracy with which laypeople can recognise voices.

Set-up of voice parades

In the arson case discussed above, Nolan was initially contacted by Detective Sergeant John McFarlane of the Metropolitan Police. As a result of the voice line-up method developed and applied in that case, the procedure and guidelines McFarlane implemented became an example of good practice, and since 2003 has been presented by the Home Office to all police forces in England and Wales as 'Advice on the use of voice identification parades'. The advice can be summarised as:

1   The officer in charge should obtain a detailed statement from the witness, containing as **much detail and description of the voice as is possible**. All descriptions of the voice given by the witness must be included in the material supplied to the relevant forensic phonetics/linguistics expert, the suspect and solicitors.

2   Under no circumstances should an attempt be made to conduct a live voice identification procedure, using live suspect and foils.

3   The identification officer should obtain a **representative sample of the suspect's voice**. Such samples might include police recorded interview tapes, during which the suspect is speaking naturally and responding to questions. Under no circumstances should the suspect be **invited to read any set text**.

4   The identification officer should obtain no less than 20 samples of speech, from **persons of similar age and ethnic, regional and social background as the suspect**. A suitable source of such material may be other police recorded interview tapes from unconnected cases.

5   The officer should ensure that all the work can be undertaken and completed within **4-6 weeks of the incident in question**, as memory degradation or 'fade' on the part of the witness has been identified as a critical factor by experts in the field.

6   The identification officer should request the services of a force-approved expert witness in phonetics/linguistics, for example, a Member of the International Association for Forensic Phonetics and Acoustics, to ensure

that the final selection and compilation of sample voices and the match with the suspect's is as accurate and balanced as possible.

(These guidelines can be accessed from: http://webarchive.nationalarchives.gov. uk/20130125102358/http://www.homeoffice.gov.uk/about-us/corporate-publications-strategy/home-office-circulars/circulars-2003/057-2003, or in Nolan 2003.)

These procedures are offered as recommendations, rather than being mandatory. Nonetheless, they offer very clear and helpful guidelines for the successful implementation of voice parades, and they were clearly developed in close communication with experts in the field. As Nolan (2003: 288) notes, however, practical difficulties remain in the setting up of voice parades. In light of contemporaneous and more recent research, there are particular points in these guidelines (bold in the list) which require further discussion.

First, people's descriptions of voices in the first instance may be unhelpful or unreliable. In contrast with identity parades, lay witnesses find it much harder to describe voices than they do faces, and 'exhibit a wide variety of subjective categories' (Künzel 1994: 48). Künzel notes that, while in some cases witnesses' descriptions are so precise that the expert only needs to convert them into scientific terminology, other subjects are unable to indicate any categories for their judgements. Second, it may not be an easy enterprise to source representative samples of the suspect's voice. The guidelines suggest that police interviews should be used, but it may be difficult to extract samples which do not include any incriminating utterances. Furthermore, a question remains over what a 'representative' speech sample is. It might be that the context in which the witness initially heard the suspect's voice is dramatically different from the controlled situation of the voice parade. For example, there is research demonstrating the effect of voice disguise and imitation on naïve speaker recognition (Schlichting and Sullivan 1997; Eriksson *et al.* 2010), suggesting that if the suspect disguised their voice during a crime, witnesses would be less likely to identify them in a voice parade. Also, while the guidelines suggest that 'under no circumstances should the suspect be invited to read any set text', recent experimental research has found that naïve speaker recognition accuracy is actually better when speakers read from a text book than if they are involved in a dialogue (Sarwar *et al.* 2014).

The guidelines are clear that the foils used in voice parades should come from people who are of similar age and ethnic, regional and social background to the suspect. In sociolinguistics it is commonly held that social factors such as age, ethnicity and gender are not determinants of how people will talk, but are resources that speakers use when creating voices (Johnstone 1996: 11). Therefore, although people may share a whole range of social characteristics; that does not mean their voices will sound the same. This problem will be partially overcome by the consultation of a forensic phonetician in deciding the appropriateness of foil samples (point 6 in the guidelines) and Nolan and Grabe (1996) outline a pre-parade experiment they ran with a group of listeners to judge the similarity of foils and suspects and to control for bias. Nolan and Grabe (1996: 92) state that the standard assumption has been that foils should be similar to the actual *suspect*. This process involves some decision regarding how similar the foils should be to the suspect, and could result in an 'ideal' line-up consisting of a set of voices so close that identification would be virtually impossible (e.g. Hollien 2002: 100). However, they point out that an alternative, derived from suggestions for eyewitness line-ups by Wells (1993), is to match foils to the witness's description of the voice of the *offender*. The issue here is the accuracy and usefulness of lay-people's description of voices.

Finally, the guidelines recommend that the voice line-ups should take place within four to six weeks of the incident in question, due to the fact that witness' memory of the voice fades, or 'lapses'. Early research, however, suggests that memory lapsing occurs very quickly; McGehee (1937) reported 87 per cent correct identification after two days, falling to 13 per cent after five months. While sooner is always better for voice parades (Hollien 2002: 102), very soon is not always possible in the forensic context. Furthermore, time pressure could exacerbate the other challenges posed by the selection of speaker samples and foils. Nevertheless, these guidelines developed by Nolan (2003) and the police offer a very useful benchmark against which practice can be measured.

Ability of laypeople to recognise voices

Rose (2002: 97) states, 'common experience suggests that untrained human listeners can and do make successful judgements about voices'. He continues: 'the natural human ability to recognise and identify voices has been accepted in courts for several centuries'. Others, however, are less optimistic. Solan and Tiersma (2005: 119) argue that 'the unreliability of earwitness identification has gone virtually unnoticed', at least by the US legal system. Hollien *et al.* (2014: 174) accept that if competent personnel are used, 'results can be both robust and reasonably accurate'. Elsewhere, however, he points out that 'some listeners are simply better at identification than others' (Hollien 2002: 102), and research has found that untrained listeners perform significantly worse than trained listeners in speaker identification (Schiller and Köster 1998).

The reason for this variability in success is that, as well as the factors affecting the organisation of voice parades discussed above, there are a wide range of factors which affect individuals' abilities to recognise voices. Firstly, it is well established that there are significant differences in recognition success depending on whether it is a familiar or an unfamiliar voice. Rose (2002: 98–99), for example, report experiments which show listeners being twice as successful in correctly recognising familiar voices. Secondly, even with familiar voices, listeners make mistakes roughly one-third of the time. Thirdly, one cannot extrapolate from these scores for average success to the likely success of a given witness being able to recognise a known voice, because there is massive individual variation; listener success in one experiment which was testing the ability to recognise 25 famous voices ranged 'all the way from totally correct (100%) to chance (46%)' (Rose 2002: 100). Witness emotion and stress can also influence their memory and recollection of events; Hollien (2002: 101) reports that subjects who have been stressed or aroused do better at recognising speakers than those who have not. Exposure to the suspect voice has also been found to affect people's abilities to recognise that voice. Listeners are better able to recognise voices they have heard for longer periods (e.g. Yarmey 1991), and those which they have been exposed to more frequently (Deffenbacher *et al.* 1989). Biological characteristics of the witness have also been found to influence their success in naïve speaker recognition. Generally speaking, women outperform men when identifying the voices of other women, people aged between 21 and 40 years are superior to older listeners, and witnesses are better at identifying the voices of people of the same ethnicity or race (Yarmey 2012: 549–50). Finally, some of the most recent research in naïve speaker recognition and earwitness accuracy has found that some types of voices are easier to identify than others. For example, Sørensen (2012) found that in a group of young men between 20 and 35 years of age, 'less common' voices, so called because their average voice pitch (fundamental frequency) is markedly higher or lower than the average of the group, are easier to identify in voice line-ups than 'common' voices.

Given the vast array of factors that can influence the accuracy and reliability of naïve speaker recognition and voice parades, some of which are beyond the control of the police officers and phoneticians, it is generally agreed that evidence obtained through earwitness testimony should be treated with caution by the courts (e.g. Nolan 2003: 228; Yarmey 2012: 556). Voice line-ups are used, however, and can produce critical evidence in a case in which they are carefully designed and controlled, and reasonable speech samples and foils are available, as demonstrated by Nolan (2003).

Conclusion

You may be wondering how you could contribute to the field of forensic phonetics. Transcription and voice parade research can be undertaken by students with a working knowledge of phonetics, and careful engagement with the frameworks and cases outlined in this chapter. To a certain extent, this is also true of speaker profiling, as work in areas such as perceptual dialectology has found that people with no background in studying linguistics at all can make accurate and nuanced geographical observations about the voices that they hear. The field of forensic speaker comparison may seem harder to penetrate, however, especially when expertise in phonetics needs to be combined with skills in computing and programming to operate acoustic analysis software. Nonetheless, for the student of linguistics, at least, forensic speaker identification offers a real-world, high-stakes application of your knowledge and understanding of phonetics and the human voice.

Further reading

Rose (2002) (chapters 2, 6, 5, 7 and 10 in that order); Hollien (2002); Jessen (2010); Watt (2010), Foulkes and French (2012); and French and Stevens (2013).

Research tasks

1 Record a friend or family member speaking with you in natural conversation. Gather some participants (who don't know the speaker) for an experiment, and have them listen to the recording a number of times. Ask them to deduce as much as they can about the speaker's 'profile' from that recording, including sex, gender, ethnicity, region, body size. How *accurate* are they? How *confident* are they? On what basis are they making their decisions? You might like to record a number of sections of different lengths, and observe whether your participants' predictions are more accurate with longer recordings. Be careful that the content of the recordings doesn't give anything away!

2 Find or create a recording of a professional mimic or impersonator producing the voice of a famous person. Then, collect authentic samples of the famous person along with other, non-professional impersonators imitating the voice. Construct a voice parade, in which you organise for participants to listen to short extracts of recordings you have for (i) the actual famous person, (ii) the professional impersonator and (iii) non-professional impersonators. Ask them to identify which recording is of the actual famous person. Are they able to tell? How confident are they, and on what basis are they making their identification? Try it with different famous people. Are some, more familiar people, easier to identify? Why?

3 Record a natural conversation between yourself and a friend or family member. Now, with that same family member, perform and record a structured interview that you have designed. The interview can be about anything, but it is important that they are answering questions that you ask them. Now, find ten participants for an experiment. Choose short sections of both the natural conversation and the interview, ideally parts that don't include your own voice. Give these sections to your participants, and ask them to compare the person's voice across the two different types of recording. Are they able to identify the voices they hear as being from the same speaker? How confident are they? What are they basing their comparison on? You might like to also run a similar test, but in which the speaker in the natural conversation and the interview have similar voices but are actually different speakers. Are your participants able to distinguish between the voices?

8   Authorship attribution

It sounds like something out of, well, a detective novel: the U.K.'s *Sunday Times* broke the news yesterday that Robert Galbraith, the 'first time' writer behind the critically acclaimed crime novel *The Cuckoo's Calling*, was, in fact, the nom de plume of Harry Potter creator J.K. Rowling.

(*Time*, 15 July 2013)

Text message analysis is becoming a powerful tool in solving crime cases. In February 2008, linguistic evidence contributed to the conviction of David Hodgson (sic) in the murder of Jenny Nicholl.

(BBC News, 8 September 2013)

Introduction

Authorship attribution is the process in which linguists set out to identify the author(s) of disputed, anonymous or questioned texts. The first epigraph above relates to the highly-publicised revelation that the novel *The Cuckoo's Calling* was written by Harry Potter creator J.K. Rowling, who had published the book under the pseudonym Robert Galbraith. This revelation came after computational linguists had compared the writing style in the novel with other work by Rowling and with three additional crime fiction writers. The comparison showed that the style in the disputed text, *The Cuckoo's Calling*, was more similar to J.K. Rowling's known style than to that of any of the other three authors. This is an example of a non-forensic application of authorship attribution. By contrast, in a forensic context, the disputed texts under analysis are potentially evidential in alleged infringements of the law or threats to security. Such texts could include abusive emails, threatening tweets, ransom notes, blackmail or extortion letters, falsified suicide notes, or text messages sent by a person acting as someone else. In both criminal and civil investigations which involve these kinds of texts, linguists can be called upon by police or legal teams to analyse the texts and provide expert witness reports, sometimes presenting their evidence in court to juries through examination and cross-examination (as discussed in Chapters 5 and 10). In most casework of this kind the situation is such that the police have in mind or may even have arrested an individual or group of individuals who they suspect to have authored the texts in question. The job of the forensic linguist is then to answer questions such as: *did this person write this text?* or, *which of these suspects is the most likely to have written this text?* The second epigraph to this chapter is from a BBC News report of the murder investigation of teenager Jenny Nicholl in 2008 which involved disputed text messages. In this case, Coulthard was asked to express an opinion on whether a series of four text messages, sent from Jenny's mobile telephone after her disappearance, had been written by her or, if not, could they have been written by her lover Hodgson. This case is discussed in more detail later in the chapter.

The task of the linguistic detective is rarely one of identifying an author from millions of candidates on the basis of the linguistic evidence alone, but rather of selecting (and, of course, deselecting) from a very small number of candidate authors, usually fewer than a dozen and in many cases only two (Coulthard 1994a, 1997; Eagleson, 1994; Grant 2013). In order to reach opinions about the authorship of written linguistic evidence, the forensic analyst requires not only the 'questioned' or 'disputed' text(s) central to the case, but also 'known' pre-crime writings from the potential author(s), gathered from written material, computers or mobile devices. Once the available data has been collected, the forensic linguist compares the linguistic styles exhibited in the disputed and known texts in order to identify whether or not they are similar enough to have been written by the same person. These comparisons are made on the basis of a range of linguistic features and using a variety of different methodological approaches. In an ideal world, there would be a substantial amount of data to work with, both disputed and known. However, the forensic world is rarely ideal, and the texts are often unhelpfully short; many of the texts which the forensic linguist is asked to examine are very short indeed – most suicide notes, ransom demands and threatening letters, for example, are well under 100 words long. At the same time, any 'known' data used for comparison would ideally consist of large sets of texts of the same text-type as the questioned documents, written in the same register and at around the same time. However, the data that forensic linguists are given for comparison is often 'any old collection of texts' (Cotterill 2010: 578) that the police or solicitors have been able to gather together, rather than a relevant or balanced comparison corpus.

A brief history of authorship attribution

The involvement of linguists in questions of authorship is comparatively recent, but there has been a recorded interest in assigning authorship for over 2,000 years; for an excellent historical survey see Love (2002: 14–31). Davis (1996) reports humorously on an early unsuccessful attempt. He tells of how in Greece, in the fourth century BC, two philosophers, Heraklides and Dionysius fell out and, in order to revenge himself, Dionysius wrote a tragedy, which he then presented as a recently rediscovered work, possibly written by Sophocles. Heraklides, who also had a reputation as a literary critic, was asked for his opinion on the authenticity of the work and, after studying it, pronounced that it had indeed been written by Sophocles. At this point Dionysius announced that he had actually written the play himself. However, Heraklides rejected the claim and stood by his initial judgement that the play was indeed written by Sophocles and produced stylistic evidence to support his attribution.

> Dionysius replied by asking, if it was genuine, how was it that the first letters of the [first eight] lines of the play were an acrostic that … spelled P-A-N-K-A-L-O-S, … the name of Dionysius' lover. Obviously, said Heraklides, it was a coincidence. At this point, Dionysius pointed out that first letters of the next consecutive lines of the play were another acrostic: they formed a couplet, which, loosely translated, went:
> Who says an old monkey's not caught in a snare?
> All it takes is the time to get him there.
> And … he invited his enemy to read the first letters of the next few lines … yet another acrostic: … 'Heraklides knows nothing whatsoever about literature'.
> When he read this, it is said, Heraklides blushed.
>
> (Davis 1996: 53–54)

The first proposal to solve questions of authorship by accessing assumed individual linguistic regularities was made by de Morgan in 1851 in a letter replying to a biblical scholar who had asked him to devise a way of deciding on the authenticity of a series of letters traditionally attributed to St Paul. De Morgan hypothesised that average word length, measured simply in terms of letters per word, would be writer-specific and virtually constant and would even survive translation (de Morgan 1882). The first person to actually test this hypothesis was Mendenhall (1887) who counted by hand the lengths of hundreds of thousands of words drawn not only from the Pauline letters, but also from works by Shakespeare and two of the major candidate authors for some of his plays, Marlowe and Bacon. While this measure discounted Bacon as a possible author, the word length scores for Marlowe's later plays correlated more closely with Shakespeare's histories, tragedies and Roman plays than did Shakespeare's own comedies. Neither Mendenhall himself nor anyone else re-used or developed the method, although he had founded what came to be called *stylometry* – the science of measuring literary style (Klarreich 2003). Stylometry is the name now given to a wide range of methodological approaches to authorship analysis in which the similarity or difference between authors' styles is statistically measured on the basis of their use of a particular set of linguistic features.

One of the earliest applications of stylometry was Mosteller and Wallace's (1964) analysis of *The Federalist Papers*, 85 essays which were published anonymously in 1787–88 designed to persuade New Yorkers to adopt the new American Constitution. The papers are now known to have been written by three authors, Alexander Hamilton, James Madison, and John Jay, but both Hamilton and Madison claimed authorship of a set of 12 of them. In an attempt to resolve the dispute, Mosteller and Wallace assumed that there would be idiolectal differences in preferences for choosing from a small set of lexical items. First they analysed a collection of texts known to have been written by Hamilton or Madison and found a number of inter-author differences. They found, for instance, that Hamilton used *upon* 18 times more frequently than Madison, who in turn used *also* twice as often as Hamilton. Among other pools of lexical features, Mosteller and Wallace used 70 high-frequency function words to test the authorship of the 12 disputed papers, ultimately assigning all 12 to Madison. This is a conclusion that coincides with the prevailing view reached independently by historians on the basis of other evidence, and one that has been supported and confirmed by more recent stylometric experiments performed on *The Federalist Papers* (Holmes and Forsyth 1995; Tweedie *et al.* 1996).

Since Mosteller and Wallace's study, stylometry has been a major pre-occupation of authorship analysis researchers. Researchers have used a wide range of linguistic features to measure similarity between texts, distinguish between authors, and identify the writers of disputed texts. Such linguistic features include: the most frequent words in a corpus (e.g. Burrows 2007), frequent word sequences (e.g. Hoover 2002), full lexical repertoires (e.g. Labbé 2007; Jockers and Witten 2010), words occurring only once in a text (hapax legomena) or twice (dislegomena) (e.g. Woolls and Coulthard 1998; Woolls 2003), syntactic part-of-speech category combinations (e.g. Hirst and Feiguina 2007). Most recently, character n-grams, that is simple sequences of letters (e.g. Koppel *et al.* 2013; Stamatatos 2013: 343), and word n-grams (Johnson and Wright 2014; Wright 2014) have been used. Grieve (2007), Koppel *et al.* (2009), and Stamatatos (2009) offer excellent surveys of the linguistic features and methodological procedures that have been used in stylometric studies of authorship.

Purely stylometric techniques are rarely applied in forensic casework, despite the amount of research that has been undertaken. Morton and Michaelson (1990) describe the first purely statistical approach to authorship to be used in court. Morton (1991) calculated the frequency of occurrence, within each sentence, of variables like the number of nouns, of words beginning with a vowel, of words consisting of three or four letters, or, most commonly, of words consisting of two or three letters (2/3lw). Each of these measurements was matched against sentence length as calculated in term of orthographic words. The results were not expressed in terms of the percentage of words of a given category per sentence; rather a calculation was made separately, both for the sentence and for the variable under consideration, of the CUmulative SUM of the deviation of both from the average for the whole text. For this reason the method itself was labelled CUSUM. Graphs were then made from the resulting scores and one superimposed on top of the other. The assumption was that as habits are constant, if one is examining the same author, the graphs for the two measurements would match each other. Morton first presented CUSUM evidence successfully in the Court of Appeal in 1991 and three more times in the next 15 months. However, subsequent empirical tests of the reliability of CUSUM (Canter and Chester 1997; Hardcastle 1997) severely attacked the accuracy of the method. Hardcastle (1997: 138) concluded after his own tests of the method that CUSUM 'shows a deplorable lack of scientific rigour and objectivity'.

Since CUSUM, stylometric techniques in authorship attribution have rarely been applied in forensic contexts. Some exceptions are experiments by Grant (2007) and Rico-Sulayes (2011) and a report of a civil case by Juola (2013). Turell (2010) reports on a case in which she provided expert evidence in a Spanish civil court case. The case involved a Catalonian tourism company which had been accused of unfairly dismissing an employee. It was alleged by the company (the plaintiff) that the employee (the defendant) had tried to extort money from them in one of a series of four disputed emails that he had supposedly sent to the company. Using strings of two and three morphological and syntactic part-of-speech categories as linguistic features, Turell ran a statistical procedure called discriminant function analysis, which involves predicting which author a text belongs to based on a range of 'predictor' linguistic variables. The disputed emails were compared with faxes known to have been written by the defendant and with a set of four anonymous emails from another case as a control set. Turell found that the disputed emails were significantly more similar to the non-disputed faxes than they were to the other email set, and that there was quite a high probability that the author of the non-disputed faxes was also the author of the disputed emails (Turell 2010: 235).

Linguistic variation and style markers

Despite the interest in statistical methods of authorship attribution, the procedures used by forensic linguistics to analyse disputed texts and make judgements about authorship that have been most commonly and successfully applied in forensic casework are those which are *stylistic* in approach. The term 'forensic stylistics' is most widely associated with American linguist Gerald McMenamin. He defines it as:

> the application of the science of linguistic stylistics to forensic contexts. [...] Forensic stylistics makes use of stylistic analysis to reach a conclusion and opinion related to the authorship of a questioned writing within the context of litigation. Stylistics is the scientific study of patterns of variation in written language. The object of study is the language of a single individual (idiolect), resulting in a description of his or her identifying linguistic characteristics.
> (McMenamin 2002: 163)

Stylistic approaches to authorship analysis operate within a paradigm of linguistic variation and involve the analyst identifying 'style markers', which McMenamin (2010: 488) defines as an author's 'choice from optional forms', which are 'the observable results of the habitual and usually unconscious choices an author makes in the process of writing'. For example, there are different ways in which writers can arrange object clause elements within a sentence (McMenamin 2010: 498):

Variation 1: I give John my estate
        S V   IO   DO
Variation 2: I give my estate to John
        S V   DO   to+IO
Variation 3: I give to John my estate
        S V   to+IO   DO

(S = Subject, V = Verb, IO = Indirect Object, DO = Direct Object)

While one author may use variation 1, another may use variation 2, and yet another may prefer variation 3. As Nini and Grant (2013: 174) point out, 'style markers' as choices from alternative forms correspond to Labov's (1966: 15) variable-variant relationship in sociolinguistics, in that different 'variants' represent different realisations of the same 'variable'. McMenamin (2002: 47, 53) argues that the linguistic choices authors make reflect their individual linguistic competence and their unique combination of linguistic knowledge, cognitive associations and extra-linguistic influences: their *idiolect*. In other words, an individual's linguistic choices can be accounted for by their unique social and communicative backgrounds, such as where they have lived, what they have read, the education they have received, the music they have listened to, the jobs they have had, the friends they speak to etc. In turn, because each person's social background is unique, this is manifest in unique linguistic choices and preferences, which are observable through the analysis of style markers. Style markers are pervasive and can be found across all levels of language. McMenamin (2010) provides examples and details of markers that have been important in cases on which he has worked, including spelling, punctuation use, morphology (such as absent inflections), lexical choices, syntax, clause relations, and features of discourse such as letter closings and sign-offs. However, McMenamin (2002: 172) emphasises that unique markers are extremely rare, and so authorship attribution requires 'the identification of an aggregate of markers', which individually may well be found in other writers, but which combined 'would unlikely be present together in any other writer'. A person's idiolectal style (Turell 2010: 217), therefore, is an aggregation of their choices across a full range of style markers (see Chapter 2).

McMenamin (2002: 181–205) exemplifies a forensic stylistic analysis with a detailed, 25-page treatment of the linguistic evidence in the famous 1996 JonBenét Ramsey murder case. Six-year-old JonBenét disappeared and was later found dead in the basement of the family home, but only after a three-page, 370-word, ransom note had been discovered in the house. Both her parents became murder suspects and McMenamin was asked to compare the ransom note with a set of their writings. An analysis of the ransom note revealed a series of idiosyncratic spellings, word divisions and ways of writing sums of money – for example, *bussiness, posession; un harmed, out smart;* S‖118,000.00 and S‖100 (where S‖ indicates that $ was written as an S with two vertical lines) – which McMenamin felt were collectively likely to be evidential. Some of these can be seen in context in the extract below:

Mr. Ramsey. Listen carefully! We are a group of individuals that represent a small foreign faction. We respect your **bussiness** but not the country that it serves. At this time we have your daughter in our **posession**. She is safe and **un harmed** and if you want her to see 1997, you must follow our instructions to the letter.

You will withdraw **S‖118,000.00** from your account. **S‖100,000** will be **S‖100 bills** and the remaining **S‖18,000** in **S‖20 bills**.

(Extract of JonBenét Ramsey ransom note from McMenamin 2002: 182)

Looking at these orthographic differences *qualitatively*, he found 15 stylistic differences between the ransom note and the father's pre-crime writing and 18 between the note and the mother's pre-crime writing. Armed with this *qualitative* evidence, he subsequently approached the question *quantitatively*. In order to do this, he compared the style features of the ransom note with a corpus of 338 typed and handwritten texts from the American Writing Project. He isolated six variables for analysis because they occurred frequently in the comparison corpus and were ones on which Mrs Ramsey, who still remained a suspect, differed from the ransom note. He calculated that the likelihood of all six co-occurring in the same text by chance was less than one in 10,000. Thus, he argued, both qualitative and quantitative measures supported the opinion that neither Mr nor Mrs Ramsey had written the ransom note.

Consistency and distinctiveness

Alongside the importance of linguistic variation in authorship attribution is the 'consistency' and 'distinctiveness' of this variation. According to Grant (2013: 473), comparative authorship analysis depends on two assumptions:

The first assumption is that there is a sufficient degree of *consistency of style* within relevant texts by an individual author. The second assumption is that this consistency of style inherent in an author's writings is *sufficiently distinctive* to discriminate the one author from other relevant authors [our emphasis].

Both of these terms require some unpacking. Given that a person's style is the combination of choices across variables, as indicated by Grant in the quotation, there is an assumption that when writing texts of the same type or genre (e.g. email, text message, tweet), then there will be an observable 'consistency' in their choices across texts. This does not have to be an absolute consistency, but should be considered in terms of degrees of consistency. Using the example of the syntactic structure above from McMenamin (2010: 498), an author may sometimes use variation 1 (S+V+IO+DO), and sometimes use variation 2 (S+V+DO+IO). What is important for the forensic linguist is that they take note of relative frequencies of alternative variants. Such degrees of consistency are important when it comes to the 'weight of evidence' that can be placed upon any style marker used in an analysis of authorship. Consider that a disputed document in a forensic case contains a consistent misspelling of the word 'neighbour' as *'nieghbor'. At the same time, the collected known writings of the suspect in the case also contain the variable 'neighbour' 30 times. Of these 30 instances of the variable, 29 are misspelt as *'nieghbor'. On the basis of these relative frequencies of correct/incorrect spellings, the linguist can infer that the suspect has acquired a different rule from that of the standard system (Corder 1973). Furthermore, the consistency with which the suspect uses the misspelt variant provides evidence that they may have also written the disputed document. This evidence is stronger than would be the case if the suspect was less consistent in their misspelling (say, if they spelt it correctly half the time in their known writing).

'Distinctiveness' refers to the extent to which the styles of two or more authors are similar or different. Grant (2010: 515) distinguishes two types of distinctiveness. First, in a forensic case it is necessary to identify not only that the candidate writers have *consistent* styles, but that they have *different* styles, this is called 'pairwise distinctiveness'. It is only possible to attribute disputed texts to one of a number of candidate authors if the candidate authors all have their own distinctive styles. If their styles are not sufficiently distinctive, then the analyst should go no further in attempting to make judgements about who wrote the disputed text. The second type is 'population-level distinctiveness'. With the example of the misspelling of 'neighbour', it might be potentially evidential that the suspect is very consistent in their use of *'nieghbor' and that this is also found in the disputed text. However, it is not known how many other people in the general population misspell 'neighbour' as *'nieghbor'. The weight of evidence is lessened if it is found that millions of other people use this misspelling; the disputed text *may* have been written by any of them, while it would be considerably strengthened if it was found that nobody else misspells the word that way. Remembering that styles are made up of a combination of features such as this, it may be that one person's writing style within a particular text type can be said to be distinctive, unusual or even unique against a reference population of writers. At the moment, this population-level distinctiveness is difficult to measure due to the lack of available population data that forensic linguists can use. However, developments in corpus linguistics discussed later in the chapter are helping the field move in that direction.

The identification of linguistic consistency and distinctiveness are exemplified and demonstrated in practice by two murder cases in the UK in which forensic linguists' analysis of disputed text messages played an important role in conviction: the cases of Jenny Nicholl and Amanda Birks.

The Jenny Nicholl case

The second epigraph to this chapter reports a case in which stylistic evidence was presented in court in Britain. In June 2005, teenager Jenny Nicholl was murdered and the main suspect was her estranged lover David Hodgson. After her disappearance, four text messages were sent from her mobile phone. Coulthard was

Table 8.1 A comparison of Jenny Nicholl and David Hodgson's stylistic choices

Variable	Nicholl's preference	Hodgson's preference
I am	im	i am
I have	ive	ave
my/myself	my/myself	me/meself
off	off	of
to	[word]2[word]	[word]2 [word]
see you	cu	cya
phone	fone	phone
shit	shit	shite
am not	'm not	aint

asked to express an opinion on whether the four text messages had been written by her, and if not, whether they could have been written by Hodgson.

The police provided Coulthard with two sets of pre-crime text messages, one set known to have been written by Nicholl, and the other known to have been written by Hodgson. These were the known writings of the two candidate authors, against which the four disputed texts could be compared. First, Coulthard performed a qualitative, descriptive, stylistic analysis of these two sets of known messages and identified a set of nine style markers which served to distinguish between the texting habits of Nicholl and Hodgson (see Table 8.1). These style markers capture elements of linguistic variation insofar as the authors' choices represent selections from alternative forms. These were choices that were consistent in the emails of the respective authors, and they resulted in the Nicholl and Hodgson having two different and distinctive text messaging styles.

Once he had identified that the two candidate authors had consistent and distinctive styles, he turned his attention to the four questioned text messages. These text messages are now in the public domain, and are reproduced and analysed in 1 to 4 below.

Text 1
Thought u wer grassing me up.mite b in trub wiv **me** dad told mum i was lving didnt giv a shit.**been2kessick** camping was great.**ave2** go **cya**

Text 2
Hi jen tell jak **i am** ok know ever 1s gona b mad tell them **i am** sorry.living in Scotland wiv my boyfriend.shitting **meself** dads gona kill me mum dont give a **shite**.hope nik didnt grass me up.keeping phone **of**.tell dad car jumps out of gear and stalls put it back in auction.tell him **i am** sorry

Text 3
Y do u h8 me i know mum does.told her i was goin.i **aint** cumin back and the pigs wont find me.**i am** happy living up here.every1 h8s me in rich only m8 i got is jak.txt u couple wks tell pigs **i am** nearly 20 **aint** cumin back they can shite off

Text 4

She got me in this shit its her fault not mine get blame 4evrything.**i am** sorry ok just **had 2 lve** shes a bitch no food in and always searching **me** room eating **me** sweets.**ave2** go ok i am very sorry x

The task for Coulthard was then to find out whether or not any of the nine style markers that were consistent and distinctive in the known messages of Nicholl and Hodgson appeared in these four disputed messages. The variables did indeed appear in the messages, and are highlighted in bold in the extracts. We can see, for example, that the variable 'I am' is realised as 'i am' (rather than 'im') consistently in the disputed texts. Looking at the style markers in Table 8.1, this is consistent with David Hodgson's preference. Similarly, in all but one instance (in Text 2) 'my/myself' is represented as 'me/meself' in the disputed texts, which was also a distinctive feature of Hodgson's style in Table 8.1. Indeed, if we continue that analysis, comparing the highlighted style markers with those in Table 8.1, it is clear that the messaging style exhibited in the questioned texts is more consistent with that of David Hodgson's known set than that of Jenny Nicholl. On this basis, Coulthard arrived at the conservative opinion that the disputed texts were inconsistent with the known text messaging style of Jenny Nicholl, and that she was unlikely to have written the messages. Meanwhile, he gave the opinion that the linguistic features identified in the disputed texts and David Hodgson's known messages were 'consistent with their having been produced by the same person' and that Hodgson was one of a small group of potential authors of the four texts. The trial concluded in February 2008 with Hodgson being convicted of murder and sentenced to life in prison.

Combining stylistics and statistics: The Amanda Birks case

Despite the success of descriptive methods such as those used by Coulthard, the stylistic approach is sometimes criticised for being too subjective, relying heavily on the intuition of the expert witness. This subjectivity refers to the linguistic features that the linguist uses for any given attribution and the attributive power they attach to such features. Also, because the identification of useful style markers happens on a case-by-case basis (that is, a marker may be useful in one case but not another), the methods may not be replicable and results may not be generalisable (Nini and Grant 2013: 176). Instead, stylometric approaches such as those mentioned earlier in this chapter, which rely on the statistical measurement of style and similarity between texts, are held by some to be more reliable. Therefore, in a legal setting, it is thought they are more suitable for providing scientific evidence for the courts, especially when considered in terms of the Daubert Criteria for the admissibility of expert evidence (e.g. Howald 2008, see also Chapter 10). However, purely statistical approaches are often of no practical use to forensic linguists (Grant 2007: 3), most often because forensic conditions are far less controlled than experimental ones; it is likely that the expert working on a case will not have sufficient known or disputed data to use solely quantitative techniques, for example. Also, despite achieving generally high rates of accuracy in identifying authors, there is often no linguistic explanation as to *why* the methods have worked (Argamon and Koppel 2013: 299).

With all of this in mind, Grant (2013) describes a case in which he developed the descriptive stylistic methodology successfully applied by Coulthard and combined it with statistical measurements of similarity between texts and authors. He presents the case of the murder of Amanda Birks in Stoke-on-Trent, UK, in January 2009. It was found that Amanda had been killed by her husband, Christopher Birks, who had subsequently attempted to disguise his wife's death by making it look as if she had died as a result of an accidental house fire. This included Christopher sending a series of text messages from his wife's mobile phone to her friends and family. The police provided Grant with a corpus of 204 text messages from Amanda Birks' mobile phone, and were suspicious that the messages sent from the phone after midday on 17 January 2009 had not been written by her. Therefore, Grant set aside all the text messages that were sent after midnight on 16 January and these became the 'disputed' messages in the case. Removing these messages left a set of 165 messages, and it was taken to be a reasonable assumption that all of these had been authored by Amanda and so were considered her 'known' writings (Grant 2013: 479) Alongside these, Grant was given a comparable set of 203 text messages from Christopher Birks' phone. The task, then, was to identify whether the writing style exhibited in the disputed messages was closer to that of Amanda's or Christopher's known writings.

Grant's first analytical step was to examine the full set of 407 text messages using *Wordsmith Tools* (Scott 2012) to identify all word forms and their spelling variants in the data. These, along with other features of text messaging (e.g. abbreviations, letter/number substitutions, spacing between words) formed an initial 'basket' of 154 features for analysis. This approach is exhaustive, systematic and replicable in identifying linguistic variation and style markers. In the interests of consistency, Grant rejected any features that appeared fewer than ten times across all of the messages. With regard to *distinctiveness*, he also only retained features which were used by one author in at least twice as many messages as the other. After these steps, Grant was left with 18 features which had 'discriminative power' for analysis, ten of which were characteristic of Amanda's style, and eight characteristic of Christopher's. These features included alternate spelling variants such as *bak* for *back*, *wud* for *would*, *wen* for *when*, and the use of digits 2 and 4 with no space before the following word.

The next stage for Grant was to statistically measure the distinctiveness of the styles of the two authors. To do this he coded each feature as being 'present' (1) or 'absent' (zero) in every text message by both authors. Pairs of messages were then compared for their arrays of 1s and zeros using Jaccard's similarity coefficient (Jaccard 1912; see Chapter 10 for a discussion of the method). This calculation produced a number between zero and 1, with zero indicating that the two text messages were entirely dissimilar in their use of the given features, and 1 indicating that they were identical. What Grant found was that messages known to have been written by Amanda Birks were more similar to other messages she had written than they were to messages Christopher had written. Similarly, Christopher's messages were more similar to each other than they were to Amanda's. Using another statistic called the Mann Whitney U test, Grant found that the similarity between pairs of messages written by the same author was statistically significant. These statistical findings, underpinned by linguistic variation, demonstrated that Amanda and Christopher had consistent and distinctive text messaging styles.

Once Grant had completed this analysis of the known texts, he turned his attention to the disputed texts. Following the same methodology, the disputed messages were coded for the presence or absence of each of the 18 style markers. Jaccard was used again, this time to measure the similarity between the disputed texts and Amanda's known messages and the disputed texts and Christopher's known messages. On the basis of that comparison, and the application of Mann Whitney, Grant (2013: 484) concluded that:

> Taken as a set, the stylistic choices made in the disputed messages show significant dissimilarity from the stylistic choices in Amanda Birks' undisputed messages but no equivalent difference can be shown for the undisputed messages of Christopher Birks.

Grant (2013: 486) then goes on to analyse each of the disputed messages individually, highlighting in each case the stylistic features which suggest the changing author of the disputed texts in such a way that explains the statistical results. In November 2009, Christopher Birks changed his previously 'not guilty' plea to 'guilty', and was given a life sentence. An initial proposal of the method used can be found in Grant (2010) and a full description of its application in this case can be found in Grant (2013).

Corpus methods in authorship attribution

Corpus linguistics has been applied in various fields of linguistic enquiry in such a way that quantitative and qualitative results can be used to complement one another (McEnery and Wilson 2001: 76–77). One of the ways in which corpora can be used to aid forensic authorship attribution is in measuring the rarity or frequency of potential style markers identified in stylistic analysis. Chaski (2005: 2) states that without databases to ground the significance of linguistic features or style markers identified in a stylistic analysis, 'the examiner's intuition about the significance of a stylistic feature can lead to methodological subjectivity and bias'. While Grant (2010; 2013) demonstrates how we can measure 'pairwise distinctiveness', the use of large corpora allows us to measure the 'population-level distinctiveness' of an individual's style markers or their idiolectal style. Turell and Gavaldà (2013: 499) use the label 'Base Rate Knowledge' for an understanding of how common or rare a feature is in a relevant population of writers. Carefully designed specialised corpora may offer the kind of relevant population data required for such an understanding, and go some way in addressing Chaski's criticism.

Recent research in forensic authorship analysis has begun to experimentally test the ways in which corpora can be used in this way. In Chapter 2 we discussed the work of Wright (2013) and Johnson and Wright (2014) which used the Enron email corpus as relevant population data. Wright (2013) found that two email greetings used by employees of Enron, 'Hello:' and 'Hey:' (with colons), were respectively 555 and 269 times more likely to appear in an email written by one particular employee than in one written by any of the other 175 employees in the dataset. Later, Johnson and Wright (2014) demonstrated that, even though *please* occurred over 11,000 times in the emails of 165 out of 176 authors in the corpus, it was still possible to identify individual and idiolectal variation within 'please'-initial word strings. For example, 'please print the message', 'please format and print' and 'please proceed with your' only occur in emails sent by one employee. Such strings, it was argued, hold population-level distinctiveness, and represent 'n-gram textbites' that can characterise an author's writing style.

Corpus linguistic methodologies have been used in forensic casework. Notably, two seminal and historically important cases involved the use of evidence derived from corpora: the cases of Derek Bentley and the Unabomber, both of which are discussed in detail below. Since then, however, and until recently, corpus methods have not been at the forefront of authorship analysis research, as emphasis has been on the development of stylometric techniques. The findings such as those from the Enron studies have implications for the methodologies applied in casework and provide a fertile ground for future research projects. We begin to think about ways in which small corpora can be developed by students in the Research Tasks at the end of this chapter.

The Derek Bentley case

It is not unusual for the expert to use more than one approach. Here is such a case, which also illustrates two complementary approaches to those texts where there is a doubt about internal consistency, in other words, where it is possible that there was multiple authorship. The evidence provided in this case combines a detailed discourse analysis with the first use of a corpus linguistic method in forensic authorship analysis work.

In November 1952, two teenagers, Derek Bentley aged 19 and Chris Craig aged 16, were seen climbing up onto the roof of a London warehouse. The police were called and surrounded the building and three unarmed officers went up to the roof to arrest the boys. Bentley immediately surrendered; Craig started shooting, wounding one policeman and killing a second. Bentley was jointly charged with murder. The trial, which lasted only two days, took place five weeks later and both were found guilty, even though Bentley had been under arrest for some considerable time when the officer was killed. Craig, because he was legally a minor, was sentenced to life imprisonment; Bentley was sentenced to death and executed shortly afterwards. Bentley's family fought for a generation to overturn the guilty verdict and were eventually successful 46 years later, in 1998. The evidence which was the basis for both Bentley's conviction and the successful appeal was in large part linguistic.

In the original trial the problem for the prosecution, in making the case against Bentley, was to demonstrate that he could indeed be guilty of murder despite being under arrest when the murder was committed. At this point it would be useful to read the statement which, it was claimed, Bentley dictated shortly after his arrest. It is presented in full below as Extract 8.1; the only changes that have been introduced, to facilitate commentary are: to number the sentences for ease of reference, to highlight negative clauses with bold and to put occurrences of 'then' in italic.

Extract 8.1 Derek Bentley's confession statement
(1) I have known Craig since I went to school. (2) We were stopped by our parents going out together, but we still continued going out with each other – I mean **we have not gone out** together until tonight. (3) I was watching television tonight (2 November 1952) and between 8 p.m. and 9 p.m. Craig called for me. (4) My mother answered the door and I heard her say that I was out. (5) I had been out earlier to the pictures and got home just after 7 p.m. (6) A little later Norman Parsley and Frank Fasey called. (7) **I did not answer the door or speak to them**. (8) My mother told me that they had called and I *then* ran out after them. (9) I walked up the road with them to the paper shop where I saw Craig standing. (10) We all talked together and *then* Norman Parsley and Frank Fazey left. (11) Chris Craig and I *then* caught a bus to Croydon. (12) We got off at West Croydon and *then* walked down the road where the toilets are – I think it is Tamworth Road.

(13) When we came to the place where you found me, Chris looked in the window. (14) There was a little iron gate at the side. (15) Chris *then* jumped over and I followed. (16) Chris *then* climbed up the drainpipe to the roof and I followed. (17) Up to *then* **Chris had not said anything.** (18) We both got out on to the flat roof at the top. (19) *Then* someone in a garden on the opposite side shone a torch up towards us. (20) Chris said: 'It's a copper, hide behind here.' (21) We hid behind a shelter arrangement on the roof. (22) We were there waiting for about ten minutes. (23) **I did not know** he was going to use the gun. (24) A plain clothes man climbed up the drainpipe and on to the roof. (25) The man said: 'I am a police officer - the place is surrounded.' (26) He caught hold of me and as we walked away Chris fired. (27) **There was nobody else** there at the time. (28) The policeman and I *then* went round a corner by a door. (29) A little later the door opened and a policeman in uniform came out. (30) Chris fired again *then* and this policeman fell down. (31) I could see that he was hurt as a lot of blood came from his forehead just above his nose. (32) The policeman dragged him round the corner behind the brickwork entrance to the door. (33) I remember I shouted something but I forgot what it was. (34**) I could not see** Chris when I shouted to him - he was behind a wall. (35) I heard some more policemen behind the door and the policeman with me said: '**I don't think** he has many more bullets left.'

(36) Chris shouted 'Oh yes I have' and he fired again. (37) I think I heard him fire three times altogether. (38) The policeman *then* pushed me down the stairs and **I did not see** any more. (39) I knew we were going to break into the place. (40) **I did not know** what we were going to get – just anything that was going. (41**) I did not have** a gun and **I did not know** Chris had one until he shot. (42) I now know that the policeman in uniform that was shot is dead. (43) I should have mentioned that after the plain clothes policeman got up the drainpipe and arrested me, another policeman in uniform followed and I heard someone call him 'Mac'. (44) He was with us when the other policeman was killed.

Bentley's barrister spelled out for the jury the two necessary pre-conditions for them to convict: they must be 'satisfied and sure'

i) that [Bentley] knew Craig had a gun and
ii) that he instigated or incited Craig to use it.

(Trow 1992: 179)

The evidence adduced by the prosecution to satisfy the jury on both points was linguistic. For point i) it was observed that in his statement, which purported to give his unaided account of the night's events, Bentley had said 'I did not know he was going to use the gun' (sentence 23). In his summing up, the judge who, because of the importance of the case was the Lord Chief Justice, made great play with this sentence, telling the jury that its positioning in the narrative of events, before the time when there was a single policeman on the roof, combined with the choice of 'the gun' (as opposed to 'a gun'), must imply that Bentley knew that Craig had a gun well before it was used. In other words 'the gun', given its position in the statement, must be taken to mean 'the gun I already knew at this point in the narrative that Craig had'. In addition, his Lordship suggested, this sentence also showed Bentley to be an unreliable witness, because he contradicted himself later, in sentence 41, by saying 'I did not know Chris had [a gun] until he shot'.

The evidence used to support point ii), that Bentley had instigated Craig to shoot, was that the police officers in their statements and in their evidence given in court, asserted that Bentley had uttered the words 'Let him have it, Chris' immediately before Craig had shot and killed the policeman. As the judge emphasised, the strength of the linguistic evidence depended essentially on the credibility of the police officers who had recorded it and sworn to its accuracy. When the case came to appeal in 1998, one of the defence strategies was to challenge the reliability of the statement. If they could throw doubt on the veracity of the police, they could mitigate the incriminating force of both the statement and the phrase 'Let him have it' which Bentley, had denied uttering and Craig said even if Bentley had said it he had not heard it. This raises the interesting speech act question. What are the necessary conditions for someone to incite? Surely, it is not sufficient to simply utter the words; inciting must involve uptake and consequent action. If Craig denied hearing, how could Bentley be accused of having incited him?

(a) Single or multiple narrators

At the time of Bentley's arrest, the police were allowed to collect verbal evidence from those accused of a crime in two ways: either *by interview*, when they were supposed to record contemporaneously, verbatim and in longhand, both their own questions and the replies they elicited, or *by statement,* when the accused was invited to write down, or, if s/he so preferred, to dictate to a police officer, their version of events. During statement-taking the police officers were supposed not to ask substantive questions.

At the trial, three police officers swore on oath that Bentley's statement was the product of unaided monologue dictation, whereas Bentley asserted that it was, in part at least, the product of dialogue, and that police questions and his replies had been conflated and reported as monologue. There is no doubt that this procedure was at that time sometimes used for producing statements. A senior police officer, involved in another murder case a year later, explained to the Court how he had himself elicited a statement from another accused in exactly this way:

> I would say 'Do you say on that Sunday you wore your shoes?' and he would say 'Yes' and it would go down as 'On that Sunday I wore my shoes'.
>
> (Hannam 1953: 156)

There are many linguistic features which suggest that Bentley's statement is not, as claimed by the police, a verbatim record (see Coulthard 1993 for a detailed discussion). Here we focus only on evidence that the statement was indeed, at least in part, produced by dialogue being converted into monologue. Firstly, the final four sentences of the statement:

> (39) I knew we were going to break into the place. (40) I did not know what we were going to get – just anything that was going. (41) I did not have a gun and I did not know Chris had one until he shot. (42) I now know that the policeman in uniform that was shot is dead.

form some kind of meta-narrative whose presence and form are most easily explained as the result of a series of clarificatory questions about Bentley's knowledge at particular points in the narrative. In searching for evidence of multiple voices elsewhere in the statement we must realise that there will always be some transformations of Q-A which will be indistinguishable from authentic dictated monologue. In the Hannam example quoted above, had we not been told that 'On that Sunday I wore my shoes' was a reduction from a Q-A, we would have had some difficulty in deducing it, although the pre-posed adverbial 'On that Sunday' is certainly a little odd.

We can begin our search for clues with the initial observation that narratives, particularly narratives of murder, are essentially accounts of what happened and to a lesser extent what was known or perceived by the narrator and thus reports of what did **not** happen or was **not** known are rare and special. There is, after all, an infinite number of things that did not happen and thus the teller needs to have some special justification for reporting any of them to the listener, in other words, there must be some evident or stated reason for them being newsworthy. (See Pagano (1994) for a discussion of the function of negative clauses in texts.)

We can see typical examples of 'normal' usage of negative reports in the sentences below, which are taken from a crucial confession statement in another famous case, that of the Bridgewater Four, which is discussed in detail in Chapter 9.

i)   Micky dumped the property but **I didn't know where**.
ii) Micky Hickey drove the van away, **I don't know where he went** to
iii) **We didn't all go together**, me and Vinny walked down first.

(Molloy's Statement)

In examples, i) and ii) the second negative clause functions as a *denial* of an inference which the listener could otherwise have reasonably derived from the first clause. Example iii) is similar but this time it is a denial of an inference which the narrator guesses the listener might have made, as there is no textual basis for the inference. In other words, such negatives are an integral part of the ongoing narrative. We find examples of negatives being used in a similar way in Bentley's statement:

(6) A little later Norman Parsley and Frank Fasey called.
(7) **I did not answer the door or speak to them**

When Bentley reported that his friends had called, the listener would reason-ably expect him to have at least talked to them and therefore again there is a quite natural denial of a reasonable expectation. Similarly:

(38) The policeman then pushed me down the stairs and **I did not see** any more

where the negative explains the end of the narrative of events, in other words, 'not seeing anything more' has a clear narrative relevance.

However, there are some negatives in Bentley's statement which have no such narrative justification, like sentence (17) below:

(16) Chris then climbed up the drainpipe to the roof and I followed.
(17) Up to then **Chris had not said anything.**
(18) We both got out on to the flat roof at the top.

Chris is not reported as beginning to talk once they got onto the roof, nor is his silence contrasted with anyone else's talking, and nor is it made significant in any other way later in the narrative. A similarly unwarranted example is:

(26) He caught hold of me and as we walked away Chris fired.
(27) **There was nobody else** there at the time.
(28) The policeman and I then went round a corner by a door.

None of the possible inferences from this denial seem to make narrative sense here – i.e. that as a result of there being no one else there (a) it must be the policeman that Craig was firing at, or (b) that it must be Craig who was doing the firing, or (c) that immediately afterwards there would be more people on the roof. So, the most reasonable explanation for the negatives in these two examples is that, at this point in the statement-taking process, a policeman asked a clarificatory question to which the answer was negative and the whole sequence was then recorded as a negative statement. The fact that some of Bentley's statement may have been elicited in this way becomes particularly important in relation to sentence (23):

(23) **I did not know** he was going to use the gun

which is the one singled out by the judge as incriminating. This sentence too would only make narrative sense if it were linked backwards or forwards to the use of a gun – in other words, if it was placed immediately preceding or following the report of a shot. However, the actual context is:

(22) We were there waiting for about ten minutes.
(23) **I did not** know he was going to use the gun.
(24) A plain clothes man climbed up the drainpipe and on to the roof.

If it is accepted that there were question/answer sequences underlying Bentley's statement, it follows that the logic and the sequencing of the information were not under his direct control. Thus, the placing of the reporting of at least some of the crucial events must depend on decisions made by the police questioner to ask his questions at those points, rather than on Bentley's reconstruction of the narrative sequence. Therefore, it follows, crucially, that the inference drawn by the judge in his summing up was unjustified. If sentence (23) is the product of a response to a police question, with its placing determined by the interrogating officer, there is no longer any conflict with Bentley's later denial 'I did not know Chris had one [a gun] until he shot'. Nor is there any significance to be attached to Bentley saying 'the gun'. All interaction uses language loosely and co-operatively and so, if the policeman had asked Bentley about 'the gun', Bentley would have assumed they both knew which gun they were talking about. In that context the sensible interpretation would be 'the gun that had been used earlier that evening' and not 'the gun that was going to be used later in the evening' in the sequence of events that made up Bentley's own narrative.

(b) A corpus-assisted analysis of register

One of the marked features of Derek Bentley's confession is the frequent use of the word 'then' in its temporal meaning – 11 occurrences in 588 words. This may not, at first, seem at all remarkable, given that Bentley is reporting a series of sequential events and that one of the obvious requirements of a witness statement is accuracy about time. However, a cursory glance at a series of other witness statements showed that Bentley's usage of 'then' was at the very least atypical, and thus a potential intrusion of a specific feature of police register, deriving from a professional concern with the accurate recording of temporal sequence.

Two small corpora were used to test this hypothesis, the first composed of three ordinary witness statements, one from a woman involved in the Bentley case itself and two from men involved in another unrelated case, totalling some 930 words of text, the second composed of three statements by police officers, two of whom were involved in the Bentley case, the third in another unrelated case, totalling some 2,270 words. The comparative results were startling: whereas in the ordinary witness statements there is only one occurrence of 'then', it occurs 29 times in the police officers' statements, that is an average of once every 78 words. Thus, Bentley's usage of temporal 'then', once every 53 words, groups his statement firmly with those produced by the police officers. In this case it was possible to check the findings from the 'ordinary witness' data against a reference corpus, the Corpus of Spoken English – a subset of the much larger COBUILD Bank of English – which, at that time, consisted of some 1.5 million running words collected from many different types of naturally occurring speech and was by far the largest spoken corpus in the world. 'Then' in all its meanings proved to occur a mere 3,164 times, that is only once every 500 words, which supported the representativeness of the witness data and the claimed specialness of the data from the police and Bentley, (cf. Fox 1993).

What was perhaps even more striking about the Bentley statement was the frequent post-positioning of the 'then's, as can be seen in the two sample sentences below, selected from a total of seven:

(15) Chris **then** jumped over and I followed.
(16) Chris **then** climbed up the drainpipe to the roof and I followed.

The opening phrases have an odd feel, because not only do ordinary speakers use 'then' much less frequently than police officers, they also use it in a structurally different way. For instance, in the COBUILD spoken data 'then I' occurred ten times more frequently than 'I then'; indeed the structure 'I then' occurred a mere nine times, in other words, only once every 165,000 words. By contrast the phrase occurs three times in Bentley's short statement, once every 194 words, a frequency almost a thousand times greater. In addition, while the 'I then' structure, as one might predict from the corpus data, did not occur at all in any of the three witness statements, there were nine occurrences in one single 980-word police statement, as many as in the entire 1.5 million word spoken corpus. Taken together, the average occurrence in the three police statements is once every 119 words. Thus, the structure 'I then' does appear to be a feature of police (written) register.

More generally, it is in fact the structure Subject (+Verb) followed by 'then' which is typical of police register; it occurs 26 times in the statements of the three officers and seven times in Bentley's own statement. Interestingly, Svartvik

(1968: 29–32) had made the same discovery, but had not actually stated it explicitly, because the analytical category he had used was the more general 'clauses with mobile relator', with a gloss to the effect that 'such clauses include *then* and *also*'. What he did not state, obviously because he did not have access to other corpora and therefore did not realise its significance, was that, in *each and every one* of the 23 examples in his corpus, the 'mobile relator' was in fact realised by 'then'.

When we turn to look at yet another corpus, the shorthand verbatim record of the oral evidence given in court during the trial of Bentley and Craig, and choose one of the police officers at random, we find him using the structure twice in successive sentences, 'shot him *then* between the eyes' and 'he was *then* charged'. In Bentley's oral evidence there are also two occurrences of 'then', but this time the 'then's occur in the normal preposed position: 'and *then* the other people moved off', 'and *then* we came back up'. Even Mr Cassels, one of the defence barristers, who might conceivably have been influenced by police reporting style, says '*Then* you'. Such examples, embedded in Bentley's statement, of the language of the police officers who had recorded it, added support to the claim that it was a jointly-authored document and so both removed the incriminating force of the phrase 'I didn't know he was going to use the gun' and undermined the credibility of the police officers on whose word depended the evidential value of the remembered utterance 'Let him have it Chris'.

In August 1998, 46 years after the event, the Lord Chief Justice, sitting with two senior colleagues, criticised his predecessor's summing-up and allowed the appeal against conviction.

The Web as corpus: The Unabomber case

Between 1978 and 1995, an American, who referred to himself as FC, sent a series of bombs, on average once a year, through the post. At first there seemed to be no pattern, but over time the FBI noticed that the victims seemed to be people working for *Un*iversities and *a*irlines and so named the unknown individual the *Una*bomber. In 1995, six national publications received a 35,000-word manuscript, entitled *Industrial Society and its Future*, from someone claiming to be the Unabomber, along with an offer to stop sending bombs if the manuscript were published.

In August 1995, the *Washington Post* published the manuscript as a supplement and three months later a man contacted the FBI saying that the document sounded as if it had been written by his brother, whom he had not seen for ten years. He cited in particular the use of the phrase 'cool-headed logician' as being his brother's terminology, or in our terms an idiolectal preference, which he had noticed and remembered. The FBI traced and arrested the brother, who was living in a wooden hut in Montana. They impounded a series of documents, including a 300-word newspaper article on the same topic as the manifesto, which had been written a decade earlier. The FBI analysed the language and claimed that there were major linguistic similarities between the 35,000 and the 300 word documents – a series of lexical and grammatical words and fixed phrases – which, they argued, was evidence of common authorship.

The defence contracted a linguist, Robin Lakoff, who counter-argued that one could attach no significance to the fact that both documents shared these items, on the grounds that anyone can use any word at any time and that consequently vocabulary shared between texts can have no diagnostic significance. Lakoff singled out 12 words and phrases for particular criticism, on the grounds that they were items that could be expected to occur in any text that, like these two, was arguing a case – *at any rate, clearly, gotten, in practice, moreover, more or less, on the other hand, presumably, propaganda, thereabouts,* and words derived from the roots *argu** and *propos**. In response, the FBI searched the internet, which in those days was a fraction of the size it is today, but even so they discovered around three million documents, which contained one or more of the 12 items. However, when they narrowed the search to only those documents which included instances of all 12 items, they found only 69. On closer inspection, every single one of these proved to be an internet version of the 35,000-word manifesto. This was a massive rejection of the defence expert's view of text creation as purely open choice, as well as a powerful example of the idiolectal habit of co-selection and an illustration of the consequent forensic possibilities that idiolectal co-selection affords for authorship attribution.

Conclusion

The field of authorship attribution has two main methodological approaches: the stylistic and the stylometric, and there is no definitive answer yet to which method works better in forensic cases (Solan 2013: 573). What is clear, however, is that the field will benefit from the combination of approaches and the development of complementary techniques; Grant's (2013) method and corpus linguistic approaches are two movements in this direction. It is here that readers of this book can contribute. Students of linguistics can use their knowledge of language variation and their analytical skills to identify consistency and distinctiveness in authors' idiolectal styles in their own corpora. Those with statistical understanding can develop ways in which such variation can be measured statistically, and students of law can help by exploring how such evidence can be presented and handled in court, an issue which is dealt with in depth in Chapter 10. For those in the field of education, the major application of such work is in the detection of plagiarism, to which we will turn in the next chapter.

Further reading

McMenamin 2002 and 2010; Grant 2010 and 2013; Turell 2010.

Research tasks

1 Below are five emails from the Enron email corpus all written by the same person. There are four candidate authors and your job as a forensic linguist is to identify which of the four is the most likely author. The first stage of analysis has been done for you: Table 8.2

Table 8.2 Consistent and distinctive style markers in four email authors

Author A	Author B
• Multiple exclamation marks • mm/dd/yy • *Hey buddy* • *Hi Team* • *name,* (same line as rest of email)	• *Month [the] number x* (e.g. *May the 25th*) • *Day, Month+Number(x)* (e.g. *Saturday, May 25th*) • *Shall* • *I am attaching*
Author C	**Author D**
• Single/double exclamation marks • month.number • Tomarrow • Probobly • *thanks,* + *first name* • *thanks,* + *full name* • *thanks! first name* • *Hey+name* • *Let me know if you have any questions* • *Let me know if you need* • *Let me know if there is anything* • *Let me know when you [guys] are available* • *Attached is*	• *Day+Month.Number* (e.g. *Saturday May.25*) • *Day-Month+Number format* (e.g. *Saturday-May 25*) • *regards* • Enron Online semantic field • *Please find attached* • *thanks + first name thanks + full name* • *name – (same line as rest of email)*

lists style markers that have been found to be consistent and distinctive in the known writings of each of the four candidates. Using these style markers, discover which of the four candidates has a style closest to that of the disputed texts.

(a)   How sweet. Its doing ok. A better question is "how's the lovelife?" That's doing ok too – although I wish I could find the perfect woman. Mine is wanting to take some trips – Maine, New York, EUROPE!!!!!

(b)   I was out yesterday afternoon but the price for that product, all in is $5.06. Let me know if you need it broken down and if you are still interested.

      Thanks,
      [First name + Surname]

(c)   Thanks for coming. It was great to have you with us last weekend. I shall ask Vin about Blackbird. I think he should get a job ASAP. Otherwisw [sic], he will go insane staying home with two aging parents.

(d)   Attached is our sample agreement. Our legal guys are standing by to answer any questions. Let me know if there is anything else that you need.

(e)   [Name],
      We have a contract extension for Sempra, 30,000/d from La Plata to I/B Link extending it from 12/31/01 to 12/31/02. Max rate. Standard language. I would like to approve this contract in your absence. Legal and Regulatory have already approved. Thanks, [First name]

2   Text messages are now used as evidence in criminal trials. Individual texting styles can differ markedly. The following message comes from a real case that will be discussed in Chapter 10:

Hiya Stuart what are you up to. I'm in so much trouble at home at the moment. Everyone hates me even you. What the hell have I done now? Why wont you just tell me. Text back please. Love Danielle. Three kisses

First, collect ten authentic text messages from a friend; analyse them and then describe the linguistic rules your friend is subconsciously following. Now try to text the above message in your friend's style. Now ask your friend and nine other people, six from your own generation and three from a different generation to text the message to you in their usual style. Analyse all 11 messages.

(a) Can you distinguish between the styles of the two generations?
(b) Can you group individuals according to their texting style, in particular the extremeness or idiosyncrasy of their abbreviations?
(c) Which of the 11 versions of the text could not have been produced by your friend and why?
(d) How close was your text message to your friend's. Were any of the differences the result of poor analysis on your part?

3 Use 'the web as corpus' to measure the frequency or rarity of a lexical string.

Stage 1. Choose any text that you have read. That might be a newspaper, an email or a text/instant message. If you use just social media it might be a Facebook status or tweet posted by one of your friends.
Stage 2. From that text, select three or four lexical strings of any length, from short combinations of two or three words, to longer strings or perhaps whole utterances.
Stage 3. Use a search engine (e.g. Google, Bing) to search for each of your lexical strings, making sure that you have enclosed the string in speech marks (" ").
Stage 4. How many results does your search return? What can you say about the rarity or frequency of that string, and in turn about the extent to which it might be idiolectal for your author? Do you find that longer strings return fewer results? In what kinds of other texts is it found, if any?
Stage 5. Imagine now a disputed document in a forensic case included one of these lexical strings. On the basis of your web results, how certain could you be that the author of the disputed text and the author of your original text was the same person? How might you present this evidence to the court? What are the potential drawbacks of this method, and how might you overcome them as the expert?

For example, with a glance down Facebook homepage I find the string "Its alryt coz it will be found soon" used by someone. A Google search for this returns zero results. Using the web as corpus in this crude way provides some evidence to suggest that this string is distinctive of that Facebook user.

9   On textual borrowing

The barge she sat in, like a burnished throne,
Burned on the water

(Antony and Cleopatra, II ii 199–200)

The chair she sat in, like a burnished throne,
Glowed on the marble

(T.S. Eliot, The Waste Land, I, 77–78)

Introduction

For differing reasons the literary critic, the copyright lawyer and the teacher, as
well, of course, as the forensic linguist, are all interested in texts which apparently borrow from other texts – particularly when the borrowing is not acknowledged. With the T.S. Eliot example, above, it is assumed that the reader will
recognise the reference to Shakespeare, but Eliot's readers were not always willing to accept that his borrowings were deliberate intertextual references, rather
than the theft of a 'well-rounded' phrase. Indeed, Eliot had to defend himself in
an interview in August 1961:

> In one of my early poems ['Cousin Nancy'] I used, without quotation marks,
> the line 'the army of unalterable law …' from a poem by George Meredith,
> and this critic accused me of having deliberately plagiarized, pinched,
> pilfered that line. Whereas, of course, the whole point was that the reader
> should recognize where it came from and contrast it with the spirit and mean-
> ing of my own poem.
>
> (quoted in Ricks 1998: 23–24)

The literary artist may be able to make this defence, that is that any competent
reader will recognise a borrowing and therefore that s/he does not need to explicitly acknowledge it, but this does raise important questions about *definition* and
differing *disciplinary conventions*. First, there is the question of definition –
whether plagiarism is defined as the simple textual phenomenon of unacknowledged borrowing, in which case Eliot was guilty, or the product of an authorial

intention to deceive, in which case Eliot can claim (truthfully or not, we can never know) to be not guilty. But the situation becomes much more complicated if the categorisation of any borrowing, as plagiarism or not, is left to each individual reader's personal assessment, because this will of necessity depend upon that reader first recognising the unmarked borrowing and then deciding whether it is either a deliberate intertextual reference or a barefaced theft. From this point of view, Eliot might be found guilty by some readers and innocent by others. The conventions of individual disciplines cross-cut the problem, because some frown on plagiarism more than others – journalists apparently feel able to borrow large chunks of text with no attribution at all, whereas academics, ever more subject to evaluation by publication and citation, are anxious to have every quotation of their words explicitly acknowledged.

Normally, of course, even in the literary field, an accusation rests on much more than a single phrase and anyone who has read *The Waste Land* will know that Eliot is a habitual borrower, but then many of us only know that because the poem has the traditional academic apparatus of source attribution provided by the author himself, in appended notes. To paraphrase, or recontextualise, into more familiar linguistic terms, what Eliot was doing in creating intertextual references was setting up a Matching Relation (see Hoey 1983, 2000) between (sections of) the two texts and so was using the quotation quite deliberately as the *constant*, in order to trigger the reader's search for the *variable*. This is what we see in the specific *Waste Land* example above, where readers are expected to bring all the associations they have built up about Shakespeare's Cleopatra and compare and contrast them with the high class prostitute who Eliot is actually describing. Seen in these terms, plagiarism occurs when a writer sets out to conceal the matching relation that their text would otherwise create with the source(s) and instead to claim the whole (piece of) text as his/her own original creation.

The history of plagiarism

Plagiarism as we know it is very much the product of two major sociolinguistic changes in the past 700 years: the move from an oral to a written culture and the wider availability of written texts following the invention of the printing press in the 1440s. When literature was oral, it existed only in performance and although much was remembered, there is no doubt that each performance of *Beowulf* was unique, with the performer altering the sequence of some half lines, omitting others and creating yet other new ones as he was reciting. No one knows who composed *Beowulf* or *The Odyssey*, nor indeed whether there ever was a single author, how many mouths the narratives passed through, how many alterations they underwent, before they were recorded in written form. Even for the few who could read, the majority of classic texts were accessed in translation, often in translations of translations, so no special status was given to the 'wording', while the ideas the texts contained were seen to belong to the community rather than to any individual owner/author.

With the arrival of printing not a lot changed, at least at first – Shakespeare did not acknowledge his sources, although he borrowed massively for his plots, but neither did anyone accuse him of plagiarism. However, the introduction of a speculator – the publisher – between the text producer and the text consumer did cause things to change. Publishers realised that they needed to defend 'their' texts in order to protect their investment – the authors themselves sold the work to the publisher and afterwards earned very little, if anything, from sales. The Licensing Act of 1662 established a register of licensed books, along with the requirement to deposit a copy of the book to be licensed, but the purpose was mainly political; even though the system was administered by the Stationers' Company, which was an association of independent publishers, they were given the power to seize any books which might contain writings attacking the Government or the Church. The original Licensing Act was repealed fairly quickly, but the Stationers' Company had realised its value and managed to have another law passed that established for its members the right of ownership over the content of the books they had published. However, it was only in 1710, with the Statute of Queen Anne, that the rights of authors were recognised and then only with a 14-year copyright. For further information, see http://www.intellectual-property. gov.uk/ std/resources/copyright/history.htm.

Universities and plagiarism

Nowadays it is not only publishers who are concerned with ownership; the academic community too is a rigorous defender of the intellectual property rights of its members. In the opinion of the editors of the highly regarded science journal, *Nature*:

> Plagiarism is the most serious of the known crimes against scholarship … it amounts to the literal theft of another's words, thereby depriving the victim not merely of the credit for … the stolen words, but of whatever thought and imagination they embody.
>
> (Maddox 1991: 13)

Universities see it as one of their functions to instil the values and procedures of the academic community into initiates. Most set out to teach their new students explicitly about plagiarism and how to avoid it and then impose penalties on those offenders who are caught, even if they are senior academics. For instance, in July 2001 the Vice Chancellor of Monash University was forced to resign when examples of frequent plagiarism were discovered in his earlier academic work and more recently politicians have resigned after being accused of plagiarising parts of their doctoral dissertations: the German Minister of Defence in 2011 and the Polish Minister of the Environment and the German Minister of Education in 2013.

Typically, universities provide written guidance on plagiarism for their students and growingly this is available on their websites, although such documents are usually unattributed. Indeed, Pennycook (1996: 213) reports that some of Stanford University's documents about plagiarism were reproduced, without attribution, by the University of Oregon, and notes ironically that there appears to be 'one set of standards for the guardians of truth and knowledge and another for those seeking entry'.

At its simplest, plagiarism, or more accurately the type of plagiarism that linguists are competent to deal with, is the theft, or unacknowledged use, of text created by another. As the University of Birmingham's website used to express it:

> Plagiarism is a form of cheating in which the student tries to pass off someone else's work as his or her own. ... Typically, substantial passages are 'lifted' verbatim from a particular source without proper attribution having been made.

However, there are two problems with the definition of plagiarism given here. First, it claims that plagiarism typically takes the form of substantial verbatim borrowings, whereas the vast majority of cases are actually texts which have been edited, even if only superficially. Second, the university seems to be committing itself to an 'intentionalist' definition – 'tries to pass off' – but this is very hard to apply in practice. However, a university can sidestep this problem by handing over the responsibility for ensuring the absence of plagiarism to the individual student. Provided all students are required to sign a 'contract', which in effect says that they know the rules for acknowledging borrowing, any student who is then discovered to have plagiarised can be assumed to have intentionally broken them. (Find the documentation produced by your own institution and compare it with that of neighbouring institutions.)

With growing frequency linguists are being asked to help academic colleagues in the detection or confirmation of student plagiarism. Any linguistically-based investigation of plagiarism is based consciously or unconsciously on the notion of *idiolect*. In other words, it is expected that any two writers writing on the same topic, even if intending to express very similar meanings, will choose an overlapping, but by no means identical, set of lexico-grammatical items to do so. Indeed, and more importantly for some of the cases we will treat below, linguists from all persuasions subscribe to some version of the 'uniqueness of utterance' principle (Chomsky 1965; Halliday 1975) and so would expect that the same person, speaking/writing on the same topic on different occasions, would make a different set of lexico-grammatical choices, (see discussion in Chapter 6). It follows from this that, in any comparison of two texts, the more similar the set of items chosen, the greater the likelihood that, rather than being composed independently, one of the texts was derived, at least in part, from the other (or, of course, that both were derived from a third text).

In many cases involving student plagiarism there is little doubt about textual guilt. The two extracts presented below are from the openings of responses to the essay question 'Discuss the kind of policy a primary school should have towards bilingualism and multilingualism' (Johnson 1997: 214). We have used **bold** to indicate all the items which student B 'shares' with student A.

Extract 9.1
A.   It is essential for all teachers to understand the history of Britain as a multiracial, multi-cultural nation. Teachers, like anyone else, can be influenced by age-old myths and beliefs. However, it is only by having an understanding of the past that we can begin to comprehend the present.

B.   In order for **teachers** to competently acknowledge the ethnic minority, **it is essential to understand the history of Britain as a multi-racial, multicultural nation. Teachers** are prone to believe popular **myths and beliefs; however, it is only by understanding** and appreciating **past** theories **that we can begin to** anticipate **the present**.

Even these short extracts provide enough evidence to question the originality of at least one of the essays, or both, of course, if a third text later proves to be the common source. When this level of sharing is also instanced in other parts of the same texts there is no room for doubt or dispute. The case of essay C (Extract 9.2), however, is not as clear-cut (items which C shares with one or both of essays A and B are highlighted).

Extract 9.2
C.   It is very important for us as educators to realize that **Britain as a nation** has become both **multi-racial** and **multi-cultural.** Clearly it is vital for **teachers** and associate teachers to ensure that **popular myths and** stereotypes held by the wider community do not **influence** their teaching. By examining British history this will assist our **understanding** and in that way be better equipped to deal with **the present** and the future.

Even though there is still a significant amount of shared lexical material here, it is evident that the largest identical sequence is only four running words long. Even so, one would still want to categorise this degree of lexical overlap, if also instanced in other parts of the text, as unacknowledged, although more sophisticated, borrowing and therefore plagiarism, even if it does not fit easily within the original Birmingham observation that 'Typically, *substantial* passages are "lifted"'. We will not discuss here the important question of whether a significant proportion of those student essays which technically fall within the textual definition of plagiarism, are really deliberate attempts to deceive. An alternative explanation is that they are the product of a writing process that is coming to be known as 'patchwriting', that is, that they are genuine, although flawed, attempts by students, who have somehow failed to acquire the academic rules for acknowledging textual borrowing, to incorporate the work of others into their own texts (see Pecorari 2002, 2010; Howard 1999a; Coulthard 2005). Patchwriting does seem to be more common among non-native speakers struggling to produce acceptable academic writing in a language they do not fully command.

Johnson's (1997) innovative solution to the detection of this form of student plagiarism or *collusion*, was to move away from a reliance on strings or sequences of words as diagnostic and concentrate simply on shared vocabulary. She decided to disregard grammatical words (*a, the, of,* etc.) altogether, as there are very few of them, although they are used very frequently, typically making up more than 40 per cent of any given text, and they are more likely to be shared anyway. So, she chose to focus on the percentage of shared individual lexical *tokens* and *types* as a better measure of derivativeness. A *token* count sums all occurrences of each lexical *type*, so in the invented sentence 'The pretty girl gave the pretty ball to the other girl' there are four lexical types – *pretty, girl, gave, ball* – but six lexical tokens with *pretty* and *girl* occurring twice.

Johnson first took the first 500 words from three non-suspect essays and calculated the amount of shared lexical vocabulary. One would expect a degree of overlap in vocabulary choice between the essays, as they were all writing, on the same topic. In fact, this control group was found to share only 13 lexical types, of which seven – *language, languages, school, children, multilingual, bilingual* and *policy* – were almost predictable, given the topic of the essay. As these words are central to the topic, they are not only shared, but also repeated frequently and thus this set of 13 shared types made up some 20 per cent of the total lexical tokens used in the three extracts. With these figures as a base line for comparison Johnson returned to the suspect essays and found that they shared 72 lexical types, which accounted for some 60 per cent of all the lexical tokens.

It is also possible to approach such texts from a different perspective and to examine how much lexical uniqueness there is. Whilst for the control group the vocabulary unique to each essay constituted between 54 and 61 per cent of the lexical tokens, two of the suspect essays had only 16 per cent of unique lexis and the third, which had appeared to the examiner to be less derivative, still had only 39 per cent. Intensive testing has shown that measures of lexical overlap successfully separate those essays which share common vocabulary simply because they are about the same topic, from those which share much more vocabulary because one or more of them is derivative (see Woolls and Coulthard 1998; Woolls 2003).

The problem for the human reader, in trying to detect such collusion, becomes evident when one discovers that none of the three colluding essays was statistically unusual when compared with any of the control essays – in other words, had the three 'guilty' essays been marked by different professors, none would have been noticed as suspicious. So, obviously, what is needed is an automated checking procedure, to enable the rapid and reliable comparison of every essay with every other one; this quickly becomes a large task as the number of essays to be compared increases, even with a comparatively small group of essays – comparing 30 essays each with every other one necessitates 435 comparisons. However, this can be done rapidly using *Copycatch Investigator* (Woolls 2015), which has computerised Johnson's original insights – it calculates the amount of shared lexis and allows the individual user to decide, depending on subject area, its quoting conventions and the length of the essay, what percentage of overlap will trigger further investigation.

Unacknowledged use of published text

More frequent than collusion are cases of a single individual making unacknowledged use of already published text. In the past, students typically borrowed from books or journal articles and had at least to write out or type the borrowed text. Now the process is much easier – the student-plagiarist can (re-)search the web, find a useful piece of text and paste it, apparently seamlessly, at least to the eye, if not to the mind, of the beholder, into his or her own text. However, although the text is physically seamless, the joins are usually evident to a skilled and careful reader, because of the clash of styles between the student's work and the 'borrowed' text(s). A clear example of such a style clash is the opening of a story written by a 12-year-old girl (Extract 9.3, all the spelling is as in the original).

> *Extract 9.3*
> *The Soldiers*
> Down in the country side an old couple husband and wife Brooklyn and Susan. When in one afternoon they were having tea they heard a drumming sound that was coming from down the lane. Brooklyn asks,
> **'What is that glorious sound which so thrills the ear?'** when Susan replied in her o sweat voice
> 'Only the scarlet soldiers, dear,'
> The soldiers are coming, The soldiers are coming. Brooklyn is confused he doesn't no what is happening.
> Mr and Mrs Waters were still having their afternoon tea when suddenly a bright light was shinning trough the window.
> **'What is that bright light I see flashing so clear over the distance so brightly**?' said Brooklyn sounding so amazed but Susan soon reassured him.

The first paragraph is unremarkable, but the second shifts dramatically, '*What is that glorious sound which so thrills the ear?*' The story then moves back to the opening style, before shifting again to '*What is that bright light I see flashing so clear over the distance so brightly?*' It is hard to believe that an author so young could write in both styles. When one meets a style clash like this in any student's work and does not recognise the source, the first response is ever more likely to be to search the internet. Many people do this laboriously by trying, as the police sometimes do in analogous circumstances, to recreate the crime, that is, in the case of plagiarism, by searching the kinds of topics that the student him/herself had probably searched. However, what the theory of idiolect and the practice of working with *Copycatch* have taught us is the importance of the distinctiveness and individuality of lexical selection and co-selection.

If proof were needed of the distinctiveness and diagnostic power of words that occur only once – *hapaxes* as they are technically labelled – it comes from successful internet searches in cases of suspected plagiarism. Experience confirms that the most economical method to use when checking the internet manually for suspected plagiarised text is to search using pairs of collocates whose individual items occur only once in the text in question – three pairs is usually sufficient. In the case of *The Soldiers*, if one takes as search terms the three pairs of collocated *hapaxes* 'thrills + ear', 'flashing + clear' and 'distance + brightly' one can see the diagnostic power of idiolectal co-selection. The single pairing 'flashing + clear' yields over 500,000 hits on Google, but combined the three pairings yield a mere 360 hits, of which the first 13, at the time we searched, all came from the same text, W.H. Auden's poem 'O What is that sound'. When we added a seventh word 'so' and searched for the phrase 'flashing so clear' the only hits returned were from Auden's poem, see the opening below with the borrowed items highlighted in bold and items added by the girl indicated in square brackets (Extract 9.4):

Extract 9.4
O what is that sound?
> O **what is that** [glorious] **sound which so thrills the ear**
>> Down in the valley drumming, drumming?
> **Only the scarlet soldiers, dear,**
>> **The soldiers** [are] **coming.**
> O **what is that** [bright] **light I see flashing so clear**
>> **Over the distance** [so] **brightly**, brightly?
> Only the sun on their weapons, dear,
>> As they step lightly.

In incorporating five lines from the poem into her prose story, the girl had simply omitted the 'O's and added the adjectives 'glorious' and 'bright', the copula 'are' and an extra adverb 'so'.

As an alternative to individual searching, British University staff now have access, through a national centre based in the Northumbria University, to a Plagiarism Detection Service which employs the American company Turnitin, www.turnitin.org, to search for sources in cases of suspected plagiarism. In most institutions assessed work is now submitted electronically and the professor receives two copies of the work, one already 'analysed' with an indication of both the percentage of text which has been identified as shared and also an indication of a pre-existing text for each of the items identified. However, at this point the work has only just started for the professor. Firstly, Turnitin does not distinguish between acknowledged and unacknowledged borrowings. Secondly, and more seriously, the program typically finds the most recent occurrence, which may itself be a borrowing, acknowledged or not, rather than the original source. This happened with one case Coulthard was involved in – the student had borrowed extensively from a single famous Wikipedia entry about Donna Haraway's famous essay *A Cyborg Manifesto*. However, it took a while to get to the original, (https://en.wikipedia.org/wiki/A_Cyborg_Manifesto), because many other texts had quoted the same entry, although less extensively than the student, so Turnitin actually provided five separate sources. Below is a small extract from the essay with the borrowings highlighted in bold. It is interesting to note that one item added to the original by the student is a page reference, (2000:313). In another case in which Coulthard was involved, a student did not simply insert page references into a text plagiarised from a fellow student, she actually invented them, which initially suggested that the other student was the plagiarist.

> She emphasizes the **problematic use and justification of Western traditions like patriarchy, colonialism, naturalism, essentialism** etc. Such **traditions allow for the** sticky **formations of taxonomies (designation of the Other) and 'antagonistic dualisms' that order Western discourse. These dualisms,** in **Haraway**'s view, '**have all been systemic to the** logics and practices of domination of women, **people of colour, nature, workers, animals**—in short, domination of **all constituted as others**, whose task is to mirror the self' (2000:313). **She** stresses **specific problematic dualisms** such as '**self/ other,** mind/body, **culture/nature, male/female, civilized/ primitive,** reality/appearance, whole/part, agent/resource, maker/made, active/passive, **right/wrong, truth/illusion, total/partial, God/man'** (2000:313). **She** adds **that these dualisms are** involved in a dialectic of apocalypse **with one another, creating paradoxical relations of domination** and dominated (chiefly **between** self, or **One, and Other**).

Plagiarism is, of course, by no means confined to the student body. Table 9.1 is a side-by-side comparison, created using the *Copycatch Investigator* program, of extracts from two texts: one the infamous 'dodgy dossier' which the British government presented to the United Nations in February 2003, shortly before the beginning of the Iraq War, claiming it as an intelligence-based analysis of Iraqi power structures; the other is an unclassified academic article, published shortly before, from which the 'dodgy dossier' had in fact been substantially plagiarised. It is clear that, in the extracts we have chosen, the only contribution from British intelligence was to 'correct' the spelling of four words from American to British English: *rumours, pre-empted, co-ordinating* and *programmes* (see Table 9.1).

Plagiarism and translation

There is a long tradition of people translating texts into other languages without acknowledgement, which, as we mentioned above, started well before there was a concept of the ownership of ideas and their textualisations and before plagiarism came to be seen as an academic sin. It is obviously more difficult to demonstrate 'plagiarism by translation' than same-language plagiarism, although one still looks in the same way for evidence of shared content and the very similar sequencing of content, which is typical of same-language plagiarism as we noticed in the Cyborg example above.

Translingual plagiarism is where 'a plagiarist takes an original work published in another language, translates it into his/her language and publishes it [as their own]', Sousa-Silva (2014: 74). The easiest occurrences to detect are where a computerised translation program has been used and strange grammatical

Table 9.1 Comparison of extracts from British secret service document on Iraq and an academic article (we are indebted to David Woolls for this comparison, which was created with the Copycatch program)

Iraq: Its Infrastructure Of Concealment, Deception And Intimidation	*Iraq's Security And Intelligence Network: A Guide And Analysis* By Ibrahim al-Marashi
UK Government release February 2003	***Middle East Review of International Affairs*, Vol 6, iii, September 2002**
Under the Political Bureau, the Operations Office implements operations against these 'enemies', including arrests, interrogations and executions.	Under the Political Bureau, the Operations Office implements operations against these 'enemies', including arrests, interrogations and executions.
Another division is the Public Opinion Office, responsible for collecting and disseminating **rumours** on behalf of the state.	Another division is the Public Opinion Office, responsible for collecting and disseminating **rumors** on behalf of the state
The operations of Special Security are numerous, particularly in suppressing domestic opposition to the regime.	The operations of Special Security are numerous, particularly in suppressing domestic opposition to the regime.
After its creation in 1984, Special Security thwarted a plot of disgruntled army officers, who objected to Saddam's management of the Iran-Iraq War.	After its creation in 1984, Special Security thwarted a plot of disgruntled army officers, who objected to Saddam's management of the Iran-Iraq War
It **pre-empted** other coups such as the January 1990 attempt by members of the Jubur tribe to assassinate him.	It **preempted** other coups such as the January 1990 attempt by members of the Jubur tribe to assassinate him
It played an active role in crushing the March 1991 Shi'a rebellion in the south of Iraq.	It played an active role in crushing the March 1991 Shi'a rebellion in the south of Iraq.
Along with General Intelligence, Special Security agents infiltrated the Kurdish enclave in the north of Iraq in August 1996, to hunt down operatives of the Iraqi opposition.	Along with General Intelligence, Special Security agents infiltrated the Kurdish enclave in the north of Iraq in August 1996, to hunt down operatives of the Iraqi opposition.
It serves as the central **co-ordinating** body between Military-Industrial Commission, Military Intelligence, General Intelligence, and the military in the covert procurement of the necessary components for Iraq's weapons of mass destruction.	It serves as the central **coordinating** body between Military-Industrial Commission, Military Intelligence, General Intelligence, and the military in the covert procurement of the necessary components for Iraq's weapons of mass destruction
During the 1991 Gulf War, it was put in charge of concealing SCUD missiles and afterwards in moving and hiding documents from UNSCOM inspections, relating to Iraq's weapons **programmes.**	During the 1991 Gulf War it was put in charge of concealing SCUD missiles (32) and afterwards in moving and hiding documents from UNSCOM inspections, relating to Iraq's weapons **programs.**

sequences and/or odd lexical choices appear. Most examples are not as severe as an account of a robbery, reported by an English visitor to have occurred 'on the overnight coach', which, in the Brazilian police report, produced by Google Translate, situated the robbery 'no treinadaor de noite' ('on the overnight (athletics) trainer'). However, good quality translingual plagiarism is still hard to detect and, as Sousa-Silva points out, (op. cit. pp. 86 ff) the main technique available to investigators is to translate suspicious phrases into the suspected language of origin and search individually. One possible automatisation, would involve linking Google Translate with Turnitin, but the variables involved would be enormous.

Perhaps of more linguistic interest are cases where we have not one, but two or more, translations of the same text for comparison purposes. One would naturally expect more similarity between two translated texts than between two original texts written on the same topic, because the linguistic choices in the translations are necessarily constrained by the wording of the original. Thus, for example, one would expect to find in translations of the same text, more shared hapaxes and even more shared phrases and consequently it is likely to be more difficult to demonstrate plagiarism.

Turell (2004) discusses a case where a Spanish translator of Shakespeare's *Julius Caesar* accused the author of a later translation of plagiarism and she outlines the linguistic strategies used to demonstrate plagiarism. Turell was fortunate in that there were two other earlier published translations, so she could compare all four translations, (using *Copycatch Gold*, Woolls 2002), each with every other one, a total of six comparisons. In this way she was able to calculate a baseline for the quantity of shared vocabulary, shared hapax words and shared hapax phrases between all the translations known to be unrelated and then compare these scores with the results for the questioned pair. The figures for shared hapaxes, a strong diagnostic feature of plagiarism as noted above, were particularly persuasive (see Table 9.2 below).

In this case, as so often in plagiarism cases, the final nail was a plagiarised mistake. For the Shakespearean phrase 'Good Morrow, Brutus' (II, I, 87) the two comparison translations had the unremarkable 'Buenos días, Bruto' ('good day'), which is a standard Spanish morning greeting. However, the plaintiff had misunderstood 'morrow' and translated the phrase as 'Buenas noches, Bruto' ('Good evening/night'), a standard Spanish evening greeting. The plagiarised translation had the same mistake.

Do people repeat themselves?

Whereas (occasional) identical strings in two texts, which are supposed to have different authors, can be indicative of unacknowledged borrowing or plagiarism,

Table 9.2 Comparisons between the four translated texts

Criterion	Five non-suspect comparisons		Suspect comparison
	Average	*Largest*	
Shared vocabulary	69.6%	75.3%	83.9%
Shared hapaxes	527	698	1,049
Shared hapax phrases	44	48	164

it is harder to argue the case when the second text is (supposedly) produced by the same author, on a different occasion, but without recourse to the first. The example is taken from a famous English murder case, dating from 1978, where one piece of strongly contested evidence was a record of a police interview with a suspect.

In this case, four men were accused, and subsequently convicted, solely on the basis of a confession made by one of them, Patrick Molloy, to the murder of a 13-year-old newspaper delivery boy, Carl Bridgewater. There was no corroborating forensic evidence and Molloy later retracted his confession, but to no avail. He admitted that he did actually say (most of) the words recorded as his confession, but insisted that he was told what to say by one policeman, while a second wrote down what he said. He also claimed that he had only made the confession after being physically and verbally abused for some considerable time, and after being shown a confession made by one of the other accused, which incriminated him in the murder.

The police denied the existence of the other man's confession, as did its claimed author and also, to reinforce the credibility of Molloy's confession, produced a contemporaneous handwritten record of an interview with Molloy, which, they asserted, had taken place immediately prior to his confession and which contained substantially the same information, expressed in words very similar to those of the confession. Molloy, however, claimed that the interview had never taken place – in his version of events he was being abused at the time the interview was said to have occurred. He counter-claimed that the interview record had been made up later on the basis of the, by then pre-existing, confession. As is evident from a cursory glance at the two extracts below (Extracts 9.5 and 9.6) which are taken, respectively, from the statement which Molloy admitted making and the interview record which he claimed was falsified, the similarities are enormous; we have highlighted them in bold.

Extract 9.5 from Molloy's statement

(17) **I had been drinking and cannot remember the exact time I was there but whilst I was upstairs I heard someone downstairs say be careful someone is coming**. (18) **I hid for a while and** after a while **I heard** a **bang** come from downstairs. (19) I knew that it was a gun being fired. (20) I went downstairs and **the three of them were still in the room**. (21) **They all looked shocked and were shouting at each other**. (22) **I heard Jimmy say, 'It went off by accident'**. (23) I looked and **on the settee** I saw the **body** of the boy. (24) **He had been shot in the head**. (25) **I was appalled and felt sick**.

Extract 9.6 from disputed interview with Molloy

P.   How long were you in there Pat?

(18)   **I had been drinking and cannot remember the exact time that I was there, but whilst I was upstairs I heard someone downstairs say 'be careful someone is coming'.**

P.   Did you hide?
(19)   Yes **I hid for a while and** then **I heard** the **bang** I have told you
            about.
P.   Carry on Pat?
(19a)   I ran out.
P.   What were the others doing?
(20)   **The three of them were still in the room.**
P.   What were they doing?
(21)   **They all looked shocked and were shouting at each other.**
P.   Who said what?
(22)   **I heard Jimmy say 'it went off by accident'.**
P.   Pat, I know this is upsetting but you appreciate that we must get to
            the bottom of this. Did you see the **boy's body**?
(23)   Yes sir, he was **on the settee.**
P.   Did you see any injury to him?
(24)   Yes sir, **he had been shot in the head.**
P.   What happened then?
(25)   **I was appalled and felt sick.**

Most linguists would agree, on the basis of such similarities, that either one of the
two documents was derived from the other or that both had been derived from a
third. However, at the time of the original trial, no linguist was called to give
evidence – in fact there were no forensic linguists practicing in Britain at the time –
so it was left to the lawyers to evaluate the linguistic significance of the similarities between the interview and the confession. As a result, the same phenomenon,
massive identity in phrasing and lexical choice, was argued by the defence to be
evidence of falsification, and by the prosecution to be evidence of the authenticity
and reliability of both texts, on the grounds that here was an example of the
accused reliably recounting the same events, in essentially the same linguistic
encoding, on two separate occasions.

   The prosecution assertion, that identity of formulation in two separate texts is
indicative of reliability, depends on two commonly held, but mistaken, beliefs:
firstly, that people can and do recount the same content in the same words on
different occasions and secondly, that people can remember and reproduce verbatim what they and others have said on some earlier occasion. The former belief
can be easily demonstrated to be false, either by recording someone attempting
to recount the same set of events on two separate occasions, or by simply asking
a witness to repeat word for word what s/he has just said. The second belief used
to have some empirical support, at least for short stretches of speech (see Keenan
et al. 1977 and Bates *et al.* 1980), but was seriously questioned by Hjelmquist
(1984) who demonstrated that, even after only a short delay, people could
remember at best 25 per cent of the gist and 5 per cent of the actual wording of
what had been said in a five minute, two-party conversation, even when they had
been a participant. Confirmatory evidence about the inability to remember even
quite short single utterances verbatim was specially commissioned from Professor
Brian Clifford and presented at the 2003 'Glasgow Ice Cream Wars' Appeal.

Clifford's experimental evidence was used to challenge successfully the claim of several police officers that they had independently remembered, some of them for over an hour, verbatim and identically, utterances made by the accused at the time of his arrest. Clifford's experiment tested subjects' ability to remember a short, 24-word utterance and found that most people were able to recall verbatim no more than 30 to 40 per cent of what they had heard (BBC News, 17 February 2004).

By the time of the Bridgewater appeal in 1997, it was possible to provide extra evidence to support the claim that identity of expression was indeed evidence that one text was derived from the other. First, as a direct result of Johnson's work on plagiarism discussed above, which demonstrated the significance of vocabulary overlap, an analysis was done of the shared vocabulary in the two Molloy texts; it became evident that the highlighting in the extracts presented above if anything actually understates the similarities between the two texts – a closer examination revealed that there was in fact not one single word in Molloy's statement, lexical or grammatical, which did not also occur in the interview record. We have only seen a similar degree of overlap on one other occasion, when two students submitted identical essays for assessment. Ironically, in this case, the computer analysis showed the degree of similarity to be only 97 per cent – the 3 per cent apparent difference was in fact made up of one student's spelling mistakes.

In the Bridgewater case there was also secondary linguistic evidence, of a different kind, to support the claim that the interview record was both falsified and based on the statement. If we assume that the police officers had indeed, as Molloy claimed, set out to create a dialogue based on the monologue statement, they would have faced the major problem of what questions to invent in order to link forward and apparently elicit the actually pre-existing answers, which they had derived from the statement. In this scenario, one would expect there to be occasions when a question did not fit entirely successfully into the text into which it had been embedded – and indeed there are.

In a developing interview, a given police question usually links backwards lexically, repeating word(s) from the previous answer. However, in designing questions to fit a pre-existing answer, there is always the danger that this question will only link forward. For example, the original statement has a two-sentence sequence:

(21)   'They all looked shocked and were shouting at each other.'
(22)   'I heard Jimmy say 'it went off by accident'

which appears, word for word, in the interview record, except that the two sentences are separated by the question 'Who said what?'. One quickly realises that, in this context, the word 'said', although it is cataphorically unremarkable – *said* links forward to *say* – it is anaphorically odd, because the men have just been described as 'shouting'; therefore one would have expected a backward-linking, anaphorically cohesive, follow-up question to be either 'What/Why were they *shouting*?' or 'Who was *shouting* (what/at whom)?'; one would certainly not predict 'who *said* what?' The choice of 'said' is a most unexpected, if not incoherent, choice – except of course for someone who already knows that the next utterance will be 'I heard Jimmy *say* …'; then it has an evident logic and strong cohesion; and even then the 'I heard' prefacing is odd.

There are also *grammatical* misfits. For example, the two-sentence sequence from the statement 'on the settee I saw the **body** of the **boy**. **He** had …' is transformed into 'Q. Did you see the **boy's body**? Yes sir, **he** was on the settee'. The authentic statement version correctly uses the pronoun 'He' because it refers back to the 'boy' in 'the body of the boy', but the reformulated version in the police interview, 'the boy's **body**', would more likely have elicited 'it' as a referent. In addition, there are examples of *verbal process* misfit: in the exchange reproduced below, the question 'what happened' requires a report of an action or an event, but in fact the response is a description of two states, also 'borrowed' from the statement:

P.   What **happened** then?
M.   I **was appalled** and **felt sick**.

Had the question been 'how did you feel', it would, of course, have been cohesive.

There was no opportunity to test the persuasiveness of this linguistic evidence in court as, a few weeks before the date of the appeal, a test was carried out on the first page of the handwritten record of Molloy's confession, using the recently developed ESDA machine (ElectroStatic Detection Apparatus). ESDA makes it possible to read the indentations on a piece of paper that were created by someone writing on another sheet which had been resting on top of it, a sheet which may no longer even exist. For more details about the machine, see Davis (1994.) At the time when Molloy's confession was taken, the police were working within a system which required them to record interviews with suspects, contemporaneously and verbatim, in handwritten form. For the production of such handwritten records there was a special first page and then the rest of the interview was recorded on continuation sheets, a pile of which was generally available in the interview room. Typically, the recording officer would take a handful of sheets from the pile and start writing on the top sheet, laying it on one side when it was full and continuing on the next sheet and so on. In so doing, the officer, without realising it, was creating multiple copies of each page that he wrote, because he was creating indentations on the page(s) below – an officer using a ballpoint pen and pressing quite hard might make indentation copies on up to three subsequent pages. ESDA enables the analyst to read this 'secret' writing, by making the indentations visible.

The ESDA traces of the Molloy confession revealed both the last few lines of the confession which, Molloy had always insisted, had been read out while he was being persuaded to make his own, and the forged signature of the supposed confessee. The credibility of the police evidence was destroyed at a stroke, the three surviving 'murderers' were released immediately and their convictions quashed shortly afterwards, without the need to present the linguistic evidence.

The evidential value of single identical strings

In the Bridgewater Four case, as we have just seen, there were a number of identical strings of words to support the claim that the interview record was derived from the statement and the claim of fabrication was supported by other linguistic evidence of a different and independent kind. We now ask how much weight can be placed on a single identical string and how important is the length of a string when assessing its evidential significance? These questions go to the heart of current thinking about uniqueness in language production and the strength of plagiarism evidence.

As Sinclair (1991) pointed out, there are two complementary assembly principles in the creation of utterances/sentences; one is the long-accepted principle that sequences are generated word by word on an 'open choice' basis. When strings are created in this way, there is, for each successive syntagmatic slot, a large number of possible, grammatically acceptable, paradigmatic fillers and thus one can easily, if not effortlessly, generate memorable grammatical, but meaningless, sequences like 'colorless green ideas sleep furiously'. The other assembly principle proposed much more recently, as a result of work with corpora, is the 'idiom principle', according to which pre-assembled (idiomatic) chunks, made up of frequent collocations and colligations, are linked together to create larger units. In practice, both principles work side by side, which means that any given short string might be produced by either principle, and therefore might be either an idiosyncratic combination or a frequently occurring fixed phrase, or indeed a combination of the two. However, the longer a sequence is, the more likely that at least some of its components have been created by the open choice principle and thus the more likely it is that the sequence as a whole will be a unique formulation. For this reason, the occurrence of long identical sequences in two texts is likely to be a product of borrowing.

The data we will use for exemplificatory purposes come from the appeal of Robert Brown in London in 2003. As in the Bridgewater Four case, here too there was a disputed statement and a disputed interview record; the difference was that Brown claimed that his statement was in reality a dialogue which had been represented as if it had been produced as a monologue. He claimed that a police officer had asked questions to which he had simply replied 'Yes' (Judge's Summing-up, p. 95, section E), and that, although the interview did occur, the record of it was made up afterwards – 'no police officer took any notes' (Judge's Summing–up, p. 93, section E).

Below are two sentences from the statement matched with items occurring in the (disputed) interview record:

i)   Statement   I asked her if I could carry her bags she said 'Yes'
       Interview   I asked her if I could carry her bags and she said 'yes'

ii)   Statement   I picked something up like an ornament
      Interview   I picked something up like an ornament

The figures below were taken in 2002 from the Google search engine. Google was used, rather than a corpus such as the *Bank of English* or the *British National Corpus*, on the grounds that it was easily accessible to any layperson, for whom the argument was specifically designed – they could go home afterwards and test the claims for themselves, provided, of course, they didn't do it on case-related data. While the above paired utterances/sentences may not seem remarkable in themselves, neither occurred even once in the hundreds of millions of texts that Google searched and, as can be seen below, even the component sequences quickly became rare occurrences:

Sequence	*Instances*
I picked	1,060,000
I picked something	780
I picked something up	362
I picked something up like	1
I picked something up like an	0
an ornament	73,700
like an ornament	896
something like an ornament	2
I asked	2,170,000
I asked her	284,000
I asked her if	86,000
I asked her if I	10,400
I asked her if I could	7,770
I asked her if I could carry	7
I asked her if I could carry her	4
I asked her if I could carry her bags	0

It is evident that 'if I could' and perhaps 'I asked her' have the characteristics of pre-assembled idioms, in Sinclair's sense, but even then their co-selection in the same sequence is rare, at 7,770 occurrences. The moment a seventh word, 'carry', was added, the odds against the sequence occurring became enormous, with only seven instances.

From evidence like this we can assert that even a sequence as short as 12 running words and many much shorter sequences, have a very high chance of being unique occurrences. Indeed, rarity scores like these begin to look like the probability scores that DNA experts proudly present in court. The next few years will tell whether courts are willing to place the same reliance on certain kinds of linguistic evidence.

Coda

As the number of texts Google searches increases, the likelihood of phrases being unique necessarily falls. Fourteen years later, on 16 November 2015, there were now 14 examples of 'I picked something up like an ornament' which seems to contradict the claim above of uniqueness, but thankfully this is a case of the exception proving the rule. What Google found was a set of 14 repetitions of the same unique utterance, either in texts that I myself had written about the case or in texts written by others reporting my analysis. And while the nine-word sequence 'I asked her if I could carry her bags' now has 20 occurrences, five of them in different linguistic contexts, the full phrase 'I asked her if I could carry her bags and she said "yes"' is still unique.

Further reading

Johnson and Woolls (2009); Pecorari (2010); Sousa-Silva (2014); Coulthard, Johnson, Kredens and Woolls (2010); Woolls (2012).

Research tasks

1 On plagiarism
Examine the official definition of plagiarism in your own institution, discover what the penalties are and study the documents that give advice to students on how to avoid plagiarising. Then devise a questionnaire to discover answers to: (i) how well do your colleagues understand the rules and know the penalties; (ii) what are their views on the penalties; and (iii) what solutions do they propose for reducing the problem?

2 Patchwriting
Here are two texts ((a) and (b)) taken from biographies of Andrew Carnegie – are the similarities sufficient to suggest *patchwriting*? If you think so, get copies of both books and check whether this is an isolated instance or a more general writing strategy.
  (a)   With all of these problems it was little short of a miracle that the 'stichting' board was ready to lay the cornerstone for the building in the summer of 1907 at the opening of the Second Hague International Conference. It then took six more years before the Palace was completed during which time there continued to be squabbles over details, modifications of architectural plans and lengthy discussions about furnishings. For ten years the Temple of Peace was a storm of controversy, but at last, on 28 August 1913, the Grand Opening ceremonies were held.

(J.F. Wall, *Andrew Carnegie*, 1970)

  (b)   The foundation stone was not laid until the summer of 1907, in nice time for the opening of the Second Hague International Conference. Actual construction of the palace took a further six years, delayed and exacerbated by constant bickering over details, specifications and materials. For an entire decade the Peace Palace was bedevilled by controversy, but finally, on 28 August 1913, the opening ceremony was performed.

(J. Mackay, *Little Boss: A Life of Andrew Carnegie*, 1997)

3 Web plagiarism
Stage 1 *Textual 'Creation' and Detection*
Work in pairs
  (i)   First create a 1,000-word essay on a topic of your choice by taking extracts from Internet texts and pasting them together – each extract must be at least 80 words long and at most 120.
  (ii) Make two versions of each 'essay' – the first with minimal sewing together. For the second spend 90 minutes making it into a readable text.

(iii) Then exchange version 2 with your partner and see how many of the extracts they can find on the Internet. Then exchange version 1 and do the same.

Stage 2 *Reflection on the process of plagiarising*
(iv) What have you learned about the detection of web plagiarism?

10 The linguist as expert witness

> It is crucial for linguists to remain outside the advocacy that attorneys are …
> required to have. Linguists must carry out their analyses in such a way that the
> same results would occur if they were working for the other side.
>
> (Shuy 2002a: 4)

> Prof Meadow wrongly stated in Mrs Clark's trial in 1999 that there was just a 'one
> in 73 million' chance that two babies from an affluent family like hers could suffer
> cot death. The actual odds were only one in 77.
>
> (*The Guardian*, Friday 15 July 2005)

On being an expert witness

Some readers may aspire to become an expert witness, so we must emphasise
at the outset that we know of only one forensic linguist and very few forensic
phoneticians who work full time as expert witnesses – for the moment at
least, it is essentially a part-time profession. The first problem is to get
contracted as no one wants to brief an expert with no experience, so often the
only way to gain entry is by first undertaking *pro bono* work. Then there is
the question of who contracts the expert; in the adversarial system it is the
lawyers of one side or the other, while in the investigative system it is typically the judge and the court, even when both sides have already commissioned expert reports.

Working as an expert witness can be a lonely profession, because the majority
of experts work alone, on occasional cases, and rarely go to court to give
evidence; most of them average fewer than ten cases a year and one court appearance every two years. For this reason, giving evidence in person in court is, for
the majority of forensic linguists, an uncommon and stressful event. As Shuy
(2002a: 5–6) observes:

> For those who have never experienced cross-examination, there is no way to
> emphasize how emotionally draining it can be. … Testifying is not for the
> weak at heart.

Nor indeed for the weak at stomach – one colleague eventually gave up, after some 25 years as an expert witness, saying he could no longer cope with vomiting before every appearance in the witness box.

There are frustrations as well. Maley (2000: 250) observes, in an excellent paper examining linguistic aspects of expert testimony, that:

> expert witnesses, particularly if they are new and inexperienced, tend to be quite unaware of the extent to which shaping and construction of evidence goes on. ... All too often they emerge frustrated from the courtroom, believing that they have not been able to give their evidence in the way they would like and that their evidence has been twisted or disbelieved.

and this despite the fact that experts are allowed speaking turns on average two to three times longer than those of other witnesses (Heffer 2005: 101).

Intending experts, ever more frequently are seeking professional training to enable them to cope more successfully with cross-examination, but even experienced experts can still struggle with two courtroom specific interactional conventions. The first is the suspension, for the lawyer, of the Gricean conversational maxim of *quality*, that is 'do not say what you believe to be false' and its converse 'say what you believe to be true', in a situation in which the experts themselves have been required to commit themselves explicitly, by oath or affirmation, to telling the truth. Novice academic experts may be deceived into thinking that they are still in an academic environment and that, if they are sufficiently coherent and persuasive, they can not only convince the cross-examiner of the correctness of their opinion, but also get overt acknowledgement. The lawyer, of course, is paid to not be convinced, or at least not to admit that s/he has been convinced.

The second convention, which disorients all witnesses, expert and lay alike, is that, whilst the examining lawyer is in one sense both the speaker and the addressor, or, as Goffman (1981: 79) puts it, 'the author of the sentiments that are being expressed and the words in which they are encoded', the court convention is that s/he is actually acting as a spokesperson for the court and simply asking questions and raising doubts on its behalf. The expert needs to remember that it is the judge and jury who need to be convinced. The physical consequence of this is that the witness is expected to treat the judge(s), and the jury, if there is one, as addressee(s) and therefore to look at and direct answers to them and not to the lawyer who is asking the questions. This can be particularly difficult in some courts, where the physical layout places the lawyer, judge and jury in such positions that the witness cannot face both the questioner and the addressee(s) at the same time. For this reason, having turned to look at the speaker/lawyer who is asking the question, the witness may fail to turn back to direct the answer to the real addressee(s) and may even be reprimanded by the judge.

Admissible evidence

We have seen in previous chapters examples of most of the areas in which forensic linguists and phoneticians feel they have something to offer as expert witnesses and in which they have been willing to write reports. We will now look at the reaction of the courts to such evidence.

For linguists wanting to move into expert witness work, the criteria vary from country to country. Up to now Australia and Britain have shared essentially the same position, which is that it is the expert rather than the method that is approved and so courts can allow opinion evidence from anyone considered to have:

> specialised knowledge based on ... training, study or experience [provided that the opinion is] wholly or substantially based on that knowledge. (Australian Evidence Act 1995, s 79)

Usually, once an expert has been accepted by one court, s/he will be accepted by other courts at the same level and rarely challenged. The expert is retained and paid by one side, but, even so, is legally responsible to the court. Indeed, since 2007, experts in Britain have been required to state explicitly in their written reports that they are aware of their duty to the court and of the necessity to make the court aware of any counter-evidence in the data they have analysed. They also must retain all working notes and any drafts or earlier versions of reports and these can be requested at any time by the court and/or the other side – the situation is radically different in the US, where the expert's loyalty is exclusively to the client and earlier drafts of reports may be deliberately destroyed.

So far, for Anglo-Australian lawyers there have been no explicit requirements, as there are in the USA following the three Daubert rulings (see below), about the nature of the expert's theoretical position, nor about the particular methodology and evidence on which the expert bases his/her opinion. So, once an expert has been retained, it is up to the court to determine, '*ad hoc,* the sufficiency of [his/her] expertise and the relevance of that expertise' (Bromby 2002: 9). As part of this process both the competence of the expert and the reliability of the method(s) s/he has used can be subjected to detailed examination in court and this can last for many hours. In one case in which Coulthard was called to give evidence, the judge sent the jury home before lunch and took the whole of the afternoon session to hear legal argument about the admissibility of his evidence and then had him examined and cross-examined for over an hour, before he eventually decided to allow him to give evidence in open court the following day. For details of the case, search for David Hodgson + *Northern Echo* 19 Feb 2008. This case is also discussed in Chapter 8.

Even after deciding to allow an expert to give evidence, the judge(s) and/or jury may decide it is not helpful, persuasive or relevant and simply ignore it and occasionally, at the end of a trial, experts are severely censured by the court and particular methodologies deemed to be unacceptable, as in: 'in our judgment, although Professor Canter is clearly an expert in his field, the evidence tendered from him was not expert evidence of a kind properly to be placed before the court' (*Gilfoyle (No 2)* [2001] 2 Cr App R 5 (57), §25).

Expert evidence can also be a grounds for appeal, as happened in the case of David Hodgson, mentioned above, when Coulthard's evidence on the authorship of text messages was challenged on the grounds that 'it was not a proper subject for expert evidence' (*R v Hodgson* [2009] EWCA Crim 742 §42). However, the judgment confirmed the acceptability of the linguistic evidence and commented that Coulthard had emphasised sufficiently clearly that it was not possible on linguistic grounds to identify the accused as 'the' author, but only one of an admittedly small group of 'possible' authors. It is relevant to remember here McMenamin's (2002: 129) observation that 'in the courtroom, qualitative evidence is more demonstrable than quantitative evidence because it is the language data that are presented'. He goes on to claim that 'qualitative results appeal to the nonmathematical but structured sense of probability held by judges and juries'.

The position of British and Australian courts on expert evidence means, as far as linguistic evidence is concerned, that almost all of the techniques and resulting expert opinions discussed in the previous four chapters are acceptable, with the exception of auditory evidence in speaker identification cases. French long ago warned that:

> despite a recent English Court of Criminal Appeal ruling (*R v. Robb* 1991) that forensic speaker identification evidence based upon auditory analysis alone is admissible in a criminal trial, its shortcomings are quite apparent. (1994: 173)

and this observation was prophetic, because a recent ruling in Northern Ireland has forbidden such unsupported evidence, although for the moment this is only 'persuasive' rather than 'binding' in the other two jurisdictions – England and Wales, and Scotland (French personal communication).

Unlike the Anglo-Australian system, the American legal system approves the technique(s) that a witness, uses rather than the witness him/herself. This topic will be resumed later in the chapter.

Expressing opinions

Once the analysis has been done and an opinion reached, the expert is faced with two communicative problems: firstly, how can s/he best explain the analysis and express the derived opinions in a report written originally for an audience of legal professionals and secondly, if later called on to give oral evidence in court, how can s/he cope with the unusual interactional rules discussed in detail in Chapter 5. McMenamin (2002: 176–78) has a useful section on report writing, while Roger Shuy's *Linguistics in the Courtroom: a Practical Guide* is very useful for those who are called to testify.

In 2002, Stuart Campbell was tried and convicted for the murder of his niece Danielle Jones. Part of the evidence against him was two short text messages sent to his phone from Danielle's phone shortly after she disappeared. The prosecution suspected that he had sent them to himself using her phone and Coulthard was asked to compare the style of the two suspect messages with a set of 70 which Danielle had sent over the previous three days; unfortunately there was no similar corpus of texts composed by Campbell to use for comparison purposes. Below is the first of the suspect messages:

HIYA STU WOT U UP 2.IM IN SO MUCH TRUBLE AT HOME AT MOMENT EVONE HATES ME EVEN U! WOT THE HELL AV I DONE NOW? Y WONT U JUST TELL ME TEXT BCK PLEASE LUV DAN XXX

This message displays a series of linguistic choices which were either absent from, or rare in, the Danielle corpus: the use of capitals rather than sentence case, the spelling of 'what' as 'wot', the spelling in full of the morpheme 'one' in 'EVONE', rather than its substitution by the numeral '1', the omission of the definite article in the abbreviation of the prepositional phrase 'AT MOMENT' and the use of the full form of the word 'text' rather than an abbreviation in the phrase TEXT BCK. The problem was how to reach and then express an opinion on the likelihood that Danielle did or did not produce this message.

Expressing opinions semantically

The majority of forensic linguists and phoneticians have traditionally felt that they were unable to express their findings statistically in terms of mathematical probability and so have chosen to express them as a semantically encoded opinion. Indeed, some experts simply express their opinion without giving any indication to the court of how to evaluate its strength, or of how that opinion fits with the two legally significant categories of 'on the balance of probabilities' and 'beyond reasonable doubt'. During the 90s and at the beginning of this century, a growing number of experts, following the lead of the British Forensic Science Service, were using a fixed semantic scale, which they attached as an Appendix to their report, to enable the reader to assess the expert's level of confidence in their opinion. All members of the International Association of Forensic Phonetics also attached a note warning that their evidence should only be used corroboratively in criminal cases, because it was their collective opinion that it was not possible to establish the identity of a speaker with absolute certainty.

At the time of the Danielle case, Coulthard was using the scale of opinions below, adapted from the scale being used at the time by members of the International Association of Forensic Phoneticians:

Most Positive

5	'I am personally *satisfied* that X is the author'
4	'It is in my view *very likely* that X is the author'
3	'It is in my view *likely* that X is the author'
2	'It is in my view *fairly likely* that X is the author'
1	'It is in my view *rather more likely than not* that X is the author'
0	'It is in my view *possible* that X is the author'
−1	'It is in my view *rather more likely than not* that X is *not* the author'

-2   'It is in my view *fairly likely* that X is *not* the author'
-3   'It is in my view *likely* that X is *not* the author'
-4'   'It is in my view *very likely* that X is *not* the author'
-5   'I am personally *satisfied* that X is the *not* author'

Most Negative

The opinion Coulthard gave was –2 on the above scale, that is that it was *fairly likely* that Danielle had *not* written the text message. Broeders (1999) suggested that what was actually happening in such cases was that:

> experts, in using degrees of probability, are actually making categorical judgements, i.e. are really saying yes or no. Even if they use a term like *probably (not)*, I think they are subjectively convinced that the suspect did or did not produce the sample material.
>
> (Broeders 1999: 237)

Broeders went on to observe that the choice of a given degree of likelihood on a scale like this is irremediably subjective, which is why two experts might reach opinions of differing strengths based on exactly the same data. Even so, he stressed that a subjective judgement should not be condemned simply because it is subjective:

> The crucial question is not whether [it] is subjective or objective, but whether it can be relied on to be correct.
>
> (Broeders 1999: 238)

Nevertheless, a growing body of opinion is opposed to the use of such semantic scales, especially because, even when they *are* accepted by a court, an unsolvable problem remains – how can one be sure that judges and juries will attach the same meanings to the labels as did the experts who chose and applied them? This point was brought home to Coulthard in a court martial where he expressed his opinion as 'very likely' on the above 11-point scale and another expert expressed her opinion as 'very strong support' on a 9-point scale. Neither was allowed to tell the judges how many points there were on their respective scales, although the defence lawyer did his best to persuade the other expert to lower her opinion from 'very strong' to 'strong'.

An added and very serious complication is that, at the end of a trial, the triers of fact themselves are not allowed the luxury of degrees of confidence; they have to work with a binary choice of 'Guilty' or 'Not Guilty'. So, however hedged the individual expert's opinion is when s/he presents it, the judge and jury have ultimately to make a categorical judgement as to whether to interpret the evidence as supportive of the prosecution or the defence case or as simply inconclusive.

Expressing opinions statistically

Broeders (1999: 238) argued that one should be worried about opinions expressed semantically, not because they are subjective, but rather because far too often the experts who use them are expressing their opinions in the wrong way. Broeders (1999: 229) and later Rose (2002) noted that an expert can offer an opinion on two apparently similar, but in fact crucially different, things: **either**, on the probability of a hypothesis – so in linguistic cases, on the hypothesis that the accused is the speaker/author – given the strength of the evidence which the expert has analysed; **or** on the probability that the evidence would occur in the form and quantity in which it does occur, given the *two* hypotheses that the accused is and, crucially also, is *not* the speaker/author.

Both authors recommend the second approach. Indeed, Rose quotes Aitken (1995: 4) in arguing that the former type of opinion, which, he says, is tantamount to deciding on the likelihood of the accused being guilty, is the exclusive role of the judges of fact and for this reason all responsible scientists must confine themselves to talking about the likelihood of the evidence. Rose supports his argument by pointing out that no expert can make an estimate of the likelihood of guilt or innocence on the basis of the linguistic evidence alone; only those with access to all the available evidence can assess the value of each piece. So, for example, a forensic handwriting colleague, after exhaustive comparisons, concluded that it was 'very likely' on the basis of the evidence he had analysed, that a disputed signature, written with a ballpoint pen, was genuine. But then, fortunately before committing his opinion to paper, he realised that the signature was dated before ballpoint pen technology had been invented.

Broeders and Rose both argue that not only is their approach logically correct, but also it has the added advantage that it enables probability to be expressed mathematically rather than semantically. Essentially the method involves first looking at the *likelihood* of the prosecution hypothesis given the raw data on each of the particular features being examined. For example, imagine an anonymous letter, which includes the non-standard spelling 'ofcourse'. In support of the prosecution hypothesis, that the accused wrote the letter, we discover that 80 per cent of a sample of attested letters written by the suspect also display this feature. However, in support of the defence hypothesis that the accused was not the author, we discover that, in the general population, writers use the feature 10 per cent of the time. How do we now assess the evidential strength of this finding; that is, that while there is a 10 per cent chance that any letter would include 'ofcourse' the chances of a letter written by the suspect including it is very much higher?

To start with, we produce a *likelihood ratio* by dividing one percentage by the other, so we divide 80 by 10 to produce a likelihood ratio of 8. So far so good. However, interpretation of the ratio is not quite so simple. It is certainly true that, as Broeders (1999: 230) expresses it, 'to the extent that the likelihood ratio exceeds 1 the evidence lends greater support to the [prosecution] hypothesis, [while] if it is smaller than 1 it supports the alternative hypothesis'. Unfortunately, that does not tell us exactly how much greater support a likelihood ratio of 8 gives – we will return to this question of interpretation below.

A major advantage of this method of expressing the weight of evidence statistically is that it allows the user to combine the likelihood ratios of several pieces of evidence, by multiplication, in order to produce a composite likelihood ratio. So, to continue our imaginary example, there might be a series of other distinctive features co-occurring in the anonymous and attested letters like 'their' spelled as 'there', 'you're' spelled as 'your' and possessive 'its' spelled as 'it's'. These features may be found in themselves to have low likelihood ratios of, respectively, 1.4, 1.5, 1.7, but when they are combined with the likelihood ratio of 8 already calculated for 'ofcourse', they produce, by multiplication, the much higher ratio of 28.56. In other words, after examining the four features, we can now say on a principled basis that it is 28 times more likely that the letter would include these four items if the suspect had written it.

One strong argument in favour of this mathematical approach is that it allows the easy incorporation of counter-indications as well. Whereas experts using the 'evidence to evaluate the hypothesis approach', as Coulthard was in the Campbell case, have to decide what weight to give to any evidence which does not support the indication of the majority of the features analysed – should they, for example, allow such evidence to reduce their opinion by one or two degrees of certainty or by none at all? By contrast, with a likelihood ratio approach, any measurement which supports the defence hypothesis, and so by definition has a likelihood ratio of less than 1, will simply reduce the cumulative ratio. So let us now imagine we add in the feature 'whose' spelled as 'who's', which has a ratio for the letters under consideration of 0.85; the cumulative ratio will now fall to 24.28.

While such a mathematical approach has obvious attractions, it does present very real problems to both phoneticians and linguists when they try to calculate the defence likelihood ratio. First, how does one establish what is a relevant comparison population of speakers or texts and how does one get access to, and then analyse, the data from that population, particularly in a world where lawyers and courts are not willing to pay for what might be thought to be basic research. At least in the area of forensic phonetics there are already agreed reference tables for such things as pitch of voice, as well as solid evidence about the effects of telephone transmission on the pitch of the first formants of vowels. In the area of linguistics there is much less reference data, although specialist corpora are being created. McMenamin, for instance (2002: 154), reports using a corpus of 742 letters for comparison purposes, while of course for some purposes (see Coulthard 1993, 1994b), evidence can be drawn from general corpora such as the Australian National Corpus, the British National Corpus, the Collins Bank of English and the Corpus of Contemporary American English.

But then, even if we are able to calculate the defence ratios, we are still not out of the trees, because we need to know how to evaluate the significance of the resulting composite likelihood ratios. And there is still the added problem of whether a lay jury can cope with likelihood ratios, or whether their use will simply introduce even greater confusion.

Rose (2002: 62) proposed solving this problem by grouping numerical likelihood ratios into five semantically labelled categories, which, he suggests, should then be transparent to the jury:

Likelihood ratio	Semantic Gloss
10,000+	Very strong
1,000–10,000	Strong
100–1,000	Moderately strong
10–100	Moderate
1–10	Limited

However, such a translation is by no means universally accepted and Professor Meadow, who was referred to in the epigraph at the beginning of the chapter, had a much more persuasive translation – he created what came to be known as 'Meadow's Law': 'one sudden infant death is a *tragedy*, two is *suspicious* and three is *murder*, unless proven otherwise'.

Even if one accepts Rose's argument for the theoretical advantages of his mathematically calculated likelihood ratio, there remain two major doubts. First, after rejecting a scale of *opinions* expressed semantically, we have ended up with a scale of *likelihoods* expressed semantically, although admittedly, in this case, if two experts agree on the facts to be considered they will necessarily agree on the likelihood ratio too. Even so, the same problem remains of whether juries can and will interpret the semantic expressions of the ratios as the expert intended. Second, we do not yet know how appropriate the labels are as glosses for the ratios, even though the category cut-off points are numerically neat.

In principle though, the judicial system should be attracted by the fact that likelihood ratios derived from a variety of types of evidence can be combined to produce a composite likelihood ratio. In an ideal Rosean world, juries would have a statistician to help them weigh all the evidence.

Despite obvious academic support for the use of likelihood ratios, it may be a long time before they get general acceptance in courts, if they ever do. *The Times* (9 May 1996: 36) reported an Appeal Court judgment (*R v Adams*) where, in the original trial, a statistician had been allowed to instruct the jury, firstly about both the Bayes theorem and the underlying likelihood ratios and then about how to create and sum the ratios in order to produce a composite ratio. The Appeal Court judges ordered a retrial and observed that, although the likelihood ratio 'might be an appropriate and useful tool for statisticians ... it was not appropriate for use in jury trials, nor as a means to assist the jury in their tasks'. After a second trial, in which the same expert was allowed to instruct a different jury in the same way, there was a second appeal, at the end of which the judges opined:

> Introducing Bayes' Theorem, or any similar method, into a criminal trial plunges the jury into inappropriate and unnecessary realms of complexity, deflecting them from their proper tasks. Reliance on evidence of this kind is a recipe for confusion, misunderstanding, and misjudgement.
>
> (Sanderson, S.M., 10 October 2006)

And that, for the moment, is the situation in the British courts: experts are still able to express opinions without relating them to probabilities or likelihood ratios. So what should linguists do when their findings cannot be appropriately presented in a mathematical way? Firstly, in 2007 a group of UK forensic phoneticians, produced a position statement (French and Harrison, 2007), in which they noted that while in principle they accepted:

> the desirability of considering the task of speaker comparison in a likelihood ratio (including Bayesian) conceptual framework ... the lack of demographic data, along with the problems of defining relevant reference populations, [were] grounds for precluding the quantitative application of this type of approach in the present context. (2007: 142)

For this reason they set the goal as that of assessing whether a particular questioned voice fitted the description of the suspect voice. Such an assessment is a two-stage process. First, the analyst assesses the voice in terms of the compatibility of its features with those of the suspect voice. In this stage there are three possible outcomes: a negative decision that the two voices are *not compatible*, in which case the voice is excluded, or that there is simply *insufficient evidence to proceed*, in which case no more analysis is undertaken, or that the voices are *compatible*. A compatible decision essentially means that it is impossible to *exclude* the voice as a potential match. Only in such cases does the analyst move on to the second stage of analysis, when the compatibility is assessed in terms of the degree of distinctiveness of the shared items, distinctiveness measured on a five point scale ranging from 'not distinctive' to 'exceptionally distinctive'. As Rose and Morrison (2009: 142) observe 'it is implied [though not statistically demonstrated] that the likelihood that the samples have been produced by the same speaker will be greater if their shared cluster of features is distinctive or unusual'

However, in 2008 the British Government appointed a former police Detective Chief Superintendant as the first Forensic Science Regulator. His brief was to 'operate independently to ensure that quality standards apply across all forensic science services' (http://police.homeoffice.gov.uk/operational-policing/forensic-science-regulator/about-the-regulator/). In 2009, the Regulator published a consultation paper on forensic practitioner registration, which recommended that an accreditation system be set up based on internationally recognised ISO standards and assessed by the UK Accreditation Service (UKAS).

At the same time, the UK Law Commission also published a consultation paper on the admissibility of expert evidence in which they observed 'We believe the current approach to the admissibility of expert evidence in criminal trials is in need of reform' (2009: iii). In their opinion:

> The [UK] criminal courts have ... adopted a policy of *laissez-faire*. In effect [they] permit the adduction of any expert evidence, so long as it is not patently unreliable, [as a consequence] juries are not denied access to evidence which might be helpful. (2009: 22)

They attributed this problem, at least in part, to a basic flaw in the system: 'there is little if any guidance for trial judges ... faced with the task of having to screen expert evidence to determine the question of admissibility' (2009: 16). The solution the Law Commission went on to propose was the creation of a new statutory test for determining the admissibility of expert evidence in criminal proceedings, which is likely to be modelled on the system currently in force in the US, the Daubert test, to which we will now turn. British forensic linguists await the outcome with great interest and in some quarters with some trepidation, after reading Tiersma and Solan (2002). If a Daubert-type system is introduced, some currently accepted methodologies may be disallowed and others may need to be modified to meet the Daubert criteria.

Daubert criteria

Rule 702 of the US Federal Rules of Evidence allows an expert to testify as a witness if:

> the testimony is based upon sufficient facts or data, [and]
> the testimony is the product of reliable principles and methods, and
> the witness has applied the principles and methods reliably to the facts of the case.

Rule 702 is designed to take account of the 1993 Daubert Ruling which dramatically changed the nature of allowable evidence and distanced the American system even further from the Anglo-Australian one. In what follows we draw substantially on Tiersma and Solan (2002) and Solan and Tiersma (2004), which readers are advised to study in their entirety.

There have been three stages in defining the admissibility of expert evidence in the US. Until 1975, the main standard for evaluating expert testimony was the Frye test, named after a ruling in a 1923 case involving the admissibility of lie detector evidence, which required there to be general acceptability of the principles and/or methodology which the expert had used:

> while courts will go a long way in admitting expert testimony deduced from a well-recognized scientific principle or discovery, the thing from which the deduction is made must be sufficiently established to have gained general acceptance in the particular field in which it belongs.
> (293 F. at 1014, as quoted in Tiersma and Solan 2002: 223)

As time went by Frye came to be seen to be too rigorous. It was argued that scientific knowledge advances by argument and dissent, so there was pressure to allow the judge and/or jury to hear opinions from both sides when there was serious academic disagreement and in 1975 the Federal Rules of Evidence were introduced with the following observation on the admissibility of expert evidence:

if scientific, technical, or other specified knowledge will assist a trier of fact to understand the evidence or to determine a fact in issue, a witness qualified as an expert by knowledge, skill, experience, training, or education, may testify thereto in the form of an opinion or otherwise.

(Rule 702 as quoted in Tiersma and Solan 2002: 223)

Even so, and confusingly, some federal courts continued to apply Frye until 1993, when the Supreme Court ruled in the case of *Daubert v Merrell Dow Pharmaceuticals*. The main argument in that appeal was over whether expert evidence could be rejected on the grounds that the experts involved had not published their work and had thereby failed to meet the Frye test. In their ruling the Supreme Court observed that 'the adjective "scientific" implies a grounding in the methods and procedures of science' and then went on to propose four criteria with which to evaluate 'scientific-ness':

1   whether the theory ... has been tested;
2   whether it has been subjected to peer review and publication;
3   the known rate of error; and
4   whether the theory is generally accepted in the scientific community.

(509 US at 593 as quoted in Tiersma and Solan 2002)

This ruling left open the question of whether it covered evidence which was descriptive rather than theoretical, but a ruling in 1999, in the case of *Kumho Tire Co. v Carmichael*, confirmed that it did:

'the general principles of Daubert' apply not only to experts offering scientific evidence, but also to experts basing their testimony on experience.

(119 S.Ct. 1173 as quoted in Tiersma and Solan 2002: 224)

So, where does that leave the American forensic linguist? On the positive side, Tiersma and Solan (2002: 221) note that:

courts have allowed linguists to testify on issues such as the probable origin of a speaker, the comprehensibility of a text, whether a particular defendant understood the Miranda warning, and the phonetic similarity of two competing trademarks.

However, in other areas the situation is more problematic, partly, perhaps, because non-linguists have claimed ownership of the labels for linguistic concepts. The Van Wyk case in 2000 seemed to set a precedent for excluding *stylistic analysis*, as the court refused to allow the expert to give evidence about the authorship of disputed documents, but, as McMenamin (2002) points out, the expert in the case had no qualifications in linguistics. McMenamin (2004) argues a strong case for the scientific nature of his own brand of forensic stylistics and therefore for its acceptability under Daubert. Indeed he demonstrates a way of expressing opinions statistically in terms of mathematically calculated probabilities, in a case study of the significant documents in the JonBenét Ramsey case (McMenamin 2004: 193–205). It appears that the linguistic area of *discourse analysis* may have suffered similar loss of credibility through a non-linguist claiming expertise. Tiersma and Solan quote a judge's observation in a 1984 case, *State v Conway*, following evidence from a psychologist, that discourse analysis is a 'discipline allowing [the expert] to determine the intent of the speaker in covertly recorded conversations', which shows just how much re-education needs to be done.

Nevertheless, it must be conceded that, in cases where conclusions depend on observations about the frequency or rarity of particular linguistic features in the texts under examination, many linguists would have considerable difficulty in stating a 'known rate of error' for their results. It is for this reason that some linguists will be forced to change their way of reaching and presenting their opinions, while others may choose to see their role more as that of 'tour guides' than opinion givers (Solan 1998).

So we have a situation where many UK linguists and phoneticians are aspiring to express their findings statistically in terms of likelihood ratios or probabilities, but are actually using a method which cannot provide the error rates which Daubert seems to see as essential. There appear to be three ways forward for this community. Firstly, the creation of more and larger databases, which will enable linguists to derive more reliable population statistics. Secondly, as it is already acknowledged that some experts are better than others, it would be possible to test the success rate of individual experts though some kind of Proficiency Testing (Solan 2012), and then to place greater reliance on their opinions – 'perhaps proficiency testing could serve as an intermediate level of validation, while a field conducts research into replicable methods' (Solan 2012: 405). Thirdly, linguists can engage in more research of the kind reported by Grant (2010) into discovering statistical methods that will enable them to express statistically the significance of their opinions.

As noted in earlier chapters, one major difficulty for forensic linguists involved with authorship attribution is that typically the amount of questioned data is small and there are no useful population statistics. In one case, Grant was faced with the problem of deciding whether the author of a series of messages, texted from a mobile phone, had changed part way through the sequence – a husband was suspected of having murdered his wife and then sent messages, from her phone to imply that she was still alive. Earlier analyses of text messages by linguists had been criticised, because it was argued that they had 'cherry-picked' the textual items they had focused on and may therefore have exaggerated the strength of their findings. Grant used a different strategy; he took all the known texts produced by husband and wife and examined all the individual components – both full words and abbreviations – classified them into three categories in terms of differential preferences: wife's preferences, shared preferences and husband's preferences, using a pre-defined frequency measure. He was then able to show that after a particular point in the temporal sequence the questioned messages changed from containing a majority of the wife's and shared choices to a majority of shared and the husband's choices (See Chapter 8).

In a recent case Coulthard was faced with a dispute about the authorship of a single email consisting of a mere 140 words. This time there were large numbers of known emails produced by the two candidate authors. Adopting and adapting the Grant methodology it was possible to show that of the 13 words and phrases in the email for which one or other of the candidate authors was the only user, 11 belonged to candidate author A and only 2 to candidate author B. Some of A's preferences are highlighted in bold in Extract 10.1 below which are taken from the disputed email. In extract 10.2 there are six lines taken from A's emails where he is seen to be using some of the same words and phrases.

Extract 10.1 (Extract from disputed email)
Strictly Private and Confidential
… We do not know the source of these rhumours, which may be from **disgruntled** (current/**former**) **employees** or unsuccessful **competitors** …
… One of the **rhumours** being **peddle**d is that becase of the delay in the finalization
… of the XXX contract, we may have **recognised** some **revenue** asso-caited with that work.
… In addition, all the cost of supporting the HIS bid to date have been **fully expensed**

Extract 10.2
Strictly Private and Confidential
… that it emanates from a **disgruntled former employee** seeking to further a particular selfish personal agenda.
… The balance of the NPfiT-related **revenue recognized …**
… there is little evidence that the malicious **rumours peddled** by the *Guardian*

Measuring success statistically

As Solan (2012) observed, in the long term 'the basic concern, in developing methods that will be acceptable in court, is to develop and test these methods outside the litigation context' (p. 404). There is already a considerable body of stylometric and algorithmic authorship research produced by computational linguists 'outside the litigation context'. As Solan (2013: 574) acknowledges, these computer scientists 'are accustomed to testing their algorithms to see how well they work and reporting the rate of error'. However, such algorithmic work is often of very little practical use in forensic contexts. One reason is that, although the algorithms are very successful in discriminating between authors, or in matching anonymised texts with a candidate author, there is so far no *linguistic* explanation for why the algorithm works. Grant (2008: 226) highlights the different interests of stylometric authorship analysts and forensic linguistic practitioners. He notes that, while in the computational discipline of text mining,

> it might be reasonable to sacrifice linguistic validity ... to discover an authorship algorithm, but, in the forensic field the analyst must be able to say why ... features they describe ... distinguish between two authors in general, and why ... they distinguish between the particular authors of the case.

The implication, as Argamon and Koppel (2013: 300, 315) accept, is that without the ability to explain algorithmic results or evidence, the task of conveying the importance of such results to non-expert judges and juries is very difficult. Furthermore, Cheng (2013: 547) states that, given the complexity and underlying assumptions of sophisticated computational algorithms, 'I worry that statistical models in this context may distort more than illuminate' and thus confuse the jury.

What is required for authorship analysis in a forensic context, therefore, is a method in which the measurement of similarity or difference between authors' styles or texts is represented statistically, but explainable in linguistic terms and also, importantly, has a known error rate. Building on Grant's proposal of Jaccard's similarity coefficient (Jaccard 1912) already mentioned in Chapter 8, and answering Solan's call for experimental work outside of litigation, Johnson and Wright (2014) describe a methodology for identifying the authors of anonymised Enron emails. Work in corpus linguistics and psycholinguistics (e.g. Schmitt *et al.* 2004; Hoey 2005; Mollin 2009) has argued that that the associations that people have created between words, or in linguistic terminology their set of personal 'collocates', are unique. On this basis, Johnson and Wright (2014) set out to capture idiolectal collocations through the use of 'n-gram textbites', that is, lexical strings between two and six words long, The method involves comparing sets of disputed and known emails on the basis of the n-gram textbites that they share and was facilitated by the use of a piece of lexical analysis software called *Jangle* (Woolls 2013). The similarity between the two sets of texts is measured statistically by the Jaccard Coefficient.

Jaccard was first introduced into forensic authorship analysis by Grant (2010: 518), when he used it to analyse text messages from the Jenny Nicholl murder case. This was a purely academic exercise, of the kind Solan recommends, to test the applicability of the software, but subsequently Jaccard-based analyses were admitted in a UK criminal trial (Grant 2013) and in a US civil case (Juola 2013). Jaccard is a binary correlation analysis in that it hinges on the simple appearance or non-appearance of a particular linguistic feature in two given samples of text, the total number of times the item appears is of no significance. Jaccard is a simple calculation (essentially a percentage) which measures the degree of similarity between any two sets of data, for example two sets of emails, by calculating the fraction of the data that is shared between the two email sets and expressing it as a proportion of all the data in the sets combined. In the case of Johnson and Wright (2014), the data considered was the number of different word sequences of a given length, (n-grams) shared between two sets of emails expressed as a proportion of all the n-grams of that length in the two sets combined. Jaccard produces results between zero and 1 (or 100%), with zero indicating complete dissimilarity and 1 indicating that the two datasets are identical. For example, if 395 different three word sequences, trigrams, were found in both the 'disputed' sample of emails and the known emails of a given author, the calculation would proceed as follows:

> Trigrams shared between the disputed and known data = 395
> Trigrams in the disputed data but not in the known data = 1,959
> Trigrams in the known data but not in the disputed data = 6,413
> Total number of trigrams in both sets of data combined = 8,767
> Jaccard = 395/8,767 = 0.045

This Jaccard score is then multiplied by 100, to show the percentage of n-grams that are shared between the two datasets, in this case 4.51 per cent. In Johnson and Wright (2014) every disputed email sample was compared with both the remaining emails of the author from whom the sample had been taken, and with the full email sets of the other 175 authors in the corpus. An attribution was considered 'successful' if the highest of the 176 Jaccard scores was the one obtained when the disputed sample and known sample had been written by the same author. This showed that the disputed sample in question was more similar to the remaining emails of the same author than it was to the emails of any of the other candidate authors.

One of the advantages of using Jaccard is that non-occurrence has no effect on the overall similarity rating (Woodhams *et al.* 2007: 18; Grant 2010: 518). In other words, in a comparison of two authors' writings, the fact that they both *do not* use a particular word n-gram does not affect their calculated level of similarity. This is a necessary feature because texts in forensic cases are often very short and so it is not surprising, (in fact it is absolutely predictable), that many n-grams will be absent from both sets of writing, and so the inclusion of such a factor would drive their similarity scores artificially high. Furthermore, given the simple nature of this calculation, and the ability for it to be applied quickly to any number of pair-wise author comparisons, it makes an attractive statistical tool for forensic linguists. Another very important advantage is that, because the shared data is considered in proportion to the union of the data, the Jaccard score is not dependent on or sensitive to dataset size, so two authors represented by varying sizes data can still be compared accurately. This is particularly important in forensic casework when there are often substantial size discrepancies between known and disputed documents.

Finally, the *Jangle* software provides the analyst with a list of all the word n-grams that are shared by the disputed and the known email sets, that is, those which account for the similarity statistic. Using this information, it was found that, for one author examined in Johnson and Wright (2014), the following

5 n-grams *please format and print the attachment*; *I will support your recommendation; please proceed with your; am OK with your proposal;* and *see the message below from,* were all distinctive and were important in attributing his disputed samples.

After testing this method on non-forensic data, an average error rate can be calculated: the number of times the correct author of the disputed emails was identified compared with the number of times an incorrect author was selected. Johnson and Wright (2014: 57), for example, found that in their experiment, strings of five words in length identified the correct author of a set of email messages totalling between 753 and 1,018 words in length with 100 per cent accuracy, an error rate of zero (note Chaski's 2001 caution with such rates). This result means that, in every single one of the ten tests used to attribute samples of this size, the correct author's known email set was scored as being most similar to the disputed sample. However, when the size of the disputed samples was reduced to 55–145 words, the success rate for five n-grams fell to 30 per cent, an error rate of 70 per cent. In seven of the ten tests using samples of this size, the correct author's known email set was *not* scored as being most similar to the disputed sample. Instead, the known emails of another author were judged most similar, and so the disputed sample was misattributed. It must of course be noted that this was an extremely rigorous test – in a forensic context there are regularly only two candidate authors and very, very rarely more than four.

Findings such as these in an experimental context satisfy the error rate criterion in Daubert. If applying five-grams as a means by which to attribute a disputed text (or set of texts) of a particular length in a case, we have some idea of how well, or badly, it has performed in experimental conditions.

Interestingly, there is no indication in Daubert as to what constitutes an acceptable error rate, and there is not yet a consensus in either the legal or the linguistic community as to 'how good is good enough' for a method of authorship attribution. That said, a number of studies (Zheng *et al.* 2006; Grieve 2007; Koppel *et al.* 2011) consider 70–75 per cent accuracy in an attribution task to be 'successful', 'satisfactory', or 'passable'. However, although 70 per cent success may well be good enough for research purposes, an error rate of three in ten is clearly unacceptable for a criminal trial.

And so, we await developments on the statistical front. However, we must never forget that, on the one hand, criminal courts work with the concept of 'beyond reasonable doubt', which does not have a defined statistical definition, although a lay juror, along with statistician A.P. Dawid (2001: 4), might be happy to equate the phrase with one chance in 100. On the other hand, one area of forensic investigation, DNA analysis, seems to be working with much higher probabilities:

> His counsel, Rebecca Poulet QC, reminded him of DNA evidence which showed his profile matched that of the attacker, with the chances of it being anyone else being one in a billion.
>
> (BBC News 17 February 2004)

Consulting and testifying as tour guides

An alternative role for the non-statistical linguist is offered by Solan (1998) who addresses a problem which is unique to experts in linguistics, the fact that the judges of fact, whether they be actual judges or jury members, are regarded by the legal system, for most purposes, to be their own experts in the area of language use and interpretation – the law is, much of the time, concerned with the meaning(s) that ordinary speakers attach to words and expressions. Even so, there is a role for the linguist, which is to explain and elucidate facts about language and usage, as a result of which judge and jury will then be in the same position as the linguist and so can make linguistically informed decisions. In Solan's words:

> my linguistic training has made me more sensitive to possible interpretations that others might not notice and I can bring these to the attention of a judge or jury. But once I point these out and illustrate them clearly, we should start on an equal footing. (p. 92)

To expand Solan's observation, linguists are not only 'experts in the nature of meaning' they are also experts in the nature of linguistic encoding at both lexico-grammatical and textual levels and so there is a role for the linguist to act as 'guide' in these areas as well, both before and during a trial.

Shuy (2002a: 8) notes that some lawyers prefer to use the linguist as consultant and not as expert witness:

> Some use my analysis as part of their opening and closing statements ... but the most common use ... is for cross-examination.

Shuy (2002a: 11–12) reports several examples of such assistance, one of them where a tape-recorded conversation with an undercover agent was being used by the prosecution to show the accused, a Mr Richards, apparently incriminating himself by referring to drug-related money. Richards counter-claimed that in this conversation he had in fact been referring to legal money, which he understood to be coming from Mexico. Shuy provided the attorney with a simple table showing how and by whom places were referred to in the conversation:

Place reference	By Agent	By Richards
Columbia(n)	7	0
Down south	5	0
Down there	1	4
Mexico	0	8

and the attorney was able to use this as a basis for aggressive cross-examination (Extract 10.3) to establish that his client had not in fact used any of the incriminating references; rather they had been fed into the conversation by the agent himself:

Extract 10.3

Q.   In all of your conversations you use the reference 'Colombian' seven times. Is it your experience that everyone from Colombia is a drug dealer?

A.   No, but these were.

Q.   I notice that you referred to the source of the money as coming from 'down south'. Is everyone from down south a drug dealer?

A.   No, but these guys were.

Q.   And did Richards ever use the expressions, 'Colombians', or 'drug dealers?'

A.   I think so.

Q.   You may think so, but would it surprise you to know that he never used these expressions?

A.   Yeah.

Q.   The tape speaks for itself. I assure you, there are none. But did Richards ever refer to a possible source of the money?

A.   I don't know.

Q.   Look at page 17 and at page 24. What does he say there?

A.   Mexico.

Shuy (2002a: 11)

One British example of the expert sensitising the lay audience comes from Coulthard's evidence in the appeal of *R v Robert Brown*. In Brown's disputed statement there occurs the phrase *my jeans and a blue Parka coat and a shirt*. The accused claimed that a monologue confession attributed to him had in fact been elicited by question and answer and transformed by the interviewing officers into monologue form. As part of his evidence in support of Brown's claim Coulthard focused on the two clauses:

I was covered in blood, my jeans and **a** blue Parka coat and **a** shirt were full of blood.

To a linguist it is clear that the phrasing of the subject of the second clause is most unnatural; no one would refer to their own clothes with the indefinite article, 'a', once they had begun a list with the possessive determiner 'my'. The most likely use of 'a' in this context would be to distinguish between 'mine' and 'not-mine'. For example, 'I looked round the room and I saw my jeans and a blue Parka coat and a shirt; they were full of blood' would be perfectly natural, but that meaning, of course, did not make any sense in a narrative where all the clothes referred to belonged to the narrator. The phrase 'a blue Parka coat and a shirt' could occur quite naturally, of course, as a result of a careless conversion of a sequence of short questions and answers into monologue form and one could see how it might have happened by looking at the following sequence taken from the record of an immediately preceding interview with Brown:

> What were you wearing?
> I had **a** blue shirt and **a** blue parka.

In this context the use of the indefinite article is normal; as just noted above, when items are introduced for the first time, the indefinite article is the natural choice. Once the oddity of the phrase and the occurrence of a similar phrase in the interview had been pointed out to the Appeal Court judges they were as competent as any linguist to draw inferences from this oddity.

A substitute prosecution witness

One of the important points that Solan makes is that, although juries and judges may well be able to analyse words, phrases and even sentences as well as any professional linguist, they may have problems with long documents or a series of related documents, because they may not be able to make the necessary links:

> Of course a jury can read the document[s]. ... But not all jurors, without help, can focus on a phrase in paragraph 24 of a contract that may have an impact on how another word should be interpreted in paragraph 55.
>
> (Solan 1998: 94)

In the Paul Blackburn appeal, already discussed above, the problem was to demonstrate to the judges the significance of the two pairs of phrases:

i)	Statement	I asked her if I could carry her bags she said 'Yes'
	Interview	I asked her if I could carry her bags and she said 'yes'
ii)	Statement	I picked something up like an ornament
	Interview	I picked something up like an ornament

As already noted in Chapter 9, linguists of most persuasions are in agreement that the likelihood of two speakers independently producing identical phrasings reduces dramatically with the length of the expression. However, the linguist's 'knowledge' is the opposite of lay belief. When faced with the problem of convincing the Appeal Court judges of the significance of the identical expressions, Coulthard chose the following procedure.

Firstly, using the Google figures discussed in Chapter 9, he set out to show that even short sequences of words can be unique encodings. Using this evidence Coulthard argued that, if there was not a single instance of anyone having ever produced the sequence 'I picked something up like an', the chances of even longer sequences occurring not once but twice in two supposedly independent documents was infinitesimal, unless, of course, one was derived from the other.

Then, to strengthen the argument, Coulthard used Google to find another case, this time one involving Lord Justice Rose, who was to preside at the trial. On typing in the words 'Lord', 'Justice', 'Rose' and 'Appeal' the first three citations he found were concerned with an Appeal by a famous British politician – Lord Archer – against his conviction for perjury. The first hit of all was:

> *Guardian Unlimited* – Special reports – Archer loses *appeal* bid
> ... was not present at today's hearing, had his application for permission to *appeal* against the conviction rejected within hours. *Lord Justice Rose*, sitting with ...
>
> (*Guardian Unlimited*, 22 July 2002)

Coulthard downloaded the full citation, which can be accessed at http://www.theguardian.com/politics/2002/jul/22/conservatives.uk and from it selected the first quotation from Lord Rose 'For reasons we will give later in the day'. Given the nature of Appeal Court judgments this seems to be an unremarkable phrase for an Appeal Court judge to use, particularly as a lot of judgments are produced some time after the verdict is announced. Yet a search returned only seven hits. Every single one of them was attributed to Lord Rose; indeed this was not because this was a favourite expression of his, they were in fact seven different reports of this same single utterance at the end of a trial.

Coulthard then took three other short phrases quoted in the article, this time from Nicholas Purnell, Lord Archer's lawyer, each of them apparently not unusual phrases for a lawyer to utter: 'the first and fundamental ground', an 'unbalancing effect on the equilibrium' of the trial and a 'substitute prosecution witness'. For these phrases Google found seven, ten and four instances respectively, but again all the instances were versions of the same single utterings. In other words all four sequences were unique.

This seemed to be a simple and efficient way of illustrating uniqueness of expression in court to non-linguists, but when Coulthard presented this illustration to the lawyers, they declined to submit it to the judges and one of them went so far as to describe it as 'whimsical'.

Further reading

Rose (2002, chapters 4 and 11); Shuy (2006); Solan, L. (2010); Tiersma and Solan (2002).

Research task

Work with a colleague.

Stage 1. Take the ten text messages you collected from your friend for Research Task 2 in Chapter 8 and add 20 more messages, ten produced by yourself and ten by another friend. Give the three sets of texts to your colleague and ask him/her to analyse the underlying rules. Then give your colleague your friend's version of the 'Hiya Stuart' text and ask him/her to identify the most likely author. At the same time you should undertake the same task using your colleague's set of texts.

Stage 2. Now choose one of the two cases and jointly write a formal expert's report, as if for a court, expressing and justifying your opinion and giving your degree of certainty using the 11-point scale presented on pages 197–8. Attach all the texts as an appendix. Remember that, even if you know who produced the texts, the linguistic evidence alone may not be strong enough to enable you to demonstrate that in court.

Stage 3. Finally exchange your joint report for one produced by another pair of colleagues. You should now take on the role of expert for the defence and test the strength of the case made in the other report, while they do the same with yours.

Stage 4. Select two other colleagues to act as courtroom lawyers who will examine and cross-examine the expert for the prosecution and then the expert for the defence. Ask the rest of the class, acting as jury, to indicate what weight they would give to the evidence.

11 Conclusion

> This sally into the relatively uncultivated field of 'forensic linguistics' has been interesting for a number of reasons ... Firstly, it has provided the linguist with one of those rare opportunities of making a contribution that might be directly useful to society ...
>
> (Svartvik 1968: preface)

Contributing to society

The quotation above contains the first written use of the phrase 'forensic linguistics'. It appears in Jan Svartvik's 1968 report about the authorship analysis he performed on statements that had been recorded in handwritten form by police officers, who claimed they were verbatim records of what was said by Timothy Evans who was a suspect in an investigation into the death of his wife and baby daughter. Svartvik observed that this application of language analysis to produce evidence for a legal process was a 'rare opportunity' for a linguist to use their skills for the benefit of society. Today, some 50 years later, the skills of forensic linguists are called on far more frequently than in Svartvik's day; indeed, as we pointed out in Chapter 6, in the last 30 years there has been a rapid growth in the frequency with which courts across the world have called upon the expertise of linguists.

As we noted in Chapter 2, whereas many forensic linguists see their role as essentially descriptive, some see themselves as working within a Critical Discourse framework, where the aim is not simply to describe but, if there seem to be problems in what has been described, to try to remedy. Here are three examples:

1   In Australia, in the 1990's, linguists highlighted the problems that Aboriginal suspects had in police stations and later in court, when legal professionals with no linguistic training decided that the Aboriginals were sufficiently competent in English to be interviewed and to give evidence without the help of an interpreter (Eades 1992). The situation has changed dramatically and now Aboriginals are standardly interviewed by police officers and examined

in court using an interpreter and courses for new judges standardly, include a lecture on the need for and use of interpreters

2   English academics have long had an easy relationship with the police, and this means that it is possible not only to engage in joint research, but also to run, courses for police officers. For instance, the Aston Centre for Forensic Linguistics has provided short courses for police officers on improving interviewing strategies and on working with an interpreter – some 35 languages are spoken in Birmingham on a daily basis.

3   In Brazil the justice system is investigative, and a large number of decisions are made on the basis of written records of interviews and of trial investigative, records which for a linguist are inadequate. In the police station the interviewer produces a written summary with the interviewee's evidence represented at best in third person indirect speech and often not represented at all; in court the judge pauses every so often and dictates a summary to a typist. There is a massive need for linguists to meet with police officers and judges to convince them of the necessity to preserve a verbatim record of what was said, through at least audio-recording. In Austinian terms, everyone wants to be able to hear the locutions and decide for themselves on the intended illocution, rather than simply to be presented with a legal professional's interpretations.

Codes of conduct

As more and more courses in forensic linguistics and forensic phonetics become available in universities across the world, a new generation of forensic linguists and potential forensic practitioners are being trained. This continued development and expansion of the field has resulted in the professional organisations of forensic linguists producing Codes of Conduct for their members, Codes which members are obliged to adhere to when providing consultancy services or expert evidence for the courts. For example, in 2004, the International Association of Forensic Phonetics and Acoustics (IAFPA) published its ten-point Code of Practice, (see: http: www.iafpa.net/), which contains guidelines about the necessary impartiality and fairness of members when undertaking casework, and the need to avoid accepting commissions to write reports in which remuneration is dependent on the outcome of the case. The Guidelines instruct members that they should not attempt to assess the psychological profiles or sincerity of speakers, and also include a number of points about methodology. IAFPA members are requested to take account of the methods available to them in casework and their appropriateness for use in the case in question, and to make explicit in their reports the methods, equipment and computer programs used, as well as any known limitations.

Much more recently, in 2013, the International Association of Forensic Linguists (IAFL) published its own Code of Practice, which lays out principles of ethical conduct to guide members who engage in forensic linguistic research, legal consulting and expert witness work, (see: http://www.iafl.org/uploads/ IAFL_Code_of_Practice_1.pdf). The content is similar to that of the IAFPA document, in that its principles relate to integrity, confidentiality and conflicts of interest. Again, a substantial emphasis is placed on the explicitness and clarity with which experts should apply and then explain their analytical methods in their reports. Experts are also encouraged to share the methods used and analyses performed in casework with other linguists, through conference presentations and publications. As well as representing efforts to consolidate the practices of forensic practitioners across the world, these Codes of Conduct provide useful principles against which forensic phonetic and forensic linguistic research can be evaluated and so, should be referred to by all teachers and students who are discussing or developing methods of analysing language as evidence.

In addition to trying to regulate themselves, there have been two major attempts by forensic linguists to regulate the behaviour of non-members. In 2004, a group of 19 linguists, from four European countries plus Australia and the USA, who were worried about how language analysis was being used to make decisions, in asylum cases, about an applicant's country of origin, produced a set of Guidelines. This document was intended to inform non-linguists involved in the asylum process about how to evaluate the quality of commissioned language analyses. In the authors' words the Guidelines were intended to:

> serve as a touchstone and reference point for [a] governments seeking to know how to conduct their investigations in a professional manner; [b] asylum applicants who have been turned down, in part because of what they believe to be incorrect assessments, based in part on language; and [c] advocates who need information about the connections between language and national origins.
>
> (https://www.essex.ac.uk/larg/resources/guidelines.aspx)

Now, a similarly constituted international group has produced a set of Guidelines, intended for the police in Australia, England, Wales and the USA, about how to communicate to non-native speakers of English their legal rights, including the rights to remain silent and to have a lawyer present. Among the recommendations are that 'All vital documents must be made available in a language the suspect can understand'; that at the very beginning of the interview the suspect 'should be provided with the opportunity to request the services of a professional interpreter'; and that 'the communication of the rights and the suspect's re-statement [of the meaning of that text] should be video-recorded', so that the court can later satisfy itself that the rights were properly understood; and, in addition, 'in the US, whether [also] they were waived knowingly, intelligently, and voluntarily' (see: http://www.aaal.org/?page=CommunicationRights).

New developments and future directions

As the use of mobile devices and related digital communication and online social networks becomes increasingly ubiquitous, so too will their abuse and misuse by criminals. At the same time, the immediacy and simplicity of voice and video recording that such devices offer means that criminal activity can be captured, either overtly or covertly, far more easily than ever before. One result may be that the courts will increasingly rely on spoken and written linguistic evidence for both the defence and the prosecution and so will rely ever more on forensic linguists and forensic phoneticians acting as expert witnesses.

It has been suggested that there is a disjointed relationship between forensic linguistics and other forensic sciences. In 2007, there was a position statement published in the *International Journal of Speech, Language and the Law* concerning the approaches to and expression of conclusions in forensic speaker comparison cases. This position statement set out explicitly to align the presentation of evidence in forensic speaker comparison cases with that in cases involving DNA evidence (French and Harrison 2007: 138), despite the obvious differences between language data and DNA. This statement was specifically related to the analysis of speech samples and the justification of a decision to express results in terms of consistency and distinctiveness, an approach discussed in more detail in Chapter 10. However, forensic author comparison of written text has yet to make similar strides towards situating itself among other forensic sciences, although, as we have seen in Chapters 8 and 10, Grant's (2013) approach in the Amanda Birks text messaging case and Johnson and Wright's analyses of the Enron email database, provide a number of examples of good practice and indications of how forensic linguistics might locate itself among the statistical sciences, although principles comparable to those adduced in the forensic speaker comparison statement are yet to be formalised in the same way.

A related possible future direction for research in the field of authorship is the creation of population data, or reference corpora, against which the distinctiveness of styles of writing can be measured, the implications of which can be seen in Chapters 8 and 10. Reference corpora have been built on a case-by-case basis by forensic linguists where necessary (Kredens and Coulthard 2012). However, a general purpose reference corpus of anonymised text messages, for example, would provide base-rate population data for the frequency or rarity of particular linguistic features. Such data would help add evidential strength to the linguistic analysis relied upon in the comparison of authors. Corpora are also important for forensic linguists working in other areas, as we have shown in Chapter 3 in relation to legal language, (e.g. Finegan 2010), and in Chapters 4 and 5, when police interviews and courtroom data were the topics of investigation. Many of the studies in these areas have been corpus-based (e.g. Heydon, 2005; MacLeod 2010, working on police interviews and Cotterill, 2003; Heffer, 2005; Johnson, 2014, analysing courtroom discourse).

Future research in forensic linguistics and law and language will also need to be based on collaborative relationships that lead to combinations of methods. This is another area in which forensic phonetics has set an example for forensic linguists to follow. As outlined in Chapter 7, the method most commonly used by forensic speech scientists across the world in casework is a mixture of auditory and acoustic phonetic analyses. Such an approach combines traditional phonetic analysis with computational and quantitative analysis. In contrast, as made clear by Solan (2013), the corresponding approaches in authorship attribution – the stylistic and the algorithmic – are not yet used to complement each other. However, recent years have seen the emergence of studies which aim to combine linguistic and statistical analysis in the comparison of author styles (e.g. Grant 2013, Johnson and Wright 2014, Nini and Grant 2014), and these offer a possible direction for future work. In Chapter 10 we noted that in 2009 the UK Law Commission suggested that the criteria for the admissibility of expert evidence in criminal trials needed reforming and proposed that 'there should be a new statutory test for determining' admissibility. We also observed that if, a rigorous US Daubert-like test were to be introduced into the UK, it would most likely result in some methods being disallowed and others being modified.

Researchers are likely to reap additional rewards and insights when they collaborate across academic fields, (for example, between forensic linguistics and corpus linguistics) and academic disciplines, as Solan and Tiersma (e.g. 2005) have so successfully done, over the last decade by combining law and language, and, most recently, Oxburgh, *et al.* (2016) with linguistics and psychology. In addition, as we showed in Chapter 2, the boundaries between forensic linguistics and other linguistic sub-fields are open; indeed, there are many intersections and complementarities and we explained how we need to incorporate insights from many of these into our analysis of texts: the triad of sociolinguistics, pragmatics and discourse analysis, along with the methodologies of corpus linguistics, critical discourse analysis, computational linguistics, auditory phonetics, promises to be a powerful combination.

As well as collaborating with each other and with practitioners from other disciplines, it is in the interests of forensic linguists to foster working relationships with legal professionals. On the one hand, as we noted in Chapter 10, expert witnesses, including forensic linguists, especially new and inexperienced ones, 'tend to be quite unaware of the extent to which shaping and construction of evidence goes on' (Maley 2000: 250). At the same time, there is a fundamental ignorance of forensic linguistics on the part of most lawyers and the legal profession in general (Gray 2010: 592). Of course, a few lawyers are also linguists and vice versa and, once they become aware of the discipline, there is also an appetite amongst lawyers to learn about ways in which forensic linguistic evidence has been and could be handled by the courts (Robson, personal communication). Gray (2010: 593) suggests that in order to achieve greater visibility, linguists should set out to publish in legal journals and to present at legal conferences. These avenues offer both experienced and new forensic linguists opportunities to establish more firmly the usefulness of linguistic evidence and its relevance to court cases.

The next generation

We are often asked: 'How can I become a forensic linguist?' or: 'Can I shadow you in my summer vacation to learn more about forensic linguistic work?' or 'What can students and teachers do to develop the field?' As we pointed out in

Chapter 10, very few linguists work full-time as experts and there is no recognised profession of forensic linguist. Most of us combine this work with our academic roles of teaching and research in universities around the world, providing consultancy as an occasional service or a more regular activity, depending on choice and experience. Coulthard, for example, was a conventional academic linguist for over 20 years before being first approached, by chance, to provide expert evidence in 1987, while Johnson taught linguistics for 12 years before her first expert witness work. However, Wright was fortunate because, while still a doctoral student, he was invited to assist Johnson on a case, obviously with the knowledge and authorisation of the court. So, our advice to aspiring forensic linguists is to first become competent descriptive linguists. As we have demonstrated in every one of the chapters in this book, forensic linguistics requires close and accurate linguistic analysis first and foremost. There is much that is yet to be discovered about how language works generally, but particularly how it works in specialised settings such as legal contexts. This was Svartvik's second point (following on from the first that we quoted in the epigraph): '[my sally into the field of forensic linguistics] has highlighted our present inadequate knowledge of how language is used in various situations'. While his first point, in relation to linguists making a contribution to society, is now increasingly a reality, it is still the case that we have inadequate knowledge about situated language use. So, becoming a better informed linguist is an important first step. Also, we must not forget that while the demand for expert witnesses is limited, some of our students and colleagues have, after completing undergraduate Masters or Doctoral degrees in Linguistics, Law, Psychology or Sociology, gone into such professions as the police, the security services, negotiation, mediation and legislative and other legal or para-legal roles, not forgetting, of course, funded post-doctoral research.

It is therefore useful to remind readers of some of the dominant themes and guiding principles of linguistic analysis that we have developed in this book and which we see as essential. In all kinds of linguistic analyses *accurate description* is crucial, as we have demonstrated in our textual analyses of extracts. Selection from and explanation of *why* particular methods and tools have been employed are also vital, with an understanding that no single approach is ever going to be suitable for all purposes; it is rather a case of making appropriate and reasoned choices. Finally, we have emphasised the importance of *audience* in legal text analysis: who the talk or text is designed for. What the language is doing and who it is for determines how it is.

Closing statement

We started this book with some real world encounters with the 'news' surrounding forensic linguistics and then introduced approaches and methods for lawyers and linguists new to forensic linguistic analysis; we have just ended the second part of the book with a chapter written for aspiring experts that provides a sketch of the work of the linguist as expert witness and discusses some of the problems involved in ensuring that the results are valid and acceptable in court. In between, our concern has been with all aspects of language use and description in legal contexts, particularly in interactions with police officers and lawyers, both within and outside the court. Our two-fold aim was: firstly, to give you a much deeper insight into the language of the legal process, from first contacts with the emergency services, through interactions with the police and legal professionals to the conclusion of the legal proceedings in court; secondly, we wanted to exemplify how language, and the forensic linguist's analysis of it, can constitute significant evidence for both prosecution and defence in criminal and civil trials.

This book represents our collaborative examination and cross-examination in two parts. We have used our experience of linguistic analysis, of teaching and of acting as expert witnesses to provide both novices and more experienced students and researchers, with practical skills, advice and encouragement, but we do not know how persuasive our advocacy has been. For the moment, the jury is out; we hope the majority find in our favour.

References

ABC News (20 February 2007) Online. Available HTTP: <http://www.abc.net.au/news/newsitems/200207/s604549.htm> (accessed 9 May 2007).

Agar, M. (1985) 'Institutional discourse', *Text,* 5(3), 147–68.

Agha, A. (2003) 'The social life of a cultural value', *Language and Communication,* 23, 231–73.

Ainsworth, J. (2008) '"You have the right to remain silent … But only if you ask for it just so": The role of linguistic ideology in American police interrogation law', *International Journal of Speech, Language and the Law,* 15(1), 1–22.

—— (2010) 'Miranda rights. Curtailing coercion in police interrogation: the failed promise of Miranda v Arizona', in M. Coulthard and A. Johnson (eds), 111–25.

Aitken, C.G.G. (1995) *Statistics and the Evaluation of Evidence for Forensic Scientists,* Chichester: John Wiley.

Alcaraz-Varó, E. (2008) 'Legal translation', in J. Gibbons and M.T. Turell (eds), *Dimensions of Forensic Linguistics,* Amsterdam: John Benjamins, 95–111.

Aldridge, M. (2010) 'Vulnerable witnesses in the Criminal Justice System', in M. Coulthard and A. Johnson (eds), 296–314.

Aldridge, M. and Wood, J. (1998) *Interviewing Children: A Guide for Child Care and Forensic Practitioners,* London: Wiley.

Amsterdam, A.G. and Bruner, J. (2000) *Minding the Law,* Cambridge, MA: Harvard University Press.

Anderson, J. (1998) *Plagiarism, Copyright Violation and other Thefts of Intellectual Property,* Jefferson, NC: McFarland.

Angélil-Carter, S. (2000) *Stolen Language? Plagiarism in Writing,* Harlow: Longman.

Anthony, L. (2014) *AntConc* 3.4, Tokyo, Japan: Waseda University, Online. Available HTTP: <//www.laurenceanthony.net/> (accessed 10 December 2015).

Archer, D. (2005) *Questions and Answers in the English Courtroom (1640–1740): A Sociopragmatic Analysis,* Amsterdam: John Benjamins.

—— (2010) 'The historical courtroom. A diachronic investigation of English courtroom practice', in M. Coulthard and A. Johnson (eds), 185–98.

Argamon, S. and Koppel, M. (2013) 'A systemic functional approach to automated authorship analysis', *Journal of Law and Policy,* 21(2), 299–316.

Atkinson, J.M. and Drew, P. (1979) *Order in Court,* London: Macmillan.

Atkinson, J.M., Heritage, J.C. and Watson, D.R. (1979) 'Suspects' rights and the standardization of interrogation procedures: a case for greater formality', *Written Evidence to the Royal Commission on Criminal Procedure,* Mimeo.

Auburn, T., Drake, S. and Willig, C. (1995) 'You punched him, didn't you?': versions of violence in accusatory interviews', *Discourse and Society,* 6(3), 354–86.

Bakhtin, M. (1981) *The Dialogic Imagination: Four Essays*, M. Holquist (ed.), trans. C. Emerson and M. Holquist, Austin, TX and London: University of Texas Press.

—— (1986) *Speech Genres and Other Late Essays*, C. Emerson and M. Holquist (eds), trans. V.W. McGee, Austin, TX: University of Texas Press.

Baldwin, J. and French, J. (1990) *Forensic Phonetics*, London: Pinter.

Bamberg, M. (2004) 'Considering counter narratives', in M. Bamberg and M. Andrews (eds), *Considering Counter Narratives: Narrating, Resisting, Making Sense*, Amsterdam: John Benjamins, 351–71.

Bank of English (2007) Online. Available HTTP: <http://www.titania.bham.ac.uk/docs/svenguide.html> (accessed 12 May 2007).

Barry, A. (1991) 'Narrative style and witness testimony', *Journal of Narrative and Life History*, 1(4), 281–93.

Bartle, A. and Dellwo, V. (2015) 'Auditory speaker discrimination by forensic phoneticians and naive listeners in voiced and whispered speech'. *The International Journal of Speech, Language and the Law*, 22(2), 229–48.

Bates, E., Kintsch, W., Fletcher, C.R. and Giulani, V. (1980) 'The role of pronominalisation and ellipsis in texts: some memorisation experiments', *Journal of Experimental Psychology: Human Learning and Memory*, 6, 676–91.

BBC Crime (10 August 2006) Crime – Case Closed – Fred West (accessed 10 August 2006).

BBC News (31 January 2000) 'Shipman jailed for 15 murders'. Online. Available HTTP: <http://news.bbc.co.uk/1/hi/uk/616692.stm> (accessed 10 August 2006).

—— (17 February 2004) Online. 'Doubt over murder trial evidence'. Available HTTP: <http://news.bbc.co.uk/1/hi/scotland/3494401.stm> (accessed 3 September 2006).

—— (17 February 2004) Online. 'Rape accused tells jury "hang me"'. Available HTTP: <http://news.bbc.co.uk/1/hi/england/3496207.stm> (accessed 3 September 2006).

—— (20 October 2005) 'Man remanded in Ripper hoax probe'. Online. Available HTTP: <http://news.bbc.co.uk/1/hi/england/4360026.stm> (accessed 10 August 2006).

—— (7 April 2006) Court rejects Da Vinci copy claim'. Online. Available HTTP: <http://news.bbc.co.uk/1/hi/entertainment/4886234.stm> (accessed 10 August 2006).

—— (8 September 2008) 'The case for forensic linguistics'. Online. Available http://news.bbc.co.uk/1/hi/sci/tech/7600769.stm (Accessed 30 September 2015).

—— (21 August 2014) 'James Foley beheading: Hunt for "British" jihadist.' Online. Available http://www.bbc.co.uk/news/uk-28876994 (Accessed 4 November 2015)

Bell, A. (1984) 'Language style as audience design', *Language in Society*, 13, 145–204.

—— (1991) 'Audience accommodation in the mass media', in H. Giles, N. Coupland and J. Coupland (eds), *Context of Accommodation: Developments in Applied Sociolinguistics*, Cambridge: Cambridge University Press, 69–102.

Bennett, W.L. and Feldman, M.S. (1981) *Reconstructing Reality in the Courtroom: Justice and Judgment in American Culture*, New Brunswick, NJ: Rutgers University Press.

Benneworth, K. (2010) 'Sexual offences. Negotiating paedophilia in the investigative interview: the construction of sexual offences against children', in M. Coulthard and A. Johnson (eds), 139–54.

Berk-Seligson, S. (1999) 'The impact of court interpreting on the coerciveness of leading questions', *Forensic Linguistics*, 6(1), 30–56.

—— (2002) *The Bilingual Courtroom: Court Interpreters in the Judicial Process*, Chicago, IL: University of Chicago Press.

—— (2009) *Coerced Confessions: The Discourse of Bilingual Police Interrogations*, Vol. 25, Berlin: Walter de Gruyter.

Bhatia, V.K. (1993) *Analysing Genre: Language Use in Professional Settings*, London: Longman.

—— (1994) 'Cognitive structuring in legislative provisions', in J. Gibbons (ed.), *Language and the Law*, London: Longman, 136–55.

—— (2004) *Worlds of Written Discourse*, London: Continuum.

—— (2010) 'Legal writing: specificity. Specification in legislative writing: accessibility, transparency, power and control', in M. Coulthard and A. Johnson (eds), 37–50.

Biber, D. (1988) *Variation across Speech and Writing*, Cambridge: Cambridge University Press.

—— (1995) *Dimensions of Register Variation. A Cross-Linguistic Comparison.* Cambridge: Cambridge University Press.

Biber, D. and Conrad, S. (2009) *Register, Genre and Style*, Cambridge: Cambridge University Press.

Blatchford, H. and Foulkes, P. (2006) 'Identification of voices in shouting', *The International Journal of Speech, Language and the Law*, 13(2), 241–254.

Bloch, B. (1948) 'A set of postulates for phonemic analysis', *Language*, 24, 3–46.

Bloomfield, L. (1926) 'A set of postulates for the science of language', *Language*, 2, 153–54.

BNC (2000) *British National Corpus*, BNC World Edition, Oxford: Humanities Computing Unit, Oxford University.

Bogoch, B. (1994) 'Power, distance and solidarity: models of professional-client interaction in an Israeli legal aid office', *Discourse and Society*, 5(1), 65–88.

Bourdieu, P. (1991) *Language and Symbolic Power,* Cambridge: Polity Press.

Brazil, D.C. (1985) *The Communicative Value of Intonation*, Birmingham: English Language Research.

Brennan, M. (1994a). 'The discourse of denial: cross-examining child victim witnesses', *Journal of Pragmatics*, 23, 71–91.

—— (1994b). 'Cross-examining children in criminal courts: child welfare under attack', in J. Gibbons (ed.), *Language and the Law*, London: Longman, 199–216.

Brennan, M. and Brennan, R.E. (1988) *Strange Language*, Wagga Wagga, NSW: Riverina Literacy Centre.

Broeders, A.P.A. (1999) 'Some observations on the use of probability scales in forensic identification', *Forensic Linguistics*, 6, ii, 228–41.

Broeders, A.P.A. and Rietveld, A.C.M. (1995) 'Speaker identification by earwitnesses', in A. Braun and J-P. Köster (eds), *Studies in Forensic Phonetics*, Trier: Wissenschaftlicher Verlag, 24–40.

Broeders, A.P.A. ms 'Forensic speech and audio analysis in forensic linguistics 1998 to 2001: a review', quoted in Rose (2002) *Forensic Speaker Identification*, London: Taylor and Francis.

Bromby, M.C. (2002) *The Role and Responsibilities of the Expert Witness within the UK Judicial System*, dissertation presented for the Diploma in Forensic Medical Science, awarded by The Worshipful Company of Apothecaries, London, Online. Available HTTP: <http://cbs1.gcal.ac.uk/law/users/~mbro/documents/DipFMSDissertation.pdf> (accessed 12 September 2006).

Buranen, L. and Roy, A.M. (eds) (1999) *Perspectives on Plagiarism and Intellectual Property in a Postmodern World*, Albany, NY: State University of New York Press.

Burrows, J. (2007) 'All the way through: Testing for authorship in different frequency strata', *Literary and Linguistic Computing,* (22)1, 27–47.

Butters, R.R. (2010) 'Trademark linguistics. Trademarks: language that one owns', in M. Coulthard and A. Johnson (eds), 351–64.

Byrne, C. and Foulkes, P. (2004) 'The "Mobile Phone Effect" on vowel formants'. *The International Journal of Speech, Language and the Law*, 11(1), 83–102.

Caldas-Coulthard, C.R. and Coulthard, M. (1996) *Texts and Practices: Readings in Critical Discourse Analysis,* London: Routledge.

Cambier-Langeveld, T. (2007) 'Current methods in forensic speaker identification: Results of a collaborative exercise'. *The International Journal of Speech, Language and the Law*, 14(2), 223–43.

—— (2010) 'The role of linguists and native speakers in language analysis for the determination of speaker origin', *The International Journal of Speech, Language and the Law*, 17(1), 67–93.

—— (2014) 'State-of-the-art in language analysis: a response to the chapter on LADO in the Oxford Handbook of Language and Law', *The International Journal of Speech, Language and the Law*, 21(2), 371–81.

Canale, M., Mougeon, R. and Klokeid, T.J. (1982) 'Remarks: forensic linguistics', *Canadian Journal of Linguistics*, 27(2), 150–5.

Canter, D.C. and Chester J. (1997) 'Investigation into the claim of weighted Cusum in authorship attribution studies', *Forensic Linguistics*, 4(2), ii, 252–61.

Cao, D. (2010) 'Legal translation. Translating legal language', in M. Coulthard and A. Johnson (eds), 78–91.

Carter, E. (2011) *Analysing Police Interviews. Laughter, Confessions and the Tape*, London: Continuum.

Charnock, Ross. (2013) 'Hart as Contextualist? Theories of Interpretation in Language and the Law', *Law and Language: Current Legal Issues*, 15, 128–50.

Chaski, C.E. (2001) 'Empirical evaluations of language-based author identification techniques', *The International Journal of Speech, Language and the Law*, 8(1), 1–65.

—— (2005) 'Who's at the keyboard? Authorship attribution in digital evidence investigations', *International Journal of Digital Evidence*, 4(1), 1–14.

Cheng, E.K. (2013) 'Being pragmatic about forensic linguistics', *Journal of Law and Policy,* 21(2), 541–50.

Child, B. (2015) 'Story of Yorkshire Ripper hoaxer "Wearside Jack" to be made into a movie', *The Guardian*, 15 June.

Chomsky, N. (1965) *Aspects of the Theory of Syntax*, Cambridge, MA: MIT Press.

Chulov, M. and Halliday, J. (2014) 'British Isis militant in James Foley video "guards foreign hostages in Syria"', *The Guardian,* 20 August 2014.

Clarity International. (2015) *Clarity. An International Association Promoting Plain Legal Language, Online*. Available HTTP: <www.clarity-international.net/> (accessed 30 November 2015).

Coke, E. (1681) *The Third Part of the Institutes of the Laws of England Concerning High Treason, and other Pleas of the Crown and Criminal Causes*, 6th edn, London: Printed by W. Rawlins, for Thomas Basset, Online. Available HTTP: <sceti.library.upenn.edu/sceti/printedbooksNew/index.cfm?TextID=coke_insts3&PagePosition=1> (accessed 1 November 2015).

College of Policing (2013): *Investigative Interviewing,* Online. Available HTTP: <https://www.app.college.police.uk/app-content/investigations/investigative-interviewing/> (accessed 1 December 2015).

Conley, J.M. and O'Barr, W.M. (1998) *Just Words: Law, Language and Power*, Chicago: University Chicago Press.

Cooley, A., Bess, C. and Rubin-Jackson, M. (as told to Tom Byrnes with Mike Walker) (1995) *Madam Foreman: A Rush to Judgment?* Beverly Hills, CA: Dove Books.

Corder, S.P. (1973) *Introducing Applied Linguistics*, Harmondsworth: Penguin.

Cotterill, J. (2000) 'Reading the rights: A cautionary tale of comprehension and comprehensibility', *Forensic Linguistics,* 7(1), 4–25.

—— (ed.) (2002) *Language in the Legal Process*, London: Palgrave.

—— (2003) *Language and Power in Court: A Linguistic Analysis of the O.J. Simpson Trial*, Basingstoke: Palgrave.

—— (2008) ' "If it doesn't fit, you must acquit": metaphor and the O.J. Simpson criminal trial', *The International Journal of Speech, Language and the Law*, 5(2), 141–58.

—— (2010) 'How to use corpus linguistics in forensic linguistics', *The Routledge Handbook of Corpus Linguistics,* London: Routledge, 578–90.

Coulthard, M. (2014) 'Have you been Warned?', in R. Casesnoves, M. Forcadell and N. Gavaldà (eds), *Ens queda la paraula. Estudis de lingüística aplicada en honor a M.Teresa Turell*, Barcelona: IULA, Universitat Pompeu Fabra, 253–64.

Coulthard, M. and Johnson, A. (eds) (2010) *The Routledge Handbook of Forensic Linguistics,* Abingdon: Routledge.

Coulthard, M. and Sousa-Silva, R. (eds) (2014–) *Language and Law – Linguagem e Direito,* Porto, Universidade de Porto.

Coulthard, M., Johnson, A., Kredens, K. and Woolls, D. (2010) 'Four forensic linguists responses to suspected plagiarism', in M. Coulthard and A. Johnson (eds), 523–38.

Coulthard, R.M. (1977) *An Introduction to Discourse Analysis*, London: Longman.

—— (1992) 'Forensic discourse analysis', in R.M. Coulthard (ed.), *Advances in Spoken Discourse Analysis*, London: Routledge, 242–57.

—— (1993) 'Beginning the study of forensic texts: corpus, concordance, collocation', in M.P. Hoey (ed.), *Data Description Discourse*, London: HarperCollins, 86–97.

—— (1994a). 'Powerful evidence for the defence: an exercise in forensic discourse analysis', in J. Gibbons (ed.), *Language and the Law*, London: Longman, 414–42.

—— (1994b). 'On the use of corpora in the analysis of forensic texts', *Forensic Linguistics*, 1(1), 27–43.

—— (1997) 'A failed appeal', *Forensic Linguistics*, 4, ii, 287–302.

—— (2004) 'Author identification, idiolect and linguistic uniqueness', *Applied Linguistics*, 25, 4, 431–47.

—— (2005) 'The linguist as expert witness', *Linguistics and the Human Sciences*, 1(1), 39–58.

Crabb, A. (2014) 'Don't patronise me darling', *The Sydney Morning Herald*, 30 November, Online. Available: HTTP: <www.smh.com.au/comment/dont-patronise-me-darling-20141127-11vvxc.html> (accessed 1 November 2015).

CRTC Decision 2006-45 (2006) Online. Available HTTP: <http://www.crtc.gc.ca/archive/ENG/Decisions/2006/dt2006-45.pdf> (accessed 12 August 2006).

Crystal, D. (2003) *Cambridge Encyclopedia of the English Language*, 2nd edn, Cambridge: Cambridge University Press.

Danet, B. and Kermish, N.C. (1978) 'Courtroom questioning: a sociolinguistic perspective', in L.N. Massery (ed.), *Psychology and Persuasion in Advocacy*, Washington, DC: Association of Trial Lawyers of America, National College of Advocacy, pp. 413–41.

Davies, B.L. (2014) 'Travelling texts: The legal-lay interface in The Highway Code', in C. Heffer, F. Rock and J. Conley. (eds), *Legal-lay Communication: Textual Travels in the Law*, Oxford: Oxford University Press, 266–87.

Davies, E. (2004) 'Register distinctions and measures of complexity in the language of legal contracts', in J. Gibbons V. Prakasam, K.V. Tirumalesh and H. Nagarajan (eds), *Language in the Law*, Hyderabad: Orient Longman, 82–99.

Davies, M. (2012) *The Corpus of Contemporary American English: 450 million words, 1990–present*, Online. Available HTTP: <//corpus.byu.edu/coca/> (accessed 1 November 2015).

Davis, T. (1994) 'ESDA and the analysis of contested contemporaneous notes of police interviews', *Forensic Linguistics*, 1(1), 71–89.

—— (1996) 'Clues and opinions: ways of looking at evidence', in H. Kniffka, R.M. Coulthard and S. Blackwell (eds), *Recent Developments in Forensic Linguistics*, Frankfurt: Peter Lang, 53–73.

Dawid, A.P. (2001) 'Bayes theorem and weighing evidence by juries', Online. Available HTTP: <http://www.ucl.ac.uk/~ucak06d/evidence/1day/ba.pdf> (accessed 12 September 2006).

de Morgan, S.E. (ed.) (1882) *Memoir of Augustus de Morgan by his wife Sophia Elizabeth de Morgan with Selections from his Letters*, London: Longmans Green and Co.

Deffenbacher, K.A., Cross, J.F., Handkins, R.E., Chance, J.E., Goldstein, A.G., Hammersley, R. and Read, J.D. (1989) 'Relevance of voice identification research to criteria for evaluating reliability of an identification', *Journal of Psychology*, 123(2), 109–119.

Drew P. and Heritage J. (eds) (1992) *Talk at Work. Interactions in Institutional Settings*, Cambridge: Cambridge University Press.

Drew, P. (1979) 'Comparative analysis of talk-in-interaction in different institutional settings: a sketch', in P. Glenn, C.D. LeBaron and J. Mandelbaum (eds), *Studies in Language and Social Interaction: In Honor of Robert Hopper*, Mahweh, NJ: Lawrence Erlbaum, 293–308.

—— (1990) 'Strategies in the contest between lawyer and witness in cross-examination', in J. Levi and A. Graffam Walker (eds), *Language in the Judicial Process*, London: Plenum, 39–64.

—— (1992) 'Contested evidence in courtroom cross-examination: the case of a trial for rape', in P. Drew and J. Heritage (eds), *Talk at Work*, Cambridge and New York: Cambridge University Press, 470–520.

Drew, P. and Walker, T. (2010) 'Citizens' emergency calls. *Requesting assistance in calls to the police*', in M. Coulthard and A. Johnson (eds), 95–110.

Dumas, B.K. (1992) 'Adequacy of cigarette package warnings: an analysis of the adequacy of federally mandated cigarette package warnings', *Tennessee Law Review*, 59, 261–304.

—— (2002) 'Reasonable doubt about reasonable doubt: assessing jury instruction adequacy in a capital case', in J. Cotterill (ed.), *Language in the Legal Process*, London: Palgrave, 246–59.

—— (2010) 'Consumer product warnings. Composition, identification, and assessment of adequacy', in M. Coulthard and A. Johnson (eds), 365–77.

Duranti, A. and Goodwin, C. (eds) (1992) *Rethinking Context: Language as an Interactive Phenomenon*, Cambridge: Cambridge University Press.

Eades, D. (1992) *Aboriginal English and the Law: Communicating with Aboriginal English-Speaking Clients. A Handbook for Legal Practitioners*, Brisbane: Queensland Law Society.

—— (1994) Forensic linguistics in Australia: an overview, *Forensic Linguistics*, 1(2), 113–32.

—— (2000) '"I don't think it's an answer to the question": Silencing Aboriginal witnesses in court', *Language in Society*, 29(2), 161–96.

—— (2002) '"Evidence given in unequivocal terms": gaining consent of Aboriginal young people in court', in J. Cotterill (ed.), *Language in the Legal Process*, London: Palgrave, 162–79.

—— (2005) 'Applied linguistics and language analysis in asylum seeker cases', *Applied Linguistics*, 26(4), 503–26.

—— (2006) 'Lexical struggle in court: Aboriginal Australians vs the state', *Journal of Sociolinguistics,* 10(2), 153–81.

—— (2008) *Courtroom Talk and Neo-Colonial Control,* Berlin: De Gruyter Mouton.

—— (2010a). 'Language analysis and asylum cases', in M. Coulthard and A. Johnson (eds), 411–22.

—— (2010b). *Sociolinguistics and the Legal Process,* Bristol: Multilingual Matters.

Eades, D. and Arends, J. (2004) 'Using language in the determination of national origin of asylum seekers: an introduction'. *The International Journal of Speech, Language and the Law*, 11(2), 179–199.

Eades, D., Fraser, H., Seigel, J., McNamara, T. and Baker, B. (2003) 'Linguistic identification in the determination of nationality: a preliminary report', *Language Policy*, 2, 179–99.

Eagleson, R. (1994) 'Forensic analysis of personal written texts: a case study', in J. Gibbons (ed.), *Language and the Law*, London: Longman, 362–73.

Eastwood, J. and Snook, B. (2010) 'Comprehending Canadian police cautions: Are the rights to silence and legal counsel understandable?', *Behavioural Sciences and the Law*, 28, 366–77.

Edwards, D. (ed.) (2007) 'Calls for help', Special issue of *Research on Language and Social Interaction*, 40(1), 1–144.

Edwards, D. and Stokoe, E. (2011) '"You don't have to answer": Lawyers'contributions in police interrogations of suspects', *Research on Language and Social Interaction*, 44(1), 21–43.

Ehrlich, S. (2001) *Representing Rape: Language and Sexual Consent*, London: Routledge.

—— (2002) '(Re)Contextualizing complainants' accounts of sexual assault', *Forensic Linguistics*, 9(2), 193–212.

—— (2007) 'Normative discourses and representations of coerced sex', in J. Cotterill (ed.) *The Language of Sexual Crime,* Basingstoke; Palgrave Macmillan, 126–38.

—— (2010) 'Rape victims. The discourse of rape trials', in M. Coulthard and A. Johnson (eds), 265–80.

Ehrlich, S. and Sidnell, J. (2006) '"I think that's not an assumption you ought to make": Challenging presuppositions in inquiry testimony', *Language in Society*, 35(5), 655–76.

Ellis, S. (1994) 'Case report: The Yorkshire Ripper enquiry, Part 1', *Forensic Linguistics* 1(2), 197–206.

Eriksson, A. (2010) 'The disguised voice: imitating accents or speech styles and impersonating individuals', in C. Llamas and D. Watt (eds), *Language and Identities*, Edinburgh: Edinburgh University Press, 86–96.

—— (2012) 'Aural/Acoustic vs. Automatic methods in Forensic Phonetic casework', in A. Neustein and H.A. Patil (eds), *Forensic Speaker Recognition: Law Enforcement and Counter-terrorism*, New York: Springer: 41–69.

Eriksson, E. Sullivan, K., Zetterholm, E., Czigler, P., Green, J., Skagerstrand, A. and van Doorn, J. (2010) 'Detection of imitated voices: who are reliable earwitnesses?', *The International Journal of Speech, Language and the Law*, 17(1), 25–44.

Fairclough, N. (1989) *Language and Power*, London: Longman.

—— (1995) *Critical Discourse Analysis: The Critical Study of Language*, London: Longman.

Felton Rosulek, L. (2010) 'Prosecution and defense closing speeches. The creation of contrasting closing arguments', in M. Coulthard and A. Johnson (eds), 218–30.

—— (2015) *Dueling Discourses. The Construction of Reality in Closing Arguments,* Oxford and New York: Oxford University Press.

Fenner, S. and Gudjonsson, G.H. (2002) 'Understanding of the current police caution (England and Wales) among suspects in police detention', *Journal of Community and Applied Social Psychology,* 12(2), 83–93.

Finegan, E. (2010) 'Legal writing: attitude and emphasis. Corpus linguistic approaches to "legal language": adverbial expression of attitude and emphasis in Supreme Court opinions', in M. Coulthard and A. Johnson (eds), 65–77.

Firth, J.P. (1957) 'A synopsis of linguistic theory 1930–1955', in F.R. Palmer (ed.), *Selected Papers of J.R. Firth 1952–1959,* London: Longman, 168–205.

Flowerdew (2004) 'The argument for using English specialized corpora to understand academic and professional language', in U. Connor and T.A. Upton (eds), *Discourse in the Professions,* Amsterdam: John Benjamins, 11–33.

Foulkes, P. and French, P. (2012) 'Forensic speaker comparison: a linguistic-acoustic perspective', in P. Tiersma and L. Solan (eds), *The Oxford Handbook of Language and Law,* Oxford: Oxford University Press, 557–72.

Fox, G. (1993) 'A comparison of "policespeak" and "normalspeak": a preliminary study', in J.M. Sinclair, M. Hoey and G. Fox (eds), *Techniques of Description: Spoken and Written Discourse,* Routledge: London, 183–95.

Frade, C. (2007) 'Power dynamics and legal English', *World Englishes,* 26(1), 48–61.

Fraser, H. (2003) 'Issues in transcription: factors affecting the reliability of transcripts as evidence in legal cases', *The International Journal of Speech, Language and the Law (Forensic Linguistics),* 10(2), 203–26.

—— (2009) 'The role of "educated native speakers" in providing language analysis for the determination of the origin of asylum seekers', *The International Journal of Speech, Language and the Law,* 16(1), 113–38.

—— (2011) 'The role of linguists and native speakers in language analysis for the determination of speaker origin: A response to Tina Cambier-Langeveld', *The International Journal of Speech, Language and the Law,* 18(1), 121–30.

—— (2014) 'Transcription of indistinct forensic recordings: Problems and solutions from the perspective of phonetic science', *Language and Law – Linguagem e Direito,* 1(2), 5–21.

Fraser, H., Stevenson, B. and Marks, T. (2011) 'Interpretation of a crisis call: persistence of a primed perception of a disputed utterance', *The International Journal of Speech, Language and the Law,* 18(2), 261–92.

French, J.P. (1994) 'An overview of forensic phonetics', *Forensic Linguistics,* 1(2), 169–81.

—— (1998) 'Mr Akbar's nearest ear versus the Lombard reflex: a case study in forensic phonetics', *Forensic Linguistics,* 5(1), 58–68.

French, J.P. and Harrison, P. (2007) 'Position statement concerning use of impressionistic likelihood terms in forensic speaker comparison cases', *The International Journal of Speech, Language and the Law,* 14(1), 137–44.

French, J.P. and Stevens, L. (2013) 'Forensic Speech Science', in M.J. Jones and R. Knight (eds), *The Bloomsbury Companion to Phonetics.* London: Bloomsbury, 183–197.

French, P., Harrison, P. and Windsor Lewis, J. (2007) 'R v John Humble: The Yorkshire Ripper hoaxer trial', *The International Journal of Speech, Language and the Law,* 13, (2), 255–73.

Galatolo, R. and Drew, P. (2006) 'Narrative expansions as defensive practices in courtroom testimony', *Text and Talk,* 26(6), 661–98.

Garfinkel, H. and Sacks, H. (1970) 'On formal structures of practical actions', in J.C. McKinney and E.A. Tiryakian (eds), *Theoretical Sociology*, New York: Appleton-CenturyCrofts, 187–238.

Garner, M. and Johnson, E. (2006) 'Operational Communication: a paradigm for applied research into police call-handling', *International Journal of Speech, Language and the Law*, 13(1), 55–75.

Garside, R., Leech, G. and Sampson, G. (eds) (1987) *The Computational Analysis of English: A Corpus-based Approach*, London: Longman.

Gibbons, J. (ed.) (1994) *Language and the Law*, London: Longman.

—— (1996) 'Distortions of the police interview process revealed by video-tape', *Forensic Linguistics*, 3(2), 289–98.

—— (2003) *Forensic Linguistics: An Introduction to Language in the Justice System*, Oxford: Blackwell.

—— (2004) 'Taking legal language seriously', in J. Gibbons, J. Prakasam, K.V. Tirumalesh and H. Nagarajan *Language in the Law*, Hyderabad: Orient Longman, 1–16.

Gibbons, J., Prakasam, V., Tirumalesh, K.V. and Nagarajan, H. (eds) (2004) *Language in the Law*, Hyderabad: Orient Longman.

Giles, H. (1973) 'Accent mobility: A model and some data', *Anthropological Linguistics*, 15, 87–105.

Giles, H., Coupland, N. and Coupland, J. (1991) 'Accommodation theory: communication, context and consequence', in H. Giles, J. Coupland and N. Coupland (eds), *Context of Accommodation: Developments in Applied Sociolinguistics*, Cambridge: Cambridge University Press, 1–68.

Goffman, E. (1964) 'The neglected situation', *American Anthropologist*, 66(6), part II (Special Issue), 133–6.

—— (1981) *Forms of Talk*, Oxford: Blackwell.

Gold, E. and French, J. P. (2011) 'International practices in forensic speaker comparison', *The International Journal of Speech, Language and the Law*, 18(2), 293–307.

Grant, T. (2007) 'Quantifying evidence in forensic authorship analysis', *International Journal of Speech Language and the Law*, 14(1), 1–25.

—— (2008) 'Approaching questions in forensic authorship analysis', in J. Gibbons and M.T. Turell (eds), *Dimensions of Forensic Linguistics*, Amsterdam: John Benjamins, 215–29.

—— (2010) 'Txt 4n6: Idiolect free authorship analysis?', in M. Coulthard and A. Johnson (eds), 508–22.

—— (2013) 'Txt 4N6: Method, consistency and distinctiveness in the analysis of SMS text messages', *Journal of Law and Policy*, 21(2), 467–94.

Grant, T., Taylor, J., Oxburgh, G. and Myklebust, T. (2016) 'Exploring types and functions of questions in police interviews', in G. Oxburgh, T. Myklebust, T. Grant, and R. Milne (eds), *Communication in Investigative and Legal Contexts: Integrated Approaches*, Wiley: Chichester, 17–38.

Gray, P.R.A. (2010) 'The future for forensic linguists in the courtroom: cross-cultural communication', in M. Coulthard and A. Johnson (eds) *The Routledge Handbook of Forensic Linguistics*. London: Routledge, 591–601.

Green, G. (1990) 'Linguistic analysis of conversation as evidence regarding the interpretation of speech events', in J.N. Levi and A.G. Walker (eds), *Language in the Judicial Process*, New York: Plenum Press, 247–77.

Grice, H.P. (1975) 'Logic and conversation', in P. Cole and J. Morgan (eds), *Syntax and Semantics III: Speech Acts*, New York: Academic Press, 41–58; reprinted in A. Jaworski and N. Coupland (eds), *The Discourse Reader*, 2nd edn, London: Routledge, 66–77.

Gries, S.Th. (2013) '50-something years of work on collocations: What is or should be next…', *International Journal of Corpus Linguistics*, 18(1), 137–65.

Grieve, J. (2007) 'Quantitative authorship attribution: An evaluation of techniques'. *Literary and Linguistic Computing,* 22(3), 251–70.

Guardian Unlimited (2002) 'Archer loses appeal bid', 22 July, Online. Available HTTP: <http://www.guardian.co.uk/archer/article/0,2763,759829,00.html> (accessed 12 September 2006).

Gudjonsson, G. (2003) *The Psychology of Interrogations and Confessions: A Handbook*, Chichester: John Wiley and Sons.

Gumperz, J. (1968) 'The speech community', in A. Duranti (ed), *Linguistic Anthropology: A Reader*, 2nd edn, Malden, MA: Blackwell Publishing, 66–73.

—— (1982) *Discourse Strategies*, Cambridge: Cambridge University Press.

—— (2003) 'Interactional Sociolinguistics: A personal perspective', in D. Schiffrin, D. Tannen and H.E. Hamilton (eds), *The Handbook of Discourse Analysis*, Oxford: Blackwell, 215–28.

Gumperz, J.J. and Hymes, D. (eds) (1964) 'The Ethnography of Communication', Special issue of *American Anthropologist*, 66(6), Part II, 137–54.

—— (1972) *Directions in Sociolinguistics: The Ethnography of Communication,* New York: Holt, Rinehart, & Winston.

Gustafsson, M. (1984) 'The syntactic features of binomial expressions in legal English', *Text*, 4(1–3), 123–41.

Hagemeyer, C. and Coulthard, M. (2015) 'On Product Warnings', *Language and Law – Linguagem e Direito*, 2(1), 53–75.

Hale, S. (1999) 'Interpreters' treatment of discourse markers in courtroom questions', *Forensic Linguistics,* 6(1), 57–82.

—— (2004) *The Discourse of Court Interpreting: Discourse Practices of the Law, the Witness and the Interpreter*, Amsterdam: John Benjamins.

—— (2010) 'Court interpreting. The need to raise the bar: Court interpreters as specialized experts', in M. Coulthard and A. Johnson (eds), 440–54.

Halldorsdottir, I. (2006) 'Orientations to law, guidelines, and codes in lawyer–client interaction', *Research on Language and Social Interaction*, 39(3), 263–301.

Halliday, M.A.K. (1973) *Language in a Social Perspective: Explorations in the Functions of Language,* London: Edward Arnold.

—— (1975) *Learning How to Mean*, London: Edward Arnold.

—— (1989) *Spoken and Written Language*, 2nd edn, Oxford: Oxford University Press.

Halliday, M.A.K. and Hasan, R. (1989) *Language, Context and Text: Aspects of Language in a Social Semiotic Perspective*, Oxford: Oxford University Press.

Halliday, M.A.K. and Matthiessen, C.M.I.M. (2014) *Halliday's Introduction to Functional Grammar*, 4th edn, Abingdon: Routledge.

Hanks, W.F. (2005) 'Explorations in the deictic field', *Current Anthropology*, 46(2), 191–220.

Hanlein, H. (1999) *Studies in Authorship Recognition: A Corpus-based Approach*, New York: Peter Lang.

Hannam (1953) extract from the court transcript of the examination of Chief Inspector Hannam in the trial of Alfred Charles Whiteway.

Hans, V. and Vidmar, N. (1986) *Judging the Jury*, New York: Plenum.

Hardcastle, R.A. (1997) 'Cusum: a credible method for the determination of authorship?', *Science and Justice*, 37(2), 129–38.

Harris, S. (1984) 'Questions as a mode of control in magistrates' courts', *International Journal of the Sociology of Language*, 49, 5–27.

—— (1989) 'Defendant resistance to power and control in court', in H. Coleman (ed), *Working with Language: A Multidisciplinary Consideration of Language Use in Work Contexts, Vol 52*, Berlin: de Gruyter, 131–64.

—— (1991) 'Evasive action: how politicians respond to questions in political interviews', in P. Scannell (ed.) *Broadcast Talk*, London: Sage, 76–99.

—— (2001) 'Fragmented narratives and multiple tellers: witness and defendant accounts in trials', *Discourse Studies*, 3(1), 53–74.

—— (2005) 'Telling stories and giving evidence: the hybridisation of narrative and non-narrative modes of discourse in a sexual assault trial', in J. Thornborrow and J. Coates (eds), *The Sociolinguistics of Narrative*, Amsterdam: John Benjamins, 215–37.

Hasan, R. (2000) 'The uses of talk', in S. Sarangi and M. Coulthard (eds), *Discourse and Social Life*, London: Longman, 30–81.

Haworth, K. (2006) 'The dynamics of power and resistance in police interview discourse', *Discourse and Society*, 17(6), 739–59.

—— (2010) 'Police interviews in the judicial process. Police interviews as evidence', in M. Coulthard and A. Johnson (eds), 169–84.

—— (2013) 'Audience design in the police interview: the interactional and judicial consequences of audience orientation', *Language in Society,* 42(1), 45–69.

Heffer, C. (2002) *Making a Case: Narrative and Paradigmatic Modes in the Legal-Lay Discourse of English Jury Trial*, unpublished PhD thesis, University of Birmingham.

—— (2005) *The Language of Jury Trial: A Corpus-aided Analysis of Legal-Lay Discourse*, Basingstoke: Palgrave Macmillan.

—— (2010) 'Narrative in the trial. Constructing crime stories in court', in M. Coulthard and A. Johnson (eds), 199–217.

Heritage, J.C. (1985) 'Analyzing news interviews: aspects of the production of talk for an overhearing audience', in T.A. van Dijk (ed.), *Handbook of Discourse Analysis, Volume 3*, New York: Academic Press, 95–119.

Heritage, J.C. and Watson, D.R. (1977) 'Recent developments in the sociology of language in Britain', *Sociolinguistics Newsletter*, 8, 2–6.

—— (1979) 'Formulations as conversational objects', in G. Psathas (ed.), *Everyday Language: Studies in Ethnomethodology*, New York: Boston University Irvington Press Inc., 123–62.

—— (1980) 'Aspects of the properties of formulations in natural conversations: some instances analysed', *Semiotica*, 30(3/4), 245–62.

Heritage, J.C., and Sorjonen, M.L. (1994) 'Constituting and maintaining activities across sequences: *and*-prefacing as a feature of question design', *Language in Society*, 1, 1–29.

Heydon, G. (2005) *The Language of Police Interviewing: A critical analysis,* Basingstoke: Palgrave Macmillan.

—— (2012) 'Helping the police with their enquiries: Enhancing the investigative interview with linguistic research', *The Police Journal*, 85(2), 101–22.

Hiltunen, R. (1984) 'Some complex types of embedding in legal English', in H. Ringbom and M. Rissanen (eds), *Proceedings from the Nordic Conference for English Studies*, np.

Hirst, G. and Feiguina, O. (2007) 'Bigrams of syntactic labels for authorship discrimination of short texts', *Literary and Linguistic Computing,* 22(4), 405–417.

Hjelmquist, E. (1984) 'Memory for conversations', *Discourse Processes*, 7, 321–36.

—— (1991) 'Recognition memory for utterances in conversations', *Scandinavian Journal of Psychology*, 29, 168–76.

Hobbs, P. (2003) '"Is that what we're here about?" A lawyer's use of impression management in a closing argument at trial', *Discourse and Society,* 14(3), 273–90.

Hoey, M. (1983) *On the Surface of Discourse,* London: George Allen & Unwin.

—— (2000) *Textual Interaction: An Introduction to Written Discourse Analysis,* London: Routledge.

—— (2005) *Lexical Priming: A New Theory of Words and Language,* London: Routledge.

Hollien, H. (1990a). 'The phonetician as expert witness', in R.W. Rieber and W.A. Stewart (eds), *The Language Scientist as Expert in the Legal Setting: Issues in Forensic Linguistics,* New York: The New York Academy of Sciences, 33–45.

—— (1990b). *The Acoustics of Crime,* London: Plenum.

—— (2002) *Forensic Voice Identification,* London: Academic Press.

Hollien, H. Huntley Bahr, R. and Harnsberger, J.D. (2014) 'Issues in Forensic Voice', *Journal of Voice,* 28(2), 170–184.

Holmes, D. I. and Forsyth, R.S. (1995) 'The Federalist revisited: New directions in authorship attribution', *Literary and Linguistic Computing,* 10(2), 111–27.

Holmes, J. (2008) *An Introduction to Sociolinguistics,* 3rd edn, Harlow: Person Education Ltd.

Holt, E. and Johnson, A. (2006) 'Formulating the facts: questions and repeats in police/suspect interviews', Paper presented at the International Conference on Conversation Analysis, Helsinki (May 2006).

—— (2010) 'Legal talk. Socio-pragmatic aspects of legal talk: police interviews and trial discourse', in M. Coulthard and A. Johnson (eds), 21–36.

Home Office (2005) *National Call Handling Standards,* Online. Available HTTP: <library.college.police.uk/docs/homeoffice/call_handling_standard.pdf> (accessed 10 December 2015).

—— (2013) *Police and Criminal Evidence Act 1984 Code C: Revised code of practice for the detention, treatment and questioning of persons by police officers.* London: The Stationery Office, Online. Available HTTP: <https://www.gov.uk/guidance/police-and-criminal-evidence-act-1984-pace-codes-of-practice> (accessed 11 December 2015).

Hoover, D. L. (2002) 'Frequent word sequences and statistical stylistics', *Literary and Linguistic Computing,* 17(2), 157–80.

Howald, B.S. (2008) 'Authorship attribution under the rules of evidence: empirical approaches – a layperson's legal system', *The International Journal of Speech, Language and the Law,* 15(2), 219–47.

Howard, R.M. (1999a). 'The new abolitionism comes to plagiarism', in L. Buranen and A.M. Roy (eds), *Perspectives on Plagiarism and Intellectual Property in a Postmodern World,* Albany, NY: State University of New York Press, 87–95.

—— (1999b). *Perspectives on Writing: Theory, Research, Practice, Vol. 2: Standing in the Shadows of Giants,* Stamford, CT: Ablex Publishing.

Hutton, C. (2014) *Word Meaning and Legal Interpretation. An Introductory Guide,* Basingstoke: Palgrave Macmillan.

Hymes, D.H. (1972) 'On communicative competence', in J. Pride and J. Holmes (eds), *Sociolinguistics,* Harmondsworth: Penguin, 269–93, reprinted under the title 'Modes of the interaction of language and social life' in C. Bratt Paulston and G.R. Tucker (2003) *Sociolinguistics: The Essential Readings,* Oxford: Blackwell, 30–47.

—— D.H. (1974) 'Ways of speaking', in R. Bauman and J. Sherzer (eds), *Explorations in the Ethnography of Speaking,* Cambridge: Cambridge University Press, 425–32.

—— (1986) 'The interaction of language and social life', in J.J. Gumperz and D.H. Hymes (eds), *Directions in Sociolinguistics: The Ethnography of Communication*, Oxford: Blackwell, 35–71.

Imbens-Bailey, A. and McCabe, A. (2000) 'The discourse of distress: A narrative analysis of emergency calls to 911', *Language and Communication*, 20(3), 275–96.

Innes, B. (2011) 'R v David Bain: a unique case in New Zealand legal and linguistic history', *The International Journal of Speech, Language and the Law* 18(1), 145–55.

Jaccard, P. (1912) 'The distribution of the Wora in the alpine zone', *The New Phytologist,* 11(2), 37–50.

Jackson, B.S. (1988) *Law, Fact and Narrative Coherence*, Roby: Deborah Charles.

—— (1995) *Making Sense in Law: Linguistic, Psychological and Semiotic Perspectives*, Liverpool: Deborah Charles.

Jacquemet, M. (1996) *Credibility in Court: Communicative Practices in the Comorra Trials*, Cambridge: Cambridge University Press.

Jaworski, A. and Coupland, N. (eds) (2006) *The Discourse Reader*, 2nd edn, London: Routledge.

Jefferson, G. (2004) 'Glossary of transcript symbols with an introduction', in G. Lerner (ed.) *Conversation Analysis: Studies from the First Generation*, Amsterdam: John Benjamins, 13–31.

Jessen, M. (2010) 'The forensic phonetician. Forensic speaker identification by experts', in M. Coulthard and A. Johnson (eds), *The Routledge Handbook of Forensic Linguistics*. London: Routledge, 378–94.

Jockers, M.L. and Witten, D.M. (2010) 'A comparative study of machine learning methods for authorship attribution', *Literary and Linguistic Computing,* 25(2), 215–23.

Johnson, A. (1997) 'Textual kidnapping: a case of plagiarism among three student texts', *Forensic Linguistics*, 4(2), 210–25.

—— (2002) '*So...*? Pragmatic implications of *So*-prefaced questions in formal police interviews', in J. Cotterill (ed.), *Language in the Legal Process*, London: Palgrave, 91– 110.

—— (2006) 'Police questioning', in Brown, K (ed.), *The Encyclopedia of Language and Linguistics*, 2nd edn, vol. 9, Oxford: Elsevier, 661–72.

—— (2008) '"From where we're sat ...": Negotiating narrative transformation through interaction in police interviews with suspects', *Text and Talk,* 28(3), Special Issue: Narratives in Context, 327–49.

—— (2013) 'Embedding police interviews in the prosecution case in the Shipman trial', in C. Heffer, F. Rock and J. Conley (eds), *Legal-lay Communication. Textual Travels in the Law*, Oxford: Oxford University Press, 147–67.

—— (2014) '"Dr Shipman told you that ...". The organizing and synthesizing power of quotation in judicial summing-up', *Language and Communication,* 36(1), 53–67.

Johnson, A. and Woolls, D. (2009) 'Who wrote this? The linguist as detective', in S. Hunston and D. Oakey (eds), *Doing Applied Linguistics*. Abingdon: Routledge, 111–18.

Johnson, A. and Wright, D. (2014) 'Identifying idiolect in forensic authorship attribution: an n-gram textbite approach', *Language and Law – Linguagem e Direito*, 1(1), 37–69.

Johnstone, B. (1996) *The Linguistic Individual: Self Expression in Language and Linguistics*. Oxford: Oxford University Press.

—— (2009) 'Pittsburghese shirts: Commodification and the enregistered urban dialect', *American Speech*, 84(2), 157–75.

Jönsson, L. and Linell, P. (1991) 'Story generations: from dialogical interviews to written reports in police interrogations', *Text*, 11, 419–40.

Juola, P. (2013) 'Stylometry and immigration: A case study', *Journal of Law and Policy*, 21(2), 287–98.

Kaplan, J.P. (1998) 'Pragmatic contributions to the interpretation of a will', *Forensic Linguistics*, 5(2), 107–26.

Kaplan, J.P., Green, G.M., Cunningham, C.D. and Levi, J.N. (1995) 'Bringing linguistics into judicial decision making: semantic analysis submitted to the US Supreme Court', *Forensic Linguistics*, 2(1), 81–98.

Keenan, J.M., MacWhinney, B. and Mayhew, D. (1977) 'Pragmatics in memory: a study of natural conversation', *Journal of Verbal Learning and Verbal Behavior*, 16, 549–60.

Kelly, F. and Harte, N. (2015) 'Forensic comparison of ageing voices from automatic and auditory perspectives', *The International Journal of Speech, Language and the Law*, 22(2), 167–202.

Kelly, L., Lovett, J. and Regan, L. (2005) 'A gap or a chasm? Attrition in reported rape cases', Home Office Research Study Online. Available HTTP: <http://www.home office.gov.uk/rds/pdfs05/hors293.pdf> (accessed 12 March 2007).

Kersta, L.A. (1962) 'Voiceprint identification', *Nature*, 196, 1253–7.

Kilgariff, A. (2007) 'BNC database and word frequency lists', Online, 24 May. Available HTTP: <http://www.kilgarriff.co.uk/bnc-readme.html> (accessed 14 December 2015).

Klarreich, E. (2003) 'Bookish math: statistical tests are unraveling knotty literary mysteries', *Science News Online*, 164, 392, Online. Available HTTP: <http://www.sciencenews. org/articles/(2003)1220/bob8.asp> (accessed 14 September 2006).

Kniffka, H. (1990) (ed.) *Texte zu Theorie und Praxis forensischer Linguistik*, Tübingen: Max Niemeyer Verlag (Linguistische Arbeiten Nr. 249).

Knight, R. (2012) *Phonetics: A Coursebook*, Cambridge: Cambridge University Press.

Knox, M. (with M. Walker) (1995) *The Private Diary of an O.J. Juror: Behind the Scenes of the Trial of the Century*, Beverly Hills, CA: Dove Books.

Koenig, B.J. (1986) 'Spectrographic voice identification: a forensic survey', letter to the editor of *Journal of the Acoustical Society of America*, 79(6), 2088–90.

Koester, A. (2010) 'Building small specialised corpora', in A. O'Keefe and M. McCarthy (eds), *The Routledge Handbook of Corpus Linguistics*, London: Routledge, 66–79.

Komter, M.L. (1994) 'Accusations and defences in courtroom interaction', *Discourse and Society*, 5(3), 165–188.

—— (1998) *Dilemmas in the Courtroom: A Study of Trials of Violent Crime in the Netherlands*, Mahwah, NJ: Lawrence Erlbaum Associates.

—— (2003) 'The interactional dynamics of eliciting a confession in a Dutch police inter-rogation', *Research on Language and Social Interaction*, 36(4), 433–70.

—— (2006) 'From talk to text: the interactional construction of a police record', *Research on Language and Social Interaction*, 39(3), 201–28.

Koppel, M., Schler, J. and Argamon, S. (2009) 'Computational methods in authorship attribution', *Journal of the American Society for Information Science and Technology* 60(1), 9–26.

—— (2011) 'Authorship attribution in the wild'. *Language Resources and Evaluation* 45(1), 83–94.

—— (2013) 'Authorship attribution: what's easy and what's hard?', *Journal of Law and Policy*, 21(2), 317–32.

Köster, O., Kehrein, R., Masthoff, K. and Boubaker, Y. H. (2012) 'The tell-tale accent: identification of regionally marked speech in German telephone conversations by forensic phoneticians', *The International Journal of Speech, Language and the Law* 19(1), 51–71.

Kredens, K. and Coulthard, M. (2012) 'Corpus linguistics in authorship identification', in *The Oxford Handbook of Language and Law*, Oxford: Oxford University Press, 504–16.

Kremer-Sadlik, T. (2004) 'How children with autism and Asperger's Syndrome respond to questions: a "naturalistic" theory of mind task', *Discourse Studies*, 6(2), 185–206.

Künzel, H.J. (1994) 'On the problem of speaker identification by victims and witnesses', *Forensic Linguistics*, 1(1), 45–58.

Kurzon, D. (1997) '"Legal Language": Varieties, genres, registers, discourses', *International Journal of Applied Linguistics*, 7(2), 110–39.

—— (2000) 'The right to understand the right of silence: a few comments', *Forensic Linguistics*, 7(2), 244–8.

—— (2001) 'The politeness of judges: American and English judicial behaviour', *Journal of Pragmatics*, 33(1), Jan, 61–85.

La Rooy, D., Heydon, G., Korkman, J. and Myklebust, T. (2015) 'Interviewing child witnesses', in G. Oxburgh, T. Myklebust, T. Grant, and R. Milne (eds), *Communication in Investigative and Legal Contexts: Integrated Approaches*. Wiley: Chichester, 57–78.

Labbé, D. (2007) 'Experiments on authorship attribution by intertextual distance in English', *Journal of Quantitative Linguistics,* 14(1), 33–80.

Labov, W. (1966). 'The linguistic variable as a structural unit', *Washington Linguistic Review*, 3, 4–22.

—— (1972a) *Language in the Inner City: Studies in the Black English Vernacular*, Philadelphia, PA: University of Pennsylvania Press.

—— (1972b) *Sociolinguistic Patterns*, Philadelphia: University of Pennsylvania Press.

Labov, W. and Fanshel, D. (1977) *Therapeutic Discourse: Psychotherapy as Conversation*, New York: Academic Press.

Larner, S. (2015) 'From intellectual challenges to established corpus techniques: introduction to the special issue on forensic linguistics', *Corpora*, 10.2, 131–43.

Lave, J. and Wenger, E. (1991) *Situated Learning: Legitimate Peripheral Participation,* Cambridge: Cambridge University Press.

Laver, J. (1980) *The Phonetic Description of Voice Quality*, Cambridge: Cambridge University Press.

Leo, R.A. (1996) 'Inside the interrogation room', *Criminal Law and Criminology*, 86, 266–303.

Levi, J.N. (1993) 'Evaluating jury comprehension of the Illinois capital sentencing instructions', *American Speech,* 68(1), 20–49.

—— (1994a) *Language and the Law: A Bibliographical Guide to Social Science Research in the USA*, Chicago, IL: American Bar Association.

—— (1994b) 'Language as evidence: the linguist as expert witness in North American Courts', *Forensic Linguistics*, 1(1), 1–26.

Levi, J.N. and Graffam Walker, A. (eds) (1990) *Language in the Judicial Process*, London: Plenum.

Levinson, S. (1992) 'Activity types and language', in P. Drew and J.C. Heritage (eds), *Talk at Work. Interaction in Institutional Settings*, Cambridge and New York: Cambridge University Press, 66–100.

Liberman, K. (1985) *Understanding Interaction in Central Australia: An Ethnomethodological Study of Australian Aboriginal People*, Boston, MA: Routledge.

Linell, P. and Jönsson, L. (1991) 'Suspect stories: perspective setting in an asymmetrical situation', in I. Markovà and K. Foppa (eds), *Asymmetries in Dialogue*, Hemel Hempstead: Harvester Wheatsheaf, 75–100.

Linfoot-Ham, K. (2006) 'Conversational maxims in encounters with law enforcement officers', *International Journal of Speech, Language and the Law*, 13(1), 23–54.

Loakes, D. (2008) 'A forensic phonetic investigation into the speech patterns of identical and non-identical twins', *The International Journal of Speech, Language and the Law*, 15(1), 97–100.

Loftus, E.F. and Palmer, J.C. (1974) 'Reconstruction of automobile destruction: An example of the interaction between language and memory,' *Journal of Verbal Learning and Verbal Behavior*, 13, 585–89.

Louw, B. (1993) 'Irony in the text or insincerity in the writer?', in M. Baker, G. Francis and E. Tognini-Bonelli (eds), *Text and Technology: In Honour of John Sinclair*, Philadelphia, PA and Amsterdam: John Benjamins, 157–76.

Love, H. (2002) *Attributing Authorship: An Introduction*, Cambridge: Cambridge University Press.

Luchjenbroers, J. (1997) '"In your own words..." Questions and answers in a supreme court trial', *Journal of Pragmatics*, 27, 477–503.

MacLeod, N. (2010) *Police Interviews with Women Reporting Rape: A Critical Discourse Analysis,* unpublished PhD thesis, Aston University, Online. Available HTTP: <eprints.aston.ac.uk/15206/> (accessed 1 December 2015).

Maddox, J. (1991) 'Another mountain from a molehill', *Nature*, 351, 13.

Maley, Y. (1994) 'The language of the law', in J. Gibbons (ed.), *Language and the Law*, London: Longman, 11–50.

—— (2000) 'The case of the long-nosed potoroo: the framing and construction of expert witness testimony', in S. Sarangi and M. Coulthard (eds), *Discourse and Social Life*, London: Longman, 246–69.

Maley, Y., Candlin, C.N., Crichton, J. and Koster, P. (1995) 'Orientations to lawyer–client interviews', *Forensic Linguistics*, 2(1), 42–55.

Marcus, P. (2013) 'Judges talking to jurors in criminal cases: Why US judges do it so differently from just about everyone else', *Arizona Journal of International and Comparative Law*, 30, 1–64.

Marlow, K., Cherryman, J. and Lewis-Williams, S. (2006) 'Improving the ability of vulnerable adults with learning disabilities through effective use of rapport to establish a free narrative', paper presented at Second International Investigative Interviewing Conference 5–7 July 2006, University of Portsmouth, UK.

Martin, J.R. (1992) *English Text*, Amsterdam: John Benjamins.

Maryns, K. (2004) 'Identifying the asylum speaker: reflections on the pitfalls of language analysis in the determination of national origin', *International Journal of Speech, Language and the Law*, 11(2), 240–60.

Matoesian, G.M. (1993) *Reproducing Rape: Domination through Talk in the Courtroom*, Cambridge: Cambridge University Press.

—— (2001) *Law and the Language of Identity: Discourse in the William Kennedy Smith Rape Trial*, Oxford: Oxford University Press.

—— (2010) 'Multimodality and forensic linguistics. Multimodal aspects of victim's narrative in direct examination', in M. Coulthard and A. Johnson (eds), 541–57.

Mayr, A. (2008) *Language and Power: An Introduction to Institutional Discourse*, London: Continuum.

McEnery, T. and Wilson, A. (2001) *Corpus Linguistics: An Introduction*, 2nd edn, Edinburgh: Edinburgh University Press.

McGehee, F. (1937) 'The reliability of the identification of the human voice', *Journal of General Psychology*, 17, 249–71.

McMenamin, G. (1993) *Forensic Stylistics*, Amsterdam: Elsevier.

—— (2002) *Forensic Linguistics: Advances in Forensic Stylistics*, London: CRC Press.

—— (2004) 'Disputed authorship in US law', *International Journal of Speech, Language and the Law,* 11(1), 73–82.

—— (2010) 'Forensic stylistics. Theory and practice of forensic stylistics', in M. Coulthard and A. Johnson (eds), 487–507.

Meikle, J. (2015) 'Police review claims of unsolved Yorkshire Ripper attacks', *The Guardian,* 6 December.

Mekhennet, S. and Goldman, A. (2015) '"Jihadi John": Islamic State killer is identified as Londoner Mohammed Emwazi', *The Washington Post,* 26 February.

Mendenhall, T.C. (1887) 'The characteristic curves of composition', *Science,* 11, 237–49.

—— (1901) 'A mechanical solution to a literary problem', *Popular Science Monthly,* 60, 97–105.

Ministry of Justice (2011) *Achieving Best Evidence in Criminal Proceedings. Guidance on Interviewing Victims and Witnesses, and Guidance on Using Special Measures,* Online. Available HTTPS: <www.cps.gov.uk/docs/best_evidence_in_criminal_proceedings. pdf> (accessed 8 December 2015).

Mollin, S. (2009) '"I entirely understand" is a Blairism: The methodology of identifying idiolectal collocations', *International Journal of Corpus Linguistics,* 14(3), 367–92.

Morrison, G. S., Sahito, F. H., Jardine, G., Djokic, D., Clavet, S., Berghs, S., Goemans Dorny, C. (2016) INTERPOL survey of the use of speaker identification by law enforcement agencies. *Forensic Science International* 263, 92–100.

Morton, A.Q. (1991) 'Proper words on proper places', Department of Computing Science Research Report, R18, University of Glasgow.

Morton, A.Q. and Michaelson, S. (1990) *The Q-Sum Plot,* internal report CSR-3-90, Department of Computer Science, University of Edinburgh.

Mosteller, F. and Wallace, D.L. (1964) *Inference and Disputed Authorship: The Federalist,* New York: Springer-Verlag.

Muir, H. (24 September 1996) 'Big Mac puts the bite on McMunchies', Online. Available HTTP: <http://www.telegraph.co.uk/htmlContent.jhtml?html=/archive/1996/09/24/ nmac24.html> (accessed 22 August 2006).

Mumby, D. and Clair, R. (1997) 'Organisational discourse', in T. van Dijk (ed.) *Discourse as Social Interaction. Discourse Studies a Multidisciplinary Introduction, Volume 2,* London: Sage, 181–205.

Munro, A. (2007) '"Reform in Law" Awarded for First Plain-Language Rewrite of Federal Civil Court Rules in 70 Years', Online. Available HTTP: <http://enewschannels. com/2007/05/12/enc1282_012728> (accessed 27 May 2007).

Nakane, I. (2014) *Interpreter-Mediated Police Interviews: A Discourse-Pragmatic Approach,* Basingstoke: Palgrave Macmillan.

Nakasone, H. and Beck, S.D. (2001) 'Forensic automatic speaker recognition', *Proc. 2001 Speaker Odyssey Speaker Recognition Workshop,* 1–6.

Newbury, P. and Johnson, A.J. (2006) 'Suspects' resistance to constraining and coercive questioning strategies in the police interview', *International Journal of Speech, Language and the Law,* 13(2), 213–40.

New York Times (22 June 2013) 'Zimmerman judge bars testimony on 911 Call'. Online. Available http://www.nytimes.com/2013/06/23/us/zimmerman-judge-bars-testimony-on-911-call.html (accessed 5 November 2015).

Ng, E.N.S. (2015) 'Judges' intervention in witness examination as a cause of omissions in interpretation in the Hong Kong courtroom', *International Journal of Speech, Language and the Law,* 22(2), 203–27.

Nini, A. and Grant, T. (2013) 'Bridging the gap between stylistic and cognitive approaches to authorship analysis using Systemic Functional Linguistics and multidimensional analysis', *The International Journal of Speech, Language and the Law,* 20(2), 173–202.

Nolan, F. (1994) 'Auditory and acoustic analysis in speaker recognition', in J. Gibbons (ed.), *Language and the Law,* London: Longman, 326–45.

—— (2003) 'A recent voice parade', *International Journal of Speech, Language and the Law,* 10(2), 277–91.

Nolan, F. and Grabe, E. (1996) 'Preparing a voice lineup', *Forensic Linguistics,* 3(1), 74–94.

Nolan, F., McDougall, K., Hudson, T. (2013) 'Effects of the telephone on perceived voice similarity: implications for voice line-ups'. *The International Journal of Speech, Language and the Law,* 20(2), 229–246.

O'Grady, G. (2013) *Key Concepts in Phonetics and Phonology.* London: Palgrave.

O'Barr, W.M. (1982) *Linguistic Evidence: Language, Power and Strategy in the Courtroom,* New York: Academic Press.

Okawara, M. (2006) *A Linguistic Analysis of some Japanese Trademark Cases,* unpublished PhD thesis, Sydney: The University of Sydney, Australia.

Oxburgh, G.E., Myklebust, T. and Grant, T. (2010) 'The question of question types in police interviews from a psychological and linguistic perspective', *International Journal of Speech Language and the Law,* 17(1), 45–66.

Oxburgh, G., Myklebust, T., Grant, T., Milne, R. (eds) (2016) *Communication in Investigative and Legal Contexts: Integrated Approaches from Forensic Psychology, Linguistics and Law Enforcement.* London: Wiley-Blackwell.

Pagano, A. (1994) 'Negatives in written text', in R.M. Coulthard (ed.), *Advances in Written Text Analysis,* London: Routledge, 250–75.

Patrick, P. (2010) 'Language variation and LADO'. In K. Zwaan, M. Verrips and P. Muysken (eds.), *Language and Origin. The role of language in European asylum procedures: a linguistic and legal survey.* Nijmegen: Wolf Legal Publishers, 73–88.

—— (2012) 'Language analysis for determination of origin: objective evidence for refugee status determination', in P. Tiersma and L. Solan (eds), *The Oxford Handbook of Language and Law.* Oxford: Oxford University Press, 533–46.

Pecorari, D.E. (2002) *Original Reproductions: An Investigation of the Source Use of Postgraduate Second Language Writers,* unpublished PhD thesis, University of Birmingham.

—— (2003) 'Good and original: plagiarism and patchwriting in academic second-language writing', *Journal of Second Language Writing,* 12, 317–45.

—— (2010) *Academic Writing and Plagiarism: A Linguistic Analysis,* London: Continuum.

Pennycook, A. (1996) 'Borrowing others' words: text, ownership, memory and plagiarism', *TESOL Quarterly,* 30, 201–30.

Philbrick, F.A. (1949) *Language and the Law: The Semantics of Forensic English,* New York: Macmillan.

Plain English Campaign (1996a) *Language on Trial,* London: Robson Books.

—— (1996b) *A–Z of Legal Words and Phrases,* High Peak: Plain English Campaign.

Prakasam, V. (2004) 'The Indian Evidence Act 1872: a lexicogrammatical study', in J. Gibbons et al. (eds), *Language in the Law,* Hyderabad: Orient Longman, 17–23.

Prince, E. (1981) 'Language and the law: a case for linguistic pragmatics', *Working Papers in Sociolinguistics,* Austin: Southwest Educational Development Laboratory, 112–60.

Projeto COMET (2007) *Projeto COrpus Multilingüe Ensino e Tradução,* Online. Available HTTP: <http:comet.fflch.usp.br/> (accessed 26 November 2015).

Quirk, R. (1982) *Style and Communication in the English Language*, London: Edward Arnold.

Quirk, R., Greenbaum, S., Leech, G. and Svartvik, J. (1985) *A Comprehensive Grammar of the English Language*. London: Longman.

Ricks, C. (1998) 'Plagiarism', British Academy lecture, 10 February 1998.

Rico-Sulayes, A. (2011) 'Statistical authorship attribution of Mexican drug trafficking online forum posts', *The International Journal of Speech, Language and the Law*, 18(1), 53–74.

Roberts, C. (2011) 'Institutional Discourse', in J. Simpson (ed.), *The Routledge Handbook of Applied Linguistics*, Abingdon: Routledge, 81–5.

Robson, J. 2015. Conversation with David Wright, 16 November.

Robertson, G. (2006) 'Comma quirk irks Rogers', *Globe and Mail*, 6 August, Online. Available HTTP: <http://www.theglobeandmail.com/> (accessed 24 August 2006).

Rock, F. (2001) 'The genesis of a witness statement', *Forensic Linguistics*, 8(2), 44–72.

—— (2007) *Communicating Rights: The Language of Arrest and Detention*, Basingstoke: Palgrave Macmillan.

—— (2010) 'Witnesses and suspects in interviews. Collecting oral evidence: the police, the public and the written word', in M. Coulthard and A. Johnson (eds), 126–38.

Rock, F., Heffer, C. and Conley, J. (2013) 'Textual travel in legal-lay communication', in C. Heffer, F. Rock and J. Conley (eds), *Legal-lay Communication. Textual Travels in the Law*, Oxford: Oxford University Press, 3–32.

Rosch, E. (1975) 'Cognitive representations of semantic categories', *Journal of Experimental Psychology: General*, 104, 192–233.

Rose, P. (2002) *Forensic Speaker Identification*, London: Taylor and Francis.

Rose, P. and Morrison, G.S. (2009) 'A response to the UK position statement on forensic speaker comparison', *International Journal of Speech, Language and the Law*, 16(1), 139–63.

Royce, T. (2005) 'Case Analysis. The negotiator and the bomber: analysing the critical role of active listening in crisis negotiations', *Negotiation Journal*, 21(1), 5–27.

Russell, S. (2002) '"Three's a crowd": shifting dynamics in the interpreted interview', in J. Cotterill (ed.), *Language in the Legal Process*, Basingstoke: Macmillan, 111–26.

Sacks, H., Schegloff, E. and Jefferson, G. (1974) 'A simplest systematics for the organization of turntaking for conversation', *Language*, 50(4), 696–735.

Sanderson, S.M. 'Bayes' theorem … a simple example', Online. Available HTTP: <http://www.herkimershideaway.org/writings/bayes.htm> (accessed 12 April 2016).

Sandhya, G.K. (2004) 'Teaching the language of the law: patterns, problems and challenges', in J. Gibbons et al. (eds), *Language in the Law*, Hyderabad: Orient Longman, 133–39.

Sarangi, S. and Roberts, C. (eds) (1999) *Talk, Work and Institutional Order: Discourse in Medical, Mediation and Management Settings*. Berlin: Walter de Gruyter.

Sarwar, F., Allwood, C.M. and Zetterholm, E. (2014) 'Earwitnesses: the type of voice lineup affects the proportion of correct identifications and the realism in confidence judgments', *The International Journal of Speech, Language and the Law*, 21(1), 139–55.

Scheffer, T. (2006) 'The microformation of criminal defense: on the lawyer's notes, speech production, and a field of presence', *Research on Language and Social Interaction*, 39(3), 303–42.

Schiel, F. and Heinrich, C. (2015) 'Disfluencies in the speech of intoxicated speakers', *The International Journal of Speech, Language and the Law*, 22(1), 19–33.

Schiffrin, D. (1985) 'Conversational coherence: The role of "well"', *Language,* 61(3), 640–67.

—— (1987) *Discourse Markers,* Cambridge: Cambridge University Press.

—— (1994) *Approaches to Discourse,* Oxford: Blackwell.

Schiller, N.O. and Köster, O. (1998) 'The ability of expert witnesses to identify voices: a comparison between trained and untrained listeners', *Forensic Linguistic,* 5(1), 1–9.

Schilling, N. and Marsters, A. (2015) 'Unmasking identity: speaker profiling for forensic linguistic purposes', *Annual Review of Applied Linguistics,* 35, 195–214.

Schlichting, F. and Sullivan, K.P.H. (1997) 'The imitated voice: a problem for voice line-ups?', *Forensic Linguistics,* 4(1), 148–65.

Schmitt, N., Grandage, S. and Adolphs, S. (2004) 'Are corpus-derived recurrent clusters psycholinguistically valid?', in N. Schmitt, (ed.), *Formulaic Sequences: Acquisition, Processing and Use,* Amsterdam: John Benjamins, 127–51.

Schweda Nicholson, N. (2010) 'Sentencing convicted murderers. Convicted murderers' allocutions or leniency pleas at sentencing hearings', in M. Coulthard and A. Johnson (eds), 231–50.

Scott, M. (2010) *Wordsmith Tools Help,* Liverpool: Lexical Analysis Software.

—— (2012) *Wordsmith Tools,* Version 6, Oxford: Oxford University Press.

Shapero, J. (2011) *The Language of Suicide Notes,* unpublished PhD thesis, University of Birmingham, Online. Available: <etheses.bham.ac.uk/1525/1/Shapero11PhD.pdf> (accessed 1 December 2015).

Shuy, R. (1993) *Language Crimes: The Use and Abuse of Language Evidence in the Courtroom,* Cambridge, MA: Blackwell.

—— (1994) 'Deceit, distress and false imprisonment: the anatomy of a car sales event', *Forensic Linguistics,* 1(2), 133–49.

—— (1998) *The Language of Confession, Interrogation and Deception,* London: Sage.

—— (2002a) 'To testify or not to testify', in J. Cotterill (ed.), *Language in the Legal Process,* London: Palgrave, 3–18.

—— (2002b) *Linguistic Battles in Trademark Disputes,* New York: Palgrave.

—— (2005) *Creating Language Crimes: How Law Enforcement Uses and Abuses Language,* Oxford: Oxford University Press.

—— (2006) *Linguistics in the Courtroom: A Practical Guide,* Oxford: Oxford University Press.

Sinclair, J.McH. (1991) *Corpus, Concordance, Collocation,* Oxford: Oxford University Press.

Simpson, J.A. and Weiner, E.S.C. (eds) (1989) *Oxford English Dictionary,* 2nd edn, additions 1993–97; J. Simpson, E. Weiner and M. Proffitt (eds) and 3rd edn (in progress), Oxford: Oxford University Press; J. Simpson (ed) OED Online, Oxford University Press, Online. Available HTTP: <http://oed. com> (accessed 27 March 2007).

Sinclair, J.McH. ms Unpublished expert opinion on the ordinary man's understanding of the word 'visa'.

Singler, J.V. (2004) 'The "linguistic" asylum interview and the linguist's evaluation of it, with special reference to applicants for Liberian political asylum in Switzerland', *International Journal of Speech, Language and the Law,* 11(2), 222–39.

Slembrouck S. (1992) 'The parliamentary Hansard "verbatim" report: the written construction of spoken discourse', *Language and Literature,* 1(2), 101–19.

Solan, L. (1993) *The Language of Judges,* Chicago, IL: University of Chicago Press.

—— (1998) 'Linguistic experts as semantic tour guides', *Forensic Linguistics,* 5(2), 87–106.

—— (2002) 'Ordinary meaning in legal interpretation', in *Pohjois-Suomen Tuomarikoulu*; reprinted in B. Pozzo (ed.) (2005) *Ordinary Language and Legal Language*, Milan: Giuffrè, 125–52.

—— (2010) 'The expert linguist meets the adversarial system', in M. Coulthard and A. Johnson (eds), 395–407.

—— (2013) 'Intuition versus algorithm: The case for forensic authorship attribution', *Journal of Law and Policy*, 21(2), 551–76.

Solan, L.M. and Tiersma, P.M. (2004) 'Author identification in American courts', *Applied Linguistics*, 25(4), 448–65.

—— (2005) *Speaking of Crime: The Language of Criminal Justice*, Chicago, IL: University of Chicago Press.

Sørensen, M.H. (2012) 'Voice line-ups: speakers' F0 values influence the reliability of voice recognitions', *The International Journal of Speech, Language and the Law*, 19(2),145–58.

Sousa-Silva, R. (2014) 'Detecting translingual plagiarism and the backlash against translation plagiarists', *Language and Law – Linguagem e Direito*, 1(1), 70–84.

Stamatatos, E. (2009) 'A survey of modern authorship attribution methods', *Journal of the American Society for Information Science and Technology*, 60(3), 538–56.

Stenström, A-B. (1984) *Questions and Responses in English Conversation*, Malmö: C.W.K. Gleerup.

Stern, S. and Wiggins, J. (2007) 'McDonald's seeks to redefine "McJob"', ft.com, Online, 19 March. Available HTTP: <http://www.ft.com/cms/s/2065c45e-d65d-11db-99b7-000b5df10621.html> (accessed 9 April 2007).

Stokoe, E. (2014) 'The Conversation Analytic Role-play Method (CARM), A method for training communication skills as an alternative to simulated role-play', *Research on Language and Social Interaction*, 47(3), 255–65.

Stokoe, E. and Edwards, D. (2010) 'Lawyers in interviews. "I advise you not to answer that question": conversation analysis, legal interaction and the analysis of lawyers' turns in police interrogations of suspects', in M. Coulthard and A. Johnson (eds), 155–68.

Stubbs, M. (1996) *Text and Corpus Analysis*, Oxford: Blackwell.

—— (2004) 'Conrad, concordance, collocation: heart of darkness or light at the end of the tunnel?', The Third Sinclair Open Lecture, University of Birmingham.

Stygall, G. (1994) *Trial Language: Discourse Processing and Discursive Formation*, Amsterdam: Benjamins.

—— (2010) 'Legal writing: complexity. Complex documents/average and not-so-average readers', in M. Coulthard and A. Johnson (eds), 51–64.

Svartvik, J. (1968) *The Evans Statements: A Case for Forensic Linguistics*, Gothenburg: University of Gothenburg Press.

Swales, J.M. (1990) *Genre Analysis: English in Academic and Research Settings*, New York: Cambridge University Press.

The Home Office (2003) 'Advice on the Use of Voice Identification Parades', Online. Available HTTP: https://www.gov.uk/government/publications/advice-on-the-use-of-voice-identification-parades (accessed 8 March 2016).

The ICE Project (2015) *International Corpus of English*, Online. Available HTTP: <ice-corpora.net/ICE/INDEX.HTM> (accessed 15 November 2015).

The Shipman Inquiry (2001) *The Shipman Inquiry*, Online. Available HTTP: <webarchive.nationalarchives.gov.uk/20090808154959/http:/www.the-shipman-inquiry.org.uk/home.asp> (accessed 14 December 2015).

The Shipman Trial Transcript (2001) *The Shipman Inquiry*, Online. Available HTTP: <webarchive.nationalarchives.gov.uk/20090808154959/http://www.the-shipman-inquiry.org.uk/trialtrans.asp> (accessed 14 December 2015).

The Test of Legal English website, Online. Available HTTP: <http://www.toles.co.uk/> (accessed 14 December 2015).

Thornborrow, J. and Coates, J. (eds) (2005) *The Sociolinguistics of Narrative*, Amsterdam: John Benjamins.

Tiersma, P. (1999) *Legal Language*, Chicago, IL: University of Chicago Press.

—— (2001) 'Textualising the law', *Forensic Linguistics*, 8(2), 73–92.

—— (2002) 'The language and law of product warnings', in J. Cotterill (ed.), *Language in the Legal Process*, London: Palgrave, 54–71.

—— (2010) 'Instructions to jurors. Redrafting California's jury instructions', in M. Coulthard and A. Johnson (eds), 251–64.

Tiersma, P. and Solan, L. (2002) 'The linguist on the witness stand: forensic linguistics in American courts', *Language*, 78, 221–39.

—— (eds) (2012) *The Oxford Handbook of Language and Law*, Oxford: Oxford University Press.

Time (15 July 2013) 'J.K. Rowling's Secret: A Forensic Linguist explains how he figured it out'. Online. Available http://entertainment.time.com/2013/07/15/j-k-rowlings-secret-a-forensic-linguist-explains-how-he-figured-it-out/ (accessed 28 September 2015).

Tkačuková, T. (2010) 'Representing oneself. Cross-examination questioning: lay people as cross-examiners', in M. Coulthard and A. Johnson (eds), 333–46.

Toolan, M. (2001) *Narrative: A Critical Linguistic Introduction*, 2nd edn, London: Routledge.

Tracy, K. and Delgadillo, E.L. (2013) 'Troubling the legal-lay distinction. Litigant briefs, oral argument, and a public hearing about same-sex marriage', in: C. Heffer, F. Rock and J. Conley (eds) *Legal-lay Communication. Textual Travels in the Law*, Oxford: Oxford University Press, 226–44.

Trow, M.J. (1929) *"Let him have it Chris"*, London: HarperCollins.

Trudgill, P. (1992) *Introducing Language and Society*, London: Penguin.

Turchie Affidavit, Online. Available HTTP: <http://www.unabombertrial.com/documents/turchie_affidavit.html> (accessed 10 October 2006).

Turell, M.T. (2004) 'Textual kidnapping revisited: the case of plagiarism in literary translation', *International Journal of Speech, Language and the Law*, 11(1), 1–26.

—— (2010) 'The use of textual, grammatical and sociolinguistic evidence in forensic text comparison', *The International Journal of Speech, Language and the Law*, 17(2), 211–50.

Turell, M.T. and Gavaldà, N. (2013) 'Towards an index of idiolectal similitude (or distance) in forensic authorship analysis', *Journal of Law and Policy*, 21(2), 495–514.

Tweedie, F.J., Singh, S., and Holmes, D.I. (1996) 'Neural network applications in stylometry: The Federalist Papers', *Computers and the Humanities*, 30(1), 1–10.

Wagner, A. and Cheng, L. (eds) (2011) *Exploring Courtroom Discourse. The Language of Power and Control*, Farnham: Ashgate.

Walker, A.G. (1993) 'Questioning young children in court: A linguistic case study', *Law and Human Behavior*, 17(1), 59–81.

Watson, R. (1976) 'Some conceptual issues in the social identifications of victims and offenders', in E.C. Viano (ed.), *Victims and Society*, Washington, DC: Visage, 60–71.

—— (1983) 'The presentation of victim and motive in discourse: the case of police interrogations and interviews', *Victimology: An International Journal*, 8(1–2), 31–52.

—— (1990) 'Some features of the elicitation of confessions in murder interrogations', in G. Psathas (ed.), *Interactional Competence, Studies in Ethnomethodology and Conversation Analysis 1*, Washington, DC: University Press of America, 263–95.

Watt, D. (2010) 'The identification of the individual through speech', in C. Llamas and D. Watt (eds), *Language and Identities*. Edinburgh: Edinburgh University Press, 76–85.

Weirich, M. (2011) *The Influence of NATURE and NURTURE on Speaker-Specific Parameters in Twins' Speech: Acoustics, Articulation and Perception*, PhD Thesis, Humboldt-Universität zu Berlin, Online. Available HTTP: http://edoc.hu-berlin.de/dissertationen/weirich-melanie-2011-11-11/PDF/weirich.pdf (accessed 8 March 2016).

Wells, G.L. (1993) 'What do we know about eyewitness identification?', *American Psychologist*, 48, 553–71.

Whalen, J. and Zimmerman, D.H. (1998) 'Observations on the display and management of emotion in naturally occurring activities: The case of 'hysteria' in calls to 9-1-1', *Social Psychology Quarterly*, 61(2), 141–59.

Whalen, J., Zimmerman, D.H. and Whalen, M.R. (1988) 'When words fail: a single case analysis', *Social Problems*, 35(4), Special Issue: Language Interaction and Social Problems, 335–62.

Whalen, M.R. and Zimmerman, D.H. (1987) 'Sequential and institutional contexts in calls for help', *Social Psychology Quarterly*, 50(2), Special Issue: Language and Social Interaction, 172–85.

Windsor Lewis, J. (1994) 'Case report: The Yorkshire Ripper enquiry: Part II', *Forensic Linguistics,* 1(2), 207–16.

Winter, E.O. and Woolls, D. (1996), 'Identifying authorship in a co-written novel', Internal report for University of Birmingham.

Woodbury, H. (1984) 'The strategic use of questions in court', *Semiotica*, 48(3/4), 197–228.

Woodhams, J., Grant, T. and Price, A.R.G. (2007) 'From marine ecology to crime analysis: improving the detection of serial sexual offences using a taxonomic similarity measure', *The Journal of Investigative Psychology and Offender Profiling*, 4(1), 17–27.

Wooffitt, R. (2005) *Conversation Analysis and Discourse Analysis: A Comparative and Critical Introduction*. London: SAGE Publications.

Woolls, D. (2002) *Copycatch Gold*, Online. Available HTTP: <http://www.cflsoftware.com/GoldFull.html> (accessed 14 December 2015).

—— (2003) 'Better tools for the trade and how to use them', *International Journal of Speech, Language and the Law*, 10(1), 102–12.

—— (2010) 'Computational forensic linguistics. Searching for similarity in large specialized corpora', in M. Coulthard and A. Johnson (eds), 576–90.

—— (2012) 'Detecting plagiarism', *The Oxford Handbook of Language and Law*, Oxford: Oxford University Press, 517–29.

—— (2013) CFL *Jaccard n-gram Lexical Evaluator. Jangle,* version 2. CFL Software Limited, Online. Available HTTP: < www.cflsoftware.com/Jangle.html> (accessed 8 March 2016).

—— (2015) *Copycatch Investigator*. CFL Software Limited, Online. Available HTTP: <cflsoftware.com/Investigator.html> (accessed 8 March 2016).

Woolls, D. and Coulthard, R.M. (1998) 'Tools for the trade', *Forensic Linguistics*, 5(1), 33–57.

Wright, D. (2013) 'Stylistic variation within genre conventions in the Enron email corpus: Developing a text-sensitive methodology for authorship research', *The International Journal of Speech, Language and the Law,* 20(1), 45–75.

—— (2014) *Stylistics Versus Statistics: A Corpus Linguistic Approach to Combining Techniques in Forensic Authorship Analysis Using Enron Emails,* unpublished PhD Thesis, University of Leeds.

Yarmey, A.D. (1991) 'Voice identification over the telephone', *Journal of Applied Social Psychology,* 21(22) 1868–1876.

—— (2003) 'Earwitness identification over the telephone and in field settings', *The International Journal of Speech, Language and the Law,* 10(1), 62–74.

—— (2012) 'Factors affecting lay persons' identification of speakers', in P. Tiersma and L. Solan (eds), *The Oxford Handbook of Language and Law,* Oxford: Oxford University Press, 547–56.

Zander, M. (1999*) Cases and Materials on the English Legal System,* 8th edn, Cambridge: Cambridge University Press.

Zheng, R. Li, J., Chen, H. and Huang, Z. (2006) 'A framework for authorship identification of online messages: Writing-style features and classification techniques', *Journal of the American Society for Information Science and Technology,* 57(3), 378–93.

Zimmerman, D.H. (1992) 'The interactional organization of calls for emergency assistance', in P. Drew and J. Heritage (eds), *Talk and Work,* Cambridge and New York: Cambridge University Press, 418–69.

Acts of Parliament

Counter-Terrorism and Security Act 2015, Online. Available HTTP: <http://www.legislation.gov.uk/ukpga/2015/6/contents> (accessed 15 December 2015).

Offences Against the Person Act 1861, Online. Available HTTP: < http://www.legislation.gov.uk/ukpga/1861> (accessed 14 December 2015).

Police and Criminal Evidence Act 1984 (PACE), Online. Available HTTP: < http://www.legislation.gov.uk/ukpga/1984> (accessed 14 December 2015).

Theft Act 1968, Online. Available HTTP: < http://www.legislation.gov.uk/ukpga/1968> (accessed 14 December 2015).

Theft (Amendment) Act 1996, Online. Available HTTP: <http://www.legislation.gov.uk/ukpga/1996 > (accessed 14 December 2015).

Legal cases

Baigent v Random House (7 April 2006) *Summary of Judgment* Online. Available HTTP: <http://www.judiciary.gov.uk/judgment_guidance/judgments/summary.htm> (accessed 27 May 2007).

The State of Western Australia v Gibson [2014] WASC 240. Available HTTP: http://www.austlii.edu.au/au/cases/wa/WASC/2014/240.html (accessed 8 March 2016).

United Biscuits Limited v Customs and Excise, VAT Tribunal LON 91/160 1991.

R v Hodgson [2009] EWCA Crim 742.

Index

Taylor & Francis eBooks

Helping you to choose the right eBooks for your Library

Add Routledge titles to your library's digital collection today. Taylor and Francis ebooks contains over 50,000 titles in the Humanities, Social Sciences, Behavioural Sciences, Built Environment and Law.

Choose from a range of subject packages or create your own!

Benefits for you

- » Free MARC records
- » COUNTER-compliant usage statistics
- » Flexible purchase and pricing options
- » All titles DRM-free.

REQUEST YOUR FREE INSTITUTIONAL TRIAL TODAY

Free Trials Available
We offer free trials to qualifying academic, corporate and government customers.

Benefits for your user

- » Off-site, anytime access via Athens or referring URL
- » Print or copy pages or chapters
- » Full content search
- » Bookmark, highlight and annotate text
- » Access to thousands of pages of quality research at the click of a button.

eCollections – Choose from over 30 subject eCollections, including:

Archaeology	Language Learning
Architecture	Law
Asian Studies	Literature
Business & Management	Media & Communication
Classical Studies	Middle East Studies
Construction	Music
Creative & Media Arts	Philosophy
Criminology & Criminal Justice	Planning
Economics	Politics
Education	Psychology & Mental Health
Energy	Religion
Engineering	Security
English Language & Linguistics	Social Work
Environment & Sustainability	Sociology
Geography	Sport
Health Studies	Theatre & Performance
History	Tourism, Hospitality & Events

For more information, pricing enquiries or to order a free trial, please contact your local sales team:
www.tandfebooks.com/page/sales

 Routledge
Taylor & Francis Group

The home of
Routledge books

www.tandfebooks.com